Daniel Easterman was born in Ireland in 1949 and educated in Belfast. He studied English at Trinity College, Dublin, followed by Persian and Arabic at Edinburgh University, and completed a Ph.D. in Persian Studies at King's College, Cambridge. A specialist in aspects of Iranian Islam, he has lived in Iran and Morocco. Between 1981 and 1986, he taught Arabic and Islamic Studies at Newcastle University. Now writing fiction full-time, he is an Honorary Fellow in the Centre for Middle East and Islamic Studies at Durham University. For several years now, he has taken a serious interest in the sociology of alternative medicine. He lives in Newcastle with his wife Beth, a practitioner and writer on homoeopathy.

By the same author

The Last Assassin
The Seventh Sanctuary
The Ninth Buddha
Brotherhood of the Tomb
Night of the Seventh Darkness

As Denis MacEoin

Islam in the Modern World
   (with Ahmad al-Shahi)
The Sources for Early Basic Doctrine and History
A People Apart: the Baha'i Community
   of Iran in the Twentieth Century

As Jonathon Aycliffe

Naomi's Room

DANIEL EASTERMAN

New Jerusalems

Reflections on Islam, fundamentalism
and the Rushdie affair

Grafton
An Imprint of HarperCollins*Publishers*

Grafton
An Imprint of HarperCollins*Publishers*
77–85 Fulham Palace Road,
Hammersmith, London W6 8JB

A Grafton Paperback Original 1992
9 8 7 6 5 4 3 2 1

A catalogue record for this book
is available from the British Library

ISBN 0 586 21672 3

Set in Baskerville

Printed in Great Britain by
HarperCollinsManufacturing Glasgow

Contents

III: MARTYRS, MOONIES AND MONKS

Introduction

If the present collection of essays and occasional pieces can be said to have a unifying theme, it is that of the making of myth: the Western myths of Islam and the exotic Orient, the Islamic myth of the decadent West, the myth of a plot centred around Salman Rushdie to denigrate and vilify the sacred personages of Islam, the utopian myths of the fundamentalist preachers and the gurus of the new religious movements, the myth of causes in whose path death is perfect freedom. Our lives are exercises in fiction, our fictions provide the mainsprings of our best and our worst actions.

The transition I have made from professional academic to full-time fiction writer, and the occasional forays I make back into the groves of academe are neither as difficult nor as inconsistent as they might at first appear. Our society has demarcated these and other roles much too severely, to the detriment of popular and 'serious' culture alike.

The academic treads a nervous path through thickets of opinion, bias and fantasy as great as any to be found in the realms of fiction. And novelists seek to anchor even their wildest flights of imagination in the intelligible and recognizable. The field of religious studies – in which I taught for several years – is, more than most, one in which fact may be separated from fancy with but the greatest of difficulty: the hopes and fears, wishes and dreams of believers re-create the 'real' world of the historian or the anthropologist in new and often grossly distorted images. And the questions and observations of academics themselves have an often unsuspected and powerful impact on the behaviour of the faithful – a process delightfully charted by Alison Lurie (another academic/novelist) in *Imaginary Friends*.

These distortions and their power to energize social and

political movements have for many years fascinated, repelled and provoked me. In my work as an academic, I have been much concerned to demythologize, debunk or otherwise call in question the assumptions on which they are based. Recently, there has been intense debate – debate touched on in these pages, in the section on Salman Rushdie – about the rights and wrongs of 'insulting' religions. Some, like the late Roald Dahl, have maintained that it is somehow improper to write in anything but respectful terms about the great faiths. I for one do not subscribe to that view. While eschewing gross or virulent or casual abuse of those things others hold sacred, I cannot believe that religious belief or action deserve a hermetically sealed chamber within which they may persist free from criticism or healthy mockery.

My reasons for that conviction are, I think, set out well enough in several of these essays. They rest, above all, on an understanding that religions can be and often are powerful forces for political action, and that the aspirations of the fanatic or the fantasies of the mystic may, without undue difficulty, be translated into immediate challenges for the rest of us. This is a view whose relevance has only recently started to be felt by the general public in Europe, where a secular consensus seemed to have disqualified religion from the arena of direct social action. The rise of Christian fundamentalism in the United States, the growth of imported cults or – as sociologists now prefer to term them – 'New Religious Movements', and, above all, the impact of the Islamic revival both in the Middle East and in Western society are all factors that have altered our perception of the role of religion in everyday life.

As a secularist, such developments give me cause for concern, a concern that centres, above all, on the tendency of religions, whatever their origin, to bypass the ordinary rules and conventions that govern social and political life. Where believers appeal to a court superior to any human tribunal, or lay claim to authority inaccessible to other men, or demand special rights merely because of their convictions, there is always a risk that ordinary political and ethical debate may be short-circuited or wholly dispensed with. Hence the need for vigilance on the part of both secularists and non-fundamentalist believers.

But if we are to perpetuate a free and open society, such vigilance should by no means be restricted to the activities of religious fundamentalists. Political extremists are obvious sources of concern. But so too are many groups often seen as inherently benign. Here again, it is only in recent years that many of us have begun to recognize the dangers of delivering too much unbridled power into the hands of specialist .groups within society at large – scientists, doctors, the military, the police, the courts, the media. We have, in particular, started to understand the risks inherent in a too ready acquiescence in the sometimes perilous 'advances' of science, not least those of medicine. As the century draws to its close, we and our children are reaping the ecological harvest of unbridled investment in all manner of scientific, medical and industrial adventures over which we had or wanted too little control.

With the end of the cold war, an ideological vacuum remains to be filled, not only in Europe, but throughout the globe. Already, events in the Gulf have demonstrated how premature it may be to think that history has come to an end or that ideology is a thing of the past. Without doubt, it is Islam that will, in the next few decades, come to play the role of communism as a rival to the ideological power of the West. But other ideologies are there as well, waiting for their opportunity in the waning of the influence of older systems: new religions, new fundamentalisms, new combinations of religious and political radicalism.

For all their faults, I still believe that the secular democracies of Western Europe offer the safest way forward for mankind. But as the century draws to an end, our freedoms and aspirations are under threat. No other issue has, I believe, been so alarming or so dangerous as the controversy surrounding Salman Rushdie and his novel, *The Satanic Verses*. For me, the whole affair has had very personal echoes, bringing together as it does the role of the novelist in weaving together strands of truth and fiction, the implications of Islamic identity for our own society, and the question of freedom of thought and expression which I had previously encountered in my days as a follower of the Baha'i religion. Salman's fate still haunts me. I believe it haunts us all. For that reason, this collection is dedicated to Salman, and, through him, to everyone whose life and thought stand threatened by the forces of obscurantism, cant and bigotry.

'Makes Rambo Look Like an Altarboy'

The trouble with thriller writers is that most of us don't look the part. Take David Morrell, the creator of Rambo: he's a mild-mannered college professor from the States. Len Deighton wears glasses and likes cooking. Ken Follett is more at home with an electric guitar than an AK47. As for myself, I left the Boy Scouts at fifteen because I thought they were getting too militaristic.

And yet old friends sit well back on the other side of the room after they've read one of my books. 'You're such a gentle man,' they say politely. 'A pacifist, more or less, an ex-academic, a cat lover. How can you write these things?' They're right too. I attended Ireland's top rugby school and never played a game of rugger; in my youth I was arrested by the military police for sticking anti-war fliers on tanks at a military exhibition; nowadays, I drive a very large and very safe Volvo, swearing volubly at all those boy racers in white Sierras flashing suicidally past in the fast lane.

Yet just last year the *Dublin Evening Herald* said of one of my books, *The Seventh Sanctuary*, that it 'makes Rambo look like an altarboy'. I took it as a personal compliment and carried a copy round in my wallet for months. It was the ultimate accolade: I was a wimp no longer.

Repressed violence? The killer instinct hidden beneath a façade of academic urbanity? Cro-Magnon man beneath Walter Mitty's skin? Perhaps. But I don't think so. Violence, like atmospheric pollution or Joan Collins, is everywhere; all I do is draw attention to the fact. After romances, thrillers and crime novels are our most popular reading. We crave violence almost as much as hot flushes.

There is, after all, a very serious side to all of this. Why does a mild individual like myself write books to make you shudder, filled with images of sudden death and random violence? The answer, in part, is that one need not be violent oneself to find one's life touched by violence.

In my own life, I've known one politician gunned down by terrorists, and innocent men and women shot or hanged in Tehran's Evin prison. A large part of my library was given to me by a religious leader ambushed and riddled with bullets in the south-east of Iran. Nearer home, my mother, brother and sister-in-law were almost killed when a terrorist bomb blew the train in which they were travelling off the rails and very nearly down a hundred-foot drop. Maybe it helps to come from Northern Ireland and to have spent half one's life studying Shi'ism in Iran. Maybe it just helps to have been born into the twentieth century.

That may explain why I choose to write about the brutality of life; but why do so many otherwise pleasant, unpsychotic individuals spend good money to read my books? Is it, perhaps, because we all live with the horror of our own vulnerability? Our plane may be the one with the hairline crack or the bomb in a suitcase, our ship the one that rolls over and sinks, our tyre the one that blows out at ninety in the Sierra lane. The sudden heart attack, the unexpected stroke, the cot death, the madman walking down our street blazing away with a Kalashnikov set on automatic: we and our loved ones are all moments from death.

I recently read an article suggesting that films like *Nightmare on Elm Street* owe their popularity among teenagers to the fact that watching them is a kind of initiation ceremony into the horror of adult life. That may be extreme, but it contains a nugget of truth. Deep down, we are all constantly afraid. Of death, of mutilation, of bereavement. In order to cope with our fears, we try to exorcize them. Primitive peoples held dances and performed sacrifices for the spirits of death and darkness. We read books and watch movies in which the horrors happen to other people, horrors we fervently hope are far worse than any real life can throw at us, trusting that our vicarious experience will somehow avert danger from ourselves.

The real horror, of course, is that nothing in books or movies can surpass reality. Nothing in literature prepared us for the Nazi death camps. Nothing in films could have warned us of

Hiroshima. Nothing we saw on our television screens about the Vietnam war even hinted at what happened so soon afterwards in the killing fields of Cambodia.

That is where I find the greatest difficulty as a writer. Broadly speaking, my novels are rooted in fact; but making the truth believable is much more difficult than making fiction plausible. In my first novel, *The Last Assassin*, I created an imaginary group of Shi'ite terrorists, all willing to commit suicide to achieve their aims. I treated the idea as a slight exaggeration of the Shi'ite desire for martyrdom. Within months of the book's publication came the first suicide raids in Lebanon; then the opening-up of minefields by suicide troops in the Iran–Iraq war; and most recently the murder of passengers in a bus driven into a ravine in Israel by a martyr-terrorist.

The final chapters of my third novel, *The Ninth Buddha*, in which the main characters enter Mongolia in the early months of 1921 to find the country under a reign of terror imposed by White Russian troops, read like something from Rambo out of Indiana Jones. My real problem in writing about those events was not to make them colourful enough; it was to tone down the historical facts enough to make them believable.

A few months ago, I had just started work on my next book, set in Brooklyn and Haiti and concerned with grisly murders carried out in connection with a voodoo cult. I began to think I was overdoing things. A few days later, I opened my morning newspaper to find a headline reading: 'Mexico drug cult rites claim 12'. That wasn't the *News of the World*; that was the *Guardian*. And the bodies they were digging up were real.

In *Brotherhood of the Tomb*, I describe a right-wing Christian sect with tentacles stretching deep inside the Vatican and the higher levels of Italian society. The cult may be my own invention; but it is not that many years since the Italian government was brought down by the discovery of P-2, a secret Masonic lodge with members drawn from the highest ranks of the military, the judiciary, the government and even the Church. Fiction can only follow fact; it can never outdo it.

So I go on being gentle in my private life and pitilessly cruel in my writing. It keeps me sane and my readers happy. And at least that's better than being a mass murderer who writes poems about teddy-bears. Isn't it?

(Originally published in the *Australian Bookseller and Publisher*, September 1989)

I

MAD MULLAS, BLIND EYES AND DEAD SHEEP

Fundamentalism East and West

Last week over dinner, a professor of politics asked me to explain the rise of neo-fundamentalism in the Islamic world. When I had finished Easterman's standard course on 'Everything you always wanted to know about Islamic revivalism but were afraid to ask', someone else (in this case a professor of psychology) remarked that he found the rise of Christian neo-fundamentalism much more disturbing. Today I read in my *Guardian* a report from Washington telling how a court in Greenville, Tennessee has ruled in favour of a fundamentalist Christian lobby which wants to have 'humanistic textbooks' removed from local schools. Even if the case goes to Washington, the chances are that right-wing Chief Justice Rehnquist will hand down a verdict backing the evangelicals. Frightened? I almost burned my Darwin.

It was no coincidence that the politics professor was the one concerned about Islamic fanaticism while it took the psychologist to identify a much more serious threat to every one of us round that cosy academic dinner table. In the West, Muslim fundamentalism is seen primarily through political spectacles: it affects oil prices, foreign policy, regional security. It can be an ugly business, especially when it erupts as terrorism or leads to the persecution of religious minorities, as in Iran. But the killings and burnings done in the name of resurgent Islam only serve to obscure the fact that what we term 'neo-fundamentalism' is really part of an ongoing expression of a religious culture that has held to the values of the Qur'an and religious law for fourteen centuries. Real Islamic fundamentalism is deeper, older and more enduring than the fanaticism that has used it as a front in the past decade.

Within the Islamic world, the Western values of rationality, liberalism, secular humanism or even nationalism were foreign importations that never penetrated deeper than the surface layer of a Western-educated ruling elite. For most Muslims in the modern period, Westernization has been a negative experience. Far from bringing an exhilarating liberation from the stagnation of a moribund culture, it has meant deep crises of identity in the face of a triumphant and generally insensitive West. For modern Muslims, 'fundamentalism' is a logical reaction against external rather than internal values. It is an assertion of the Islamic self-image, and in that sense it is genuinely fundamental to the society in which it is located. As a Western liberal, I may not like it, but I feel obliged to live with it as an essential element in the self-determination of a major segment of the human race.

Christian fundamentalism as typified by the 'Moral Majority' in the United States is a very different animal. Scientific rationalism, liberalism, religious toleration, social pluralism, feminism – all the things the Bible-thumpers of Hawkins County find so offensive – are essentially creations of Western civilization during the past few centuries. Other societies have fostered such values from time to time, of course – we have no monopoly on reason or tolerance or individualism – but they have become peculiarly characteristic of our own society in the modern era.

And that, I think, is why my colleague from psychology was so perturbed. The current wave of fundamentalism – with its bigotry, self-righteousness and widespread cant – is not a precise parallel to its Islamic counterpart. It is a powerful reminder of just how thin the veneer of rationality may be in any society. Some people simply cannot bear the strain of having to tolerate people unlike themselves and views unlike their own. In Hawkins County, they are condemning fairy tales and school texts that give credence to evolutionary theory. Homosexuality, feminism, non-Christian religions, even vegetarianism – all offend their so-called 'Christian' sensitivities.

And their greatest weapon is the very liberalism they despise so much, because they come to court as men and women whose deepest beliefs have been 'ridiculed' and offended by our open society. So accustomed are we to defend the rights of others – racial minorities against racism, women against male chauvinism, and, indeed, religious communities against bigotry – that we lose sight of an important difference in the case of religious fundamentalists (and, more recently, Muslims in the West calling for the banning of *The Satanic Verses*). They are not asking for the right to believe what they choose to believe or practise what they choose to practise – they have that right already. What they are demanding is that the courts should legislate to allow them to thrust their beliefs down the throats of the rest of us.

Given time and sufficient weakness on the part of the liberal establishment, it will not be long before the fundamentalist backlash begins to bring to the surface all the concealed irrationalities, fears and bigotries that lurk beneath the façade of Western society. From gays and vegetarians it is not such a big step to Jews, blacks, Asians . . . and anyone else the evangelical fancy may choose. Perhaps I am an alarmist. But the last time I said this sort of thing was in 1977. In Tehran.

(First published as 'The Fundamental
Business of Backlash and Bigotry' in the
Guardian, 15 December 1986)

Islamic Fundamentalism: Middle Eastern and Global Considerations

Following the first round of last year's presidential elections in France, the vice-president of the National Committee of Jewish Frenchmen – a Jewish group supporting the policies of the right-wing leader, Jean-Marie LePen – expressed his delight at the unexpected success of the National Front.

'There is no racial problem in France,' he stated. 'The problem is finding ways not to be destroyed by the rise of Islam . . . On the one hand, we have a Judaeo-Christian culture. On the other, we see a Muslim civilization based on the Koran and deformed by the rise of violent fundamentalism.'[1]

There is a particular irony in the fact that the above statement was made by a Jew who had just cast his vote for a neo-fascist presidential candidate in support of his expressed policy to expel all Arabs from French soil. One hears the obvious echoes: Graeco-Roman and Teutonic civilization threatened by the corruption of Jewish *untermenschen*, Christendom assaulted by the hordes of Saracen unbelievers, fish and chips ousted by mutton tikka and chicken chow mein.

But the greatest irony lies in the fact that there are other, less detectable echoes, echoes that we fail to hear because they are, as often as not, spoken in our own voices. Divest our anti-Islamic Frenchman of his right-wing credentials, and his words may strike more chords in liberal hearts than we may like to admit.

Most of us like to think that, Clause 28 apart, we have come a long way towards a more tolerant society. We know that racial and other forms of prejudice still exist, but they are more muted, less public than before. In fact, racial stereotyping is alive and well and living in the pages of our newspapers, on our

[1] *Guardian*, 26 April 1988, p. 8.

television and cinema screens, and in the foreign policies of our governments.

From popular films like *The Jewel of the Nile* or *Harem* to considered actions like the American bombing of Libya, our society acquiesces in a mindless and dangerous racism that puts our own liberal values seriously at risk. For Hollywood, Arabs are still rather dim and sex-crazed creatures dressed in army-surplus bed-linen. For Ronald Reagan – or do I mean Hollywood again? – they are all terrorists or 'mad dogs', and it doesn't really matter which ones you drop your bombs on.

Think of the stereotypes: Arabs as terrorists or oil-rich sheikhs, Iranians as crazed mullas and Hezbollahi thugs, Muslims in general as fanatics, Muslim clerics as obscurantists, Islam as a religion of hate. Oh, and just for good measure, Afghan mujahedeen as brave freedom fighters driving the atheistic commies out of their homeland to make way for God-fearing American advisers and Coca Cola.

Edward Said has analyzed in exquisite detail contemporary Western media treatment of Islam and Muslims in his incisive study, *Covering Islam* – a follow-up to his earlier, epoch-making analysis of orientalism. I have no intention of trying to repeat, much less to improve on what he has written there. But I commend his study to you.

Central to current perceptions of Islam – since roughly the outbreak of the Islamic Revolution in Iran, back in 1978 – has been the phenomenon of what is generally referred to as 'Islamic fundamentalism' or 'the resurgence of Islam' or 'the return to Islam'. Whereas Islam was portrayed throughout the last century and for much of this as backward, passive, decadent and in a state of permanent decline, the recent backlash against the West in Islamic countries has generated new images. Images of uncontrollable aggression, mindless fanaticism and consciously sustained irrationalism.

Muslims are no longer powerless and colourful denizens of our overseas colonies, but the inhabitants of independent nations made rich by the sale of oil, rendered powerful by their strategic position, and determined to reject or revalue the ideologies and systems of the once-dominant West. More terrible still, they – the Muslims – are here among us, building mosques on our street corners, sending veiled women out on shopping forays to our supermarkets, and painting indecipherable graffiti on the walls of our public lavatories and metro stations. And all of this – this ingratitude, this betrayal of what was never really a trust, this dreadful self-assertion – can, it seems, be laid at the door of something called 'Islamic fundamentalism' or, if you prefer, 'fundamentalist Islam'.

Understand 'Islamic fundamentalism' and you will have understood everything about the Islamic world today – that seems to be the new received wisdom. Unfortunately, like most concepts of the kind, Islamic fundamentalism turns out not to be so easily defined, controlled or understood as we would wish. This is not to say that there is not a phenomenon – of course, there is – just that it is far from as simple, as uniform, or as easily pigeonholed as the platitudes of our media would have us believe.

Said puts this problem very well:

> Far from being a uniform or even a coherent movement, 'the return to Islam' embodies a number of political actualities. For the United States it represents an image of disruption to be resisted at some times, encouraged at others. We speak of the anticommunist Saudi Muslims, of the valiant Muslim rebels of Afghanistan, of 'reasonable' Muslims like Sadat, the Saudi royal family, and Zia al-Haqq. Yet we also rail at Khomeini's Islamic militants and Qaddafi's Islamic 'Third Way', and in our morbid fascination with Islamic punishment (as administered by Khalkali) we paradoxically strengthen its power as an authority-maintaining device. In Egypt the Muslim Brotherhood, in Saudi Arabia the Muslim militants who took the Medina mosque, in Syria the Islamic Brotherhoods and Vanguards who oppose the Baath Party regime, in Iran the Islamic Mujahideen, as well as the Fedayeen and the liberals: these make up a small part of what is an adversarial current through the nation, although we know very little about it. In addition, the various Muslim nationalities whose identities have been blocked in various post-colonial states clamor for their Islam. And beneath all this – in madrasas, mosques, clubs, brotherhoods, guilds, parties, universities, movements, villages, and urban centers all through the Islamic world – surge still more varieties of Islam, many of them claiming to guide their members back to 'the true Islam'.[2]

---

[2] Edward W. Said, *Covering Islam*, London, Routledge & Kegan Paul, 1981, p. 60.

The term 'fundamentalism' itself creates more problems than it solves. Translation is always a thorny subject, especially when one moves into areas like philosophy or religion. It seems very easy, when speaking of an alien religion and culture like Islam, to use words and expressions from our own heritage, terms like 'orthodoxy' or 'church' or 'heresy' or 'clergy'. But try putting any of those words into Arabic or Persian or Turkish and see what happens.

'Fundamentalism' presents the same sort of difficulty. Originally, it refers to the belief that the Bible possesses complete infallibility as the revealed Word of God, the term being derived from a series of tracts, entitled *The Fundamentals*, published in the United States between 1909 and 1915. So how do we express that in Islamic terms? Well, we could start by reading 'Qur'an' for 'Bible' and go on from there. But that would not get us very far. Nobody in the Islamic world has ever seriously questioned that the Qur'an is the revealed Word of God, not even a radical breakaway group like the Baha'is. The infallibility of the Qur'an is not at issue.

Actually, when Muslim writers deal with what we so loosely term 'fundamentalism', they use a variety of related terms that carry very different connotations. Among these are *islah* ('reform' or 'reformism'), *tajdid* ('renewal', sometimes translated 'modernism'), *salafiyya* (the doctrine of returning to the ways of the first generation of Muslims, the Salaf), and *nahda* ('renaissance'). More recently, a different set of concepts has come into play: *takfir* (the pronouncement that someone or something is un-Islamic), *hijra* (the movement, both physical and mental, away from unbelief), and *da'wa* (the summoning of others to Islam or back to its proper implementation).

I do not propose to deal with any of these in detail. But you will see right away that there are real conceptual problems here. 'Reform' sounds far removed from what we have been led to expect from 'fundamentalism' or 'fanaticism' – and yet it often involves attitudes and practices that would seem positively reactionary from a liberal Western viewpoint.

Perhaps the worst thing about the term 'fundamentalism' is that it implies religious narrow-mindedness and little else. Certainly, the narrow-mindedness is there. But most radical Muslim writers are on to bigger issues – social and political questions that our own home-bred fundamentalists are only now waking up to.

The fact is that, throughout the Islamic world, religious revivalism is inextricably bound up with a whole host of other forces and demands: anti-imperialism, neo-nationalism, cultural assertiveness, class warfare, ecological and socialist responses to industrialization, and, above all, the simple search for a post-colonial identity.

But to say that Islam as a religion has become a vehicle for needs, values and discontents that are secular in origin is to miss the point and to misunderstand the true nature of Islamic movements for renewal. Modern Islamic writers have not just dreamed up a religio-social package out of nothing. To say that Islam is a comprehensive system for all human affairs from government to personal hygiene is no heretical innovation out of the bedtime ruminations of Imam Khomeini but a truism with its roots in the earliest period.

Ernest Gellner writes:

> Islam is the blueprint of a social order. It holds that a set of rules exists, eternal, divinely ordained, and independent of the will of men, which defines the proper ordering of society. . . . Thus there is in principle no call or justification for an internal separation of society into two parts, of which one would be closer to the deity than the other.

Reality has usually been at several removes from the ideal, but that has only encouraged louder and more vehement calls for a return to the imagined golden age of the original Islamic order, to the shining world of that 'first generation' of the Prophet and his companions.

Islamic idealism was for a long time fortified by the reality of Islamic success. God had not merely popped in for a visit: his hand was visible everywhere – in the success of Muslim arms, in the glories of Muslim civilization, in the vitality of the Muslim faith itself. History had become the handmaid of piety, and worldly success the seal of divine approval. There were setbacks, of course – the Crusades, the devastating Mongol invasions, the loss of Spain – but in general the idealists could feel confident of ultimate victory.

The eighteenth and nineteenth centuries changed all that. In the words of Wilfred Cantwell Smith:

> The fundamental malaise of modern Islam is a sense that something has gone wrong with Islamic history. The fundamental problem of modern Muslims is how to rehabilitate that history: to set it going again in full vigour, so that Islamic society may once again flourish as a divinely-guided society should and must. The fundamental spiritual crisis of Islam in the twentieth century stems from an awareness that something is awry between the religion which God has appointed and the historical development of the world which He controls.

Now, I suppose a lot of our own fundamentalists would say much the same thing: the world has turned away from God, the secular humanists have turned Christian societies into cesspits of vice and ungodliness, the time for a reckoning is at hand. But there is a radical difference, of course: the changes in our own society were not brought about by alien secularists working from outside to subvert the godly traditions of their ancestors (unless, of course, you subscribe to the thesis of Reds under every godfearing bed). Many of the great social advances of the modern West owed as much to Christian liberals as to freethinkers and humanists.

Not so in the Islamic world. There, the idealists could join forces (for a time at least) with even secular Marxists in denouncing the influence of the West in undermining the traditions and values of their own society. From the nineteenth century, the impact of the Western powers on the Islamic heartlands was devastating. Almost overnight, new forms of social organization, new values, new economic forces, new intellectual standards started to replace those of the past.

Western occupation and penetration of the Islamic world dealt a massive blow to the idealists. For reasons that had little or nothing to do with the spread of Western imperialism, the eighteenth and nineteenth centuries saw the rise of a number of powerful movements aiming at the wholesale Islamicization of society: Wahhabism in the Arabian Peninsula, the Sanusiyya and Tijaniyya in North Africa, Babism in Iran. But once the Western powers – notably France and Britain – came on the scene, the strength of traditional Islam was enormously weakened. Overnight, new forms of organization, new scales of values, new social forces started to replace those of the past.

Christian missions made little headway among Muslims. Islam was too well organized, too articulate – too civilized, if you like – to respond favourably to the missionary appeal. This meant that the impact of the West was secular rather than religious. But since, as we have noted, even secular matters came under religious aegis, changes in such areas deeply affected faith itself.

Thus, the introduction of Western law codes undermined the jurisdiction of the *shari'a* or religious law; new schools and universities based on Western models destroyed the monopoly of the clergy in education; the emancipation of women challenged a patriarchal system based on religious norms; the forcible conversion to Western dress (as in Turkey under Atatürk and Iran under Reza Shah) was seen as a direct attack on religious laws dictating proper clothing for a believer; modern banking methods outraged Islamic principles regarding usury.

There was no end to the ways in which Western penetration threatened the traditional values of Islamic society. When Atatürk banned religious orders or Reza Shah massacred members of the Shi'i clergy, the assault was direct. When universities instructed students in the methods of scientific enquiry, it was subtle and potentially more destructive. What was worse for many people was the fact that the severest attacks on religious values came, not from Westerners themselves, but from internal reformers who had adopted a Western outlook and espoused Western methods.

There was support for these changes, of course. Reform was needed in almost every area of life. But support meant imitation, and imitation meant passivity. Even some of the most ardent exponents of reform could see that something was wrong. Change was not merely improvement of the existing system, it was radical excision of the familiar and its replacement with the alien and the untried.

Secularization was rapid and profoundly out of pace with the heart of society. I do not wish to be misunderstood: nothing could please me more than to see society's total secularization. The problem is that you cannot force other people's pace. The process of secularizing Islamic societies has different connotations and different results from that of secularizing our own.

The secular world-view is part of our heritage: pressing for it alters but in no way distorts our social values. In the case of the Islamic world, however, secular values are still alien values, and pressure for them forms part of the implicit racism and chauvinism that inform so much of the colonial and post-colonial experience.

After early attempts to naturalize Western values, Islamic countries saw their cultures and traditions steadily eroded by foreign ideas and institutions. They responded by stressing a new-found nationalism, itself a cultural value imported wholesale from Europe. But nationalism went hand in hand with secularism and the continued pressure to conform to Western ways of thought. Arab nationalism, Turkish nationalism, Iranian nationalism, even the Islamic nationalism of Pakistan all proved powerless to stem the tide of Coca Cola, Levi's and Bananarama.

Those are trivial examples, of course. But even in those matters where our sympathies might lie with Westernization, the realities might give us pause. Take the case of women's emancipation. The veil is a vivid symbol of all that you and I detest. But listen to this anecdote from Malise Ruthven, describing an incident he once witnessed in Egypt:

> I myself once watched, with fascinated embarrassment, as a tall young woman, possibly American, bra-less and clad in a sleeveless shirt, wearing shorts which exposed the upper portions of her thighs, purchased some mangoes from a stallholder, a dignified young peasant clad in the traditional galabiya. This woman – I reflected – is sexually assaulting the man, though she may not realize it. Her garb was a systematic violation of all the sartorial codes governing male–female relations in traditional Islamic society. Only the extreme boorishness of super-power arrogance could produce such a display as this.

I do not wish to defend those criminals masquerading as defenders of morality who throw acid in the faces of unveiled women, or the perverted justice that pays half the compensation to an injured woman that it does to an injured man. Nor have I any desire to provide moral succour to those who see in the West and its values nothing but unmitigated evil and who do whatever they can to eradicate all forms of Western influence without distinction. But I do not see how the promotion of Western ideals can be furthered by insensitivity or arrogance.

I have no doubt that we stand on the verge of a new ideological struggle of considerable complexity. That the West and Islam are set on a collision course is manifest. But neither 'the West' nor 'Islam' are homogeneous. We have our home-bred fundamentalists, they their secularists. Increasingly large numbers of Westerners live and work in Muslim countries, more and more Muslims have made their homes in Europe and North America. It seems to me inevitable that all these strands will, in some measure, exert influences one on another. In the end, new cultures will emerge, both here and in the Middle East. If we can be said to have a duty as secularists, it must be to work for conditions under which these changes may take place with the least friction and the minimum of violence.

(Originally delivered as a lecture at the South Place Ethical Society on 22 May 1988, with additional material from an article published in the *New Humanist*, 102:3, 1987, pp.6–7)

What is Fundamental to Islam?

All societies resist change. Change of any kind, whether good or bad, it makes no difference, since goodness or badness may be determined only after the event. Change is, by definition, undesirable, inasmuch as it forces the individual or the group to meet the unknown head-on. Better to stick with what we know than trust ourselves to the untried and untested. And yet all societies, like all individuals, must undergo some measure of flux, whether they like it or not.

Some societies, like some individuals, have been more successful than others in their ability or their determination to resist the shock of the new, whether introduced from without or advocated from within: Confucian China, with its formalized structures of learning and government; Tokugawa Japan, with its enforced seclusion of the country from all contact with foreigners; lamaistic Tibet, remote, virtually impregnable to outsiders, ruled by priest-kings deemed reincarnations of their predecessors, the past returning, as it were, in each generation to impose the most thoroughgoing conservatism on all aspects of life; twentieth-century Oman, with its restrictions on travel and its bans on medicine, radios, music, dancing, spectacles, trousers, cigarettes and books.

But for the fiercest resistance to the new, one need look no further than religion. Small religious communities in particular have been among the most successful in resisting change – Hassidic Jews, Mennonites, Shakers, Amish and any number of monastic orders have retained the dress, the lifestyle, the techniques and even the language of former generations. Such communities are, in effect, living museums, achieving almost thoughtlessly what the designers of Beamish and the Jorvik Centre have only dreamed of. The Amish do not change their wide-brimmed hats for baseball caps at the weekend, nor do Franciscan monks go home to watch 'Dallas' at the end of the working day. These people are living in the past as much as it is possible for any human being to do.

Religious sects and orders have an extraordinary ability – and a pressing need – to fossilize parts of their past. Language in particular, normally so vulnerable to change, becomes a realm set apart and dedicated to an extreme conservatism. Witness the preservation of the Latin liturgy in the Catholic Church; the use of Coptic prayers by Arabic-speaking Christians in Egypt or Syriac by the Syrian Church; and the preservation of ancient Pahlavi in the Zoroastrian ritual of Iran and India.

For all that, there can be no better example of linguistic conservatism than the extraordinary conservation of seventh-century Arabic. The Arabic of the Qur'an has not merely been preserved – it is virtually identical with the language of modern novels and newspapers. If you have ever struggled with Sweet's Anglo-Saxon Grammar or ploughed your weary way through *Beowulf*, you will know just how much English has changed in that same period. Or French. Or German. Or almost any language you care to name. But a basic course in what is generally termed Modern Literary Arabic will enable a beginner, with little extra effort, to read the Qur'an itself.

Unlike the Vedas or the Avesta, the sacred text of Islam has not been preserved in aspic, recited and studied only by a specialized elite. All Muslim children are taught its recitation from an early age. Many learn it by heart. And any modern Arab hearing it recited can, in large measure, understand it. It is the language, not the book, that has been preserved.

Few religions have confronted the problem of change so passionately or with so much anguish as Islam. Judaism is the only other great example. The reason is simple enough. As I have explained more than once in these pages, Islam is not just a religion, but an all-embracing way of life. It has always been possible, for example, for Christians to adapt their secular behaviour without necessarily modifying their religious beliefs or rituals, or feeling that, in so doing, they have somehow compromised their faith. Equally, it has been possible for tiny communities to preserve an entire mode of life, religious and secular together – but at the high cost of isolation from the world at large.

For the majority of Muslims, neither of these options has ever been viable. True, some Islamic societies like Oman, Yemen or Saudi Arabia have, in varying degrees, tried to barricade themselves against the modern world by means of a self-imposed quarantine; but in the end such tactics have proved impotent against commercial, diplomatic and military forces that have brought the world not only to the doorstep of such enclaves, but inside their very walls. The recent war in the Gulf illustrated this more vividly than any other single event since Francis Younghusband's famous expedition carried modern rifles to Tibet in 1904.

Islam rests upon an understanding of what is and what is not *sunna*, that is to say, of what follows or does not follow the code of behaviour laid down – supposedly – by the very first Muslim community, a community built and guided by the Prophet himself. Innovation – *bid'a* – is the nearest thing to our Western notion of heresy, for to innovate is, by definition, to depart from what is *sunna*. 'Whoso introduces into our cause things not already belonging to it is an apostate,' announces one saying attributed to the Prophet. Another states that 'the most truthful communication is the Book of God, the best guidance is that of Muhammad, and the worst of all things are innovations: every innovation is heresy, every heresy is error, and every error leads to hell'.

I have argued that 'fundamentalism' is not a term that may easily be translated into any Islamic language – not, at least, to cover the kinds of activities normally defined as fundamentalist. 'Reform', 'renewal', 'renaissance' are, as we have seen, much closer to the terminology actually used by 'fundamentalist' Muslims themselves. Unfortunately, using such terms only confuses things further. We are not dealing here with a religious reformation in the European sense. Far otherwise.

It is not, argue the new thinkers of Islam, that the faith has grown out of touch with the times and is in need of an overhaul. The times have nothing to do with it: God's revelation is not moulded to fit the changing patterns and fluctuating whims of human behaviour. Quite the reverse.

Islam itself is not, its followers believe, a new faith, even though Muhammad is the latest of God's messengers and the Qur'an the most recent of His books. There has always been a religion of

Islam, from the time of Adam to the present day: 'We believe in God, and in what has been revealed to us and revealed to Abraham, Ishmael, Isaac and Jacob, and to the Tribes of Israel, and what was given to Moses and Jesus and the Prophets by their Lord.' In the figure of Abraham, the Qur'an discovers a purity of faith later distorted by Jewish and Christian divines: 'Abraham was, in truth, not a Jew, nor was he a Christian. But he was a Muslim, a man of pure faith.' It is this pure faith, this *islam* or submission to God, that has been repeatedly revealed to men and as often corrupted by them.

The final revelation took place with the appearance of Muhammad, through whom the ancient faith was sent down in its perfect form. And it is precisely here that the crisis of Islam may be said to have its roots. For, if Muhammad did indeed bring the eternal faith, purified from dross, sent down straight from heaven in its final, absolute and unalterable form, what on earth are we to make of the obvious falling away that there has been since then, the manifest failure of God's last community to withstand the forces of corruption, pride and faithlessness?

This question – or some variation on it – has plagued Muslims since the earliest period. With Muhammad's death, the Islamic community quickly fell to bickering and worse. Muslims died at the hands of Muslims. The Prophet's grandson Husayn was waylaid, surrounded and beheaded by forces sent by the ruling Caliph. God's perfect society was militarily successful, but internally divided and morally bankrupt.

Pace the Baha'is and Ahmadis, Islam leaves no opening for a fresh revelation of God's truth – all are, at least, agreed on that. Even to contemplate such a reopening is to be guilty of the most flagrant heresy. Muhammad was the 'Last of the Prophets', the *khatam al-anbiya*'. 'There shall be no prophet after me,' he is said to have declared, and his followers have for centuries sought to live with the consequences of that finality.

If there are to be no more prophets, if there can be no further inspiration from on high (and I leave aside here the more complicated positions of Shi'ites and the Sufis), what is to be done with a faith no longer in its pristine (and rather short-lived) purity and with a community so much fallen by the wayside?

The answer is simple, in the preaching if not the practice: bring the community back to its roots, return the feet of the believers to the path laid down by the Prophet, reinvent the wheel of the law. There is a prophetic saying which states that, in every age, God will send learned men to purify the faith from corruption. Each century has, by convention, had its *mujaddid*, its renewer of the faith – even if there has often been disagreement as to his identity.

New demands, new circumstances do not call for the modification of Islam, but rather for the reassertion of its basic values and the proper implementation of its ordinances – for a return to the *sunna*. That, in grossly simplified form, is what every Muslim reformer since the last century has sought to achieve. That is what modern 'fundamentalism' is all about.

Misleading though it is in some respects, the term 'fundamentalism' is not wholly inappropriate to Islam. There are in mainstream Islam three recognized fundamentals of the faith – *usul al-din* – namely, the oneness of God, prophethood and resurrection. There is, however, nothing particularly Islamic about these, not, at least, until they are defined and explicated. Judaism and Christianity between them embrace all three concepts as fully as Islam, even though their emphases are necessarily different. What marks off Islam is not so much the emphasis on God's oneness as its opposition to *shirk* – any belief or activity that may compromise that oneness. Modern fundamentalism has little enough to say about prophethood or resurrection, but its writers turn again and again to the question of God's singleness and the need to protect it from all taints of association.

The Japanese writer Toshihiko Izutsu speaks of the 'grand moral dichotomy' of the Qur'an, a dichotomy rooted in a division of the world between belief and unbelief, between the proclamation of God's oneness and denial of it. Belief in God, in a single, transcendent God, is, for the Qur'an, the yardstick by which all things and all actions are weighed in the balance. From this basic, irreducible dichotomy follow a series of lesser, but none the less vital, secondary dichotomies, of which three are central to any understanding of what Islam is about: knowledge and ignorance, guidance and error, and the division already mentioned, *sunna* and heretical innovation.

Knowledge lies at the very heart of Islam. True knowledge, God-given knowledge, knowledge of right and wrong. There is no legend of a Tree of the knowledge of good and evil, no serpentiform tempter, no apple, no fall from grace. According to Franz Rosenthal, 'Knowledge *is* Islam.' Without the knowledge God sends down via His prophets and His books, men would live in a state of ignorance, mere animals devoid of reason or goodness, forever deprived of the hope of the Beatific vision.

Originally, the term *jahiliyya* was used to designate the age of barbarism in which the Arabs dwelt before the coming of Islam. In recent fundamentalist writing, however, the concept has been expanded and brought forward to refer to anything that lies outside the sphere of true Islam-centred knowledge, as revealed in the Qur'an and the Prophetic Traditions. Radical Egyptian Muslims, including the Islamicist militants responsible for the assassination of Sadat and related cliques known collectively as the *jama'at islamiyya*, followed their martyred mentor Sayyid Qutb (d. 1966) in describing the state as a *jahili* state. To be *jahili* is to be barbarian, non-Islamic, unredeemed. All sciences, art, literature or entertainment, all pursuits or images or thoughts that are not Islamic, that are not founded in the Qur'an and rooted fast in the *sunna* (here meaning the recorded deeds and words of the Prophet that define what is proper) belong, by definition, to the realm of *al-jahiliyya*. Whatever is *jahili* must be shunned, condemned and, if possible, destroyed.

Qutb writes in *Ma'alim fi'l-tariq*:

> Nowadays, the entire world lives in a state of *jahiliyya* as far as the source from which it draws the rules of its mode of existence is concerned, a *jahiliyya* that is not changed one whit by material comfort and scientific inventions ... Any society that is not Muslim is *jahiliyya* ... as is any society in which something other than God alone is worshipped ... Thus, we must include in this category all the societies that now exist on earth.[1]

In speaking of Islam and *jahiliyya* in these terms, Sayyid Qutb and his imitators were simply reviving and intensifying an earlier conceptualization of the way in which the world is divided. Traditional theory, basing itself on the Qur'anic dichotomy between belief and unbelief, cut the world plainly into two realms: the Realm (or House) of Islam (*Dar al-Islam*) and the Realm of

---

[1] Quoted by Gilles Kepel, *The Prophet and Pharaoh*, trans. Jon Rothschild, al Saqi Books, London, 1985, pp. 44, 47.

Unbelief (*Dar al-Kufr*) or Realm of War (*Dar al-Harb*). Some modernists, faced with what was to them an impossible dilemma of living in a state whose rulers had betrayed the faith and let the Realm of Islam sink back into the condition of pre-Islamic barbarism, opted to take themselves and their followers bodily out of *jahili* society. Thus were born several extremist groups in Egypt, including the celebrated Society of Muslims, better known as *Takfir wa Hijra*.

This movement earned its popular name by the emphasis its followers placed on two related imperatives – that of declaring the society around it part of the Realm of Unbelief (a declaration known as *takfir*) and that of retreating from that realm to an enclave of true Islamicity. *Takfir* literally means 'to pronounce someone an unbeliever', and its use comes very close to that of excommunication in Christianity. Beginning with rulers who had, they believed, passed outside the bounds of belief, extremist members of the Muslim Brotherhood came to condemn the masses as unbelievers, on account of their obedience to apostates.

Retreat from unbelief is known in Arabic as *hijra*, roughly translatable as 'emigration'. *Hijra* is a central Islamic concept in its own right. When, in the year 622, the Prophet abandoned his native Mecca (whose inhabitants had, save for a few, rejected his message) and travelled with his followers to the more receptive climate of neighbouring Yathrib (later Medina), they performed a *hijra*. Later, this act of emigration, this elected separation from unbelief, became the moment from which the Islamic era would be dated.

The importance of the *hijra* and its close relationship to the dichotomies of belief and unbelief, knowledge and ignorance, cannot be stressed too much. By leaving Mecca and its pagan clans behind, Muhammad brought himself to a town where he could organize his new religion without interference. Within a short period he had become the ruler of Yathrib (henceforth Madinat al-Nabi, the City of the Prophet), and by his death ten years after the *hijra* he had established the first Islamic state on a firm footing.

To fundamentalists, the act of *hijra* is one that must be re-enacted throughout Islamic history until the day when a true Muslim state can be established throughout the world and the believers united in a single *umma*, a homogeneous community of faith and divinely sanctioned action. Whether this act of emigration be external (as in the cases of the Egyptian group above, whose members withdrew to small communes in Cairo and other cities, or the Wahhabi Ikhwan of early twentieth-century Arabia, who established *hijra* encampments in the desert) or internal (by inward acts of withdrawal from the values and practices of the world), it is an essential part of the modern Muslim experience, above all in areas where believers live in the heart of unbelief – here in Europe, for example, or in Islamic states thought to have gone bad.

Jahiliyya (barbarism) and *jahl* (ignorance), both derived from the same Arabic root (*j h l*) are related semantically to another root, *j w l*, which has connotations of wandering, of going round in circles. *'Ilm* or knowledge comes from the same root as *'alam*, a signpost. To possess right knowledge is to know the way, to follow the straight path, to be guided in the trackless desert of the world. Terms for guidance, pathways, or roads are among the most common and important in Islamic religious writing.

Sunna, the code of proper behaviour (and the basis for the term Sunni), actually means a beaten track laid down by one's ancestors. *Shari'a*, the term for the revealed law, comes from a root conveying the idea of an open road. A school of religious law or theology is a *madhhab* a 'way'. Sufi orders are *tariqat* or 'paths', their heads *murshids* or 'guides'. Throughout the Qur'an, close links are forged between the book (in which God's message is revealed), the guidance it contains, and sure knowledge. The unbelievers, the people of ignorance, are led astray by their passions, whereas the believers are on a straight path: 'those who have surrendered [i.e. become Muslims] have chosen the right way'.

Why are guidance and knowledge so central to the Islamic world-view? What about grace? What of love? Just as Islam has no concept of original sin, so it has no need for vicarious sacrifice to redeem men. God demands nothing more from His creatures than that they acknowledge their belief in His singleness and in the mission of His Prophet, and that they follow, singly and communally, the laws and ordinances He has given them. To do all this, however imperfectly, is to be assured of salvation.

The crucial thing here is the individual's responsibility to obey the *shari'a*. The burden of the law is meaningless if men are not informed of it. Hence the need for knowledge of what is right and wrong, for guidance to the open road of the law, with its clearly marked signposts and warning signs, for a divine proof that all these things are true. For Sunni Muslims, the Qur'an is God's proof, its verses 'signs' for the discerning. For Shi'ites, the proof is the Imam, an individual descended from the Prophet and endowed with superhuman faculties.

It is, I think, in the realm of knowledge that the modern world poses its greatest threat to Islam, a threat that has not gone unrecognized by Muslim theorists. The greatness of the modern West lies less in its superior scientific and technological knowledge than in the way that knowledge has been acquired and developed. Its roots are in the spirit of scientific scepticism, in the institutionalization of the right to question received wisdom, from the laws of physics to the regulations of the state or the dogmas of the established church.

Western man has for several centuries now doubted and questioned everything, but far from growing weaker as a result, his civilization has – materially, at least – gone from strength to strength. Much modern Muslim writing tries to play down the triumph of the West by emphasizing the dark side of the European and North American experience, the inner angst of a bankrupt civilization on the verge of collapse. The problem is that Islam itself is peculiarly vulnerable on this score. There is very little point in sneering at the material success of others if at the same time one measures one's own achievements by precisely the same criteria: the unprecedented triumph of Muslim arms, the glories of the Abbasid, Andalusian or Mughal empires, the scientific advances of the Islamic Middle Ages, the contribution of Islam to the arts and sciences of Western Europe from the time of the Crusades.

So here is a thorny dilemma indeed. Knowledge acquired through doubt has proved more powerful in creating material prosperity than revealed knowledge or divine guidance. Muslims may possess the true scripture and an exact index of God's will in all its detail, but they can still be brought low by unbelievers – those very unbelievers whose abasement at the hands of Islam was once a proof that God was on the Muslim side. That is not the way things are supposed to work.

One of the chief responses to this dilemma – and one that is destined, I believe, to have dire consequences for any revival of Islamic civilization in the future – has been the advocacy of the Islamization of knowledge in the curricula of all Muslim schools, colleges and universities. 'Islamic universities' have been established in a number of countries, conferences have been held at assorted venues, and there are journals such as *Muslim Education, Islamic Science* and *The American Journal of Islamic Social Sciences* in which the process of Islamization is regularly discussed. The new model of Islamic education 'seeks to impart knowledge, not only about the traditional religious sciences but also about social and natural sciences within an Islamic framework' and 'aims at teaching all the modern sciences within an Islamic perspective'.

All sorts of proposals have been made, and many implemented in countries like Iran and Saudi Arabia, to ensure that the sciences are taught in a manner that is in strict conformity with the revealed (and, by implication, superior) knowledge of the Quranic text. Particular emphasis has been placed on Islamizing the social sciences, for it is here that 'western scholarship has succeeded in making the furthest inroads into the Muslim mind'. As one Muslim writer expresses it: 'Western treatment of history, anthropology, political science, philosophy, psychology, sociology and economics has done more damage to the Islamic identity and character of Muslim society than other science.'[2]

The implications of such an approach are simply delineated in the following passage from the author just quoted:

> Whereas a Muslim sociologist must learn modern methods to study and analyse the evolutionary cultural modes and behavioural patterns of a given society, he should not necessarily accept western methodologies. To give a concrete example, he must learn and benefit from the methods of conducting different kinds of surveys – sample statistical and door-to-door – to collect reliable data on any given problem, but the criteria and methodology to analyse the data and make deductions will have to be evolved by the Muslim sociologist in the light of the Muslim umma [community] and the values laid down by the Qur'an and the Sunnah.[3]

[2] S. M. Zaman, 'Islamization and Strategies for Change', in Abdullah Omar Naseef (ed.), *Today's Problems, Tomorrow's Solutions*, Marsell, London and New York, 1988, p. 64.
[3] Ibid., p. 65.

To appreciate the force of that proposal, simply substitute 'Church' for 'umma', 'Bible' for 'Qur'an', and 'sound doctrine' for 'Sunnah'.

My reservations about this whole approach are ample. They are based on a broadly Popperian understanding of scientific method. Popper would see the fallacy in this argument at a glance. The problem is that of misleading answers to the question 'where does our knowledge come from?' Islam, as an authoritarian system, is more concerned with the legitimacy of the sources of knowledge than with the quality of the knowledge itself.

In Popper's words:

The traditional systems of epistemology may be said to result from yes-answers or no-answers to questions about the sources of our knowledge. *They never challenge these questions, or dispute their legitimacy*, the questions are taken as perfectly natural, and nobody seems to see any harm in them.

This is quite interesting, for these questions are clearly authoritarian in spirit. They can be compared with that traditional question of political theory, 'Who should rule?', which begs for an authoritarian answer such as 'the best', or 'the wisest', or 'the people', or 'the majority' ... This political question is wrongly put and the answers which it elicits are paradoxical ... It should be replaced by a completely different question such as *'How can we organize our political institutions so that bad or incompetent rulers ... cannot do too much damage?'*

The question about the sources of our knowledge can be replaced in a similar way. It has always been asked in the spirit of: 'What are the best sources of our knowledge – the most reliable ones, those which will not lead us into error, and those to which we can and must turn, in case of doubt, as the last court of appeal?' I propose to assume, instead, that no such ideal sources exist – no more than ideal rulers – and that *all* 'sources' are liable to lead us into error at times. And I propose to replace, therefore, the question of the sources of our knowledge by the entirely different question: *'How can we hope to detect and eliminate error?'*

The question of the sources of our knowledge, like so many authoritarian questions, is a *genetic* one. It asks for the origin of our knowledge, in the belief that knowledge may legitimize itself by its pedigree. The nobility of the racially pure knowledge, the untainted knowledge, the knowledge which derives from the highest authority, if possible from God; these are the (often unconscious) metaphysical ideas behind the question. My modified question, 'How can we hope to detect error?' may be said to derive from the view that such pure, untainted and certain sources do not exist, and that questions of origin or of purity should not be confounded with questions of validity, or of truth.[4]

Lest this lengthy quotation seem something of a distraction from our theme, I would draw the reader's attention to the fact that Islam has laid a peculiar stress on the genetic character of knowledge. There is, first of all, the miraculous nature of the Quranic text, a 'reading' taken by the Archangel Gabriel from a heavenly tablet co-eternal with God and transmitted verbatim to mankind through the mouthpiece of the Prophet.

It has been suggested by more than one Christian writer that the doctrine of the origin of the Qur'an presents a close parallel to the Christian doctrine of the Virgin Birth. Like Mary, Muhammad is deemed to have been a virgin: not sexually, but intellectually, in that he was *ummi*, 'unlettered' and yet gave birth to a book. It is critical to the whole temper of Islamic epistemology that he be deemed never to have tampered in the slightest way with the pristine Word of God as represented in the Qur'an as we now possess it. That is why the original 'Satanic Verses' story – that Muhammad had inadvertently allowed Satan to interpolate words of his own into the divine text – was such a hot potato, and why Salman Rushdie's reworking of it touched such a raw nerve.

But this genetic quality of Islamic knowledge does not stop with the Qur'an. In the first centuries of Islam, when collections were gradually being made of the *ahadith* or stories relating the words and doings of the Prophet, the chief criterion for the acceptance or rejection of any given narration was its genetic purity. Chains of narrators were drawn up – X was told by Y that Y's father had told him that, when he was a boy, Z had related to him that he had heard from his grandfather that the Prophet had said . . . – and subjected to the closest scrutiny. The canonical texts of these traditions, once established, were regarded as assured by the purity of the chains that linked them, through three or more generations, to the Prophet and his companions.

When, therefore, we are told that a Muslim sociologist must

---

[4] Karl Popper, 'Sources of Knowledge and Ignorance', in *Conjectures and Refutations: The Growth of Scientific Knowledge*, 4th (rev.) edn., Routledge, London and Henley, 1972, pp. 25–6.

have recourse, in the final instance, to 'the values laid down by the Qur'an and the Sunnah' (where 'Sunnah' is used for 'Prophetic Traditions'), we are, in effect, instructed that human knowledge, however gained, must be subjected to the approval or disapproval of knowledge gained from purer sources. Trust in an infallible source of knowledge is placed before the demands of scepticism (or what Popper calls 'critical rationalism') in the face of facts as they present themselves in research.

The point I am trying to make here is that any attempt to place a theological straitjacket on learning in the Islamic world must end in disaster. Science does not advance through replication of the known, but by the inculcation of a spirit of free, iconoclastic and deliberate enquiry underpinned by doubt at every turn. 'Normal science' (to use Thomas Kuhn's phrase for the day-to-day operation of science within a particular paradigm) may get on well enough by working with a fairly fixed set of 'laws' and 'facts'; but breakthroughs, particularly major ones that replace one paradigm with another, come about as a result of hard questioning of established wisdom.

Tragically, religious fundamentalism and scientific orthodoxy have much in common. This makes it the more possible that an Islam desperate for moral and intellectual certainty, in what it sees as a quagmire of sceptical confusion, will opt for precisely the kind of scientific and general education that is least likely to lead to any radical exploration of new ideas or the abandonment of fixed prejudices. Provided Western educational systems are not further eroded by politically motivated attempts to undermine their tradition of free enquiry and the unrestricted questioning of authority,[5] we are likely to go on fostering precisely the sort of intellectual climate in which fresh ideas will flourish and radical advances be made. 'Islamic science', by contrast, may in time

[5] There are currently two chief threats to the autonomy of academic enquiry in Europe and North America. The first comes from right-wing attempts to restrict academic freedom by abolishing tenure within universities and by making financial viability the sole criterion of the value of research. The second comes from no less disturbing attempts by groups on the left to insist that the content of syllabi be 'politically correct', replacing 'white, male, Western' texts and ideas with works by non-white, female representatives of other cultures regardless of their real significance in history as a whole.

become synonymous with stagnation, acceptance of authority, and imitation – exactly as happened to Islamic philosophy and science generally after about the twelfth century. Should that prove to be the case, it is hard to see how Muslims are ever to break free of their current dilemma.

One way out – and one widely anticipated by fundamentalist writers – is through the apocalyptic scenario of a wholesale breakdown in Western civilization. This may not be an unrealistic hope, but it is one rooted more in hatred of an old rival and a wish to see him get sand kicked in his face than in any very genuine desire to see civilization itself preserved. It is a negative hope, and one more likely to be disappointed than realized.

Even if the modern West collapses – as all civilizations must – there is no guarantee that Islam will rise above the ashes to inherit the earth. It is all the more likely that, rather than undergo an apocalyptic disaster, Western civilization will evolve into a more broadly-based international civilization to which the Far East in particular will make important contributions. Rather than seeking the revival of an outdated civilizational model, Muslims must, if they are to play any meaningful role in this new international culture, abandon all notions of superiority and the ultimate Islamization of mankind.

In the extract quoted above, Popper made an interesting transition from authoritarian questions about the ideal ruler to questions about the sources of knowledge. It is well worth reversing that transition, to see how Islam has posed questions about knowledge in terms of questions about the leadership of the community.

In order to receive pure knowledge of how to conduct one's relations with God or with one's fellow men, it is deemed essential, as we have seen, to have recourse to a pure source. But in Islamic doctrine, the role of a prophet does not end with the revelation of God's word. Prophets also bring laws and the framework for social organization. They establish *ummas* or religio-political communities as matrixes in which God's will may be performed.

Ahistorical though this may be in the cases of Abraham, Moses or Jesus, there is no doubt that Muhammad did create a small theocratic state which, by the time of his death, extended far through the Arabian peninsula and was on the verge of expanding its borders beyond it – as, indeed, it did within not many decades. Muhammad's death presented this nascent state with a major crisis, for much uncertainty existed as to how he wished his community to be led after him.

There is no need to enter here into the massive complications to which this single crisis led. The simple fact is that the Muslim community split along what were at first purely political lines, laying the basis for the numerous sectarian divisions that plagued its early centuries. One party argued for the succession of the Prophet's son-in-law and cousin 'Ali, seeking in a pure blood-line a resolution of the question of who was best suited to rule. This eventually developed into the broad movement of the Shi'a, whose mainstream stressed not only the right of the descendants of the Prophet to political rule, but their close contact with God, whereby they possessed direct access to divine knowledge.

The Shi'a termed their claimants Imams, that is, the ones who precede others on the path. In Shi'ite literature, they are explicitly described as 'guides', as 'gates', and even as direct paths to God. The Sunnis, for their part, named the first of their leaders 'the rightly-guided Caliphs', men who, though they may not have received direct inspiration from God, were none the less guided by him in their direction of the community.

Themes of knowledge, guidance and leadership thus combine in Islam in the search for the ideal ruler. This longing for leadership rooted in the two chief preoccupations of the faith reached its apogee in the political theorizing of Imam Khomeini, above all in his best-known book, *Wilayat al-faqih* (*Government of the Jurist*). The clergy or *ulama* (literally, 'knowers') have received particular attention in Shi'ite theory as heirs of the Imams and the repositories of their wisdom and knowledge. Khomeini carried several centuries of theorizing to their logical conclusion by arguing that only the *ulama* could prove the rightful rulers of an Islamic state, whose constitution would be the Qur'an and *sunna*.

Although Sunni Islam has never granted its clergy the status awarded the Shi'ite *ulama*, one of the chief requirements in Muslim rulers, whether Caliphs or ordinary kings, has been that they ensure the preservation of proper religious knowledge and the implementation of the religious law. In the modern period, it has been precisely the failure of rulers like Muhammad Shah,

Sadat or Atatürk to implement the *shariʿa* or to protect the religious establishment that has led to their condemnation by fundamentalist writers.

And this is precisely where Islamic radicalism, in its desire to link the government of a modern state with control over the sources of knowledge, presents the most serious threat to a successful resolution of the problem of adjustment to the modern world. It is extremely difficult in the modern world to contain knowledge within approved channels. Governments everywhere try to do just that, of course, not least within the Muslim world, but their task grows more and more difficult with every advance in modern communications. Satellite television, fax machines, videos and computers have all, in their way, revolutionized access to ideas and information. The potential in such technologies was recognized by the Shiʿite radicals who distributed cassette tapes of the exiled Khomeini through Iran in the days before the revolution.

If sermons can be taped and videoed, so can the lectures of secularists. The entire text of *The Satanic Verses* would fit snugly on to a few microfiches or a compact disc.

This argument cuts both ways, of course, and I am deeply conscious of that fact. As I have proposed elsewhere, modern technology makes possible a degree of social and intellectual control that was only dreamed of by the fundamentalists of the past. Borders can be closed and wavelengths jammed, telephones tapped and, for all I know, computer modems deactivated. But to say that is to return us to where we began, to the closed societies of Tibet and Oman. The real challenge to Islam, in a changing world, is not whether it can shut itself up again in a physical, intellectual and spiritual box, but whether it is capable of undergoing positive, thoughtful and meaningful change both within its heart and in its relations with the rest of mankind.

The Boundaries of Faith and Ignorance

In the course of a recent interview, the Aqa Khan told the Pakistani author, Akbar Ahmed, currently visiting professor at Selwyn College, Cambridge:

> Islam remains undeveloped in Western education and there-fore not understood. 'They teach about Judaism, they teach Christianity, but they don't teach Islam. There's hardly a Western country I know of where the primary or secondary education has Islam as an ongoing offering to students.' The same applies to the centres of higher learning . . .[1]

The Aqa Khan, we are told, is worried that the Western media 'tend to depict Muslims negatively'. He believes that the West cannot afford to ignore Islam: 'With Islam encompassing such a large area of the world with significant populations, Western society can no longer survive in its own interest by being ill-informed or misinformed about the Islamic world . . . There is [what] I would call a "knowledge vacuum". It is hurting everyone.'

Why does Professor Ahmed, a scholar of wide experience and no little insight, peddle such nonsense? Why does he, like an increasing number of Muslim writers, seem to think that the answer to ignorance about Islam is the perpetuation of further ignorance about the West? For many years now, Islam, along with other religions, has featured in the educational curricula of most Western countries. In Britain, Islamic studies form part of GCSE and A-level Religious Studies courses. In higher education, Islam may be studied in numerous institutions in the context of

[1] *Guardian*, 8 August 1991, p.17.

Religious Studies, Middle East Studies or in its own right. We could have more, of course we could, but it is misleading in the extreme to suggest that Islam is not or cannot be studied in the West.

Is it really surprising that children here are taught more about the Old and New Testaments than they are about the Qur'an or the Bhagavad Gita, given the central role of the Bible and Christianity in forming Western culture? Knowledge of the Qur'an and other holy books is important, and I would never suggest otherwise; but it would be ludicrous to give them an educational role equal to texts that have coloured European thought for almost two millennia. This is not the same as suggesting that children should be indoctrinated in the beliefs of Christianity – or, for that matter, any other religion – merely to recognize the unique cultural influence in the West of Jewish and Christian images, values and institutions.

Exactly the same thing happens in the Islamic world, where Islam is, frankly, even more central to school and university curricula than Christianity here. Indeed, I cannot think of anywhere in the Muslim East where Christianity or Judaism can be studied in their own right or in anything but the form given them in the Qur'an and Islamic tradition. Where are the centres for Jewish and Christian Studies in Islamic universities? In how many Muslim schools is the Bible studied? In how many Muslim countries can it even be bought openly?

The output of serious academic publications about Islam has grown in the West to the dimensions of a small industry. The same cannot be said for serious work on Western religion within Islam. Looking through the catalogue of a large and respectable Arabic-language bookseller and publisher, almost the only works on Judaism and Christianity I can find have titles like: 'A Refutation of Judaism and Christianity', 'Today's Jews are not Jews', 'The Threat of World Jewry', or 'A Refutation of the Torah'.

Ignorance about the West and Christianity, virulent anti-Semitism, and general cultural myopia are as much dangers in the Islamic world as misconceptions about Islam are in the West. We, at least, are more conscious of our ignorance than we were. What would help enormously is for Muslim leaders and writers to stop carping about how misunderstood they are and to confront with greater honesty the fact that there is ignorance on both sides. If there is a 'knowledge vacuum', it exists there as well as here.

What started as a legitimate and necessary exercise in cultural criticism – the identification of Western myths about Islam under the heading of 'orientalism' – has now become a one-sided tirade, in which Westerners are permanently assigned the roles of myth-makers, plotters, bigots and crusaders. Islam is always misunderstood, the West always misunderstands. Muslims are always misrepresented, Westerners are ever portrayed as conscious manipulators of the lives and destinies of others. There is no middle ground, no meeting place where both sides may admit their errors and progress to new levels of mutual understanding. In the end, the growing obsession with how Muslims and Islam are seen by outsiders and the parallel failure to admit, even to see, that Muslims are themselves makers of myths and wilful distorters of facts, is likely to prove a greater obstacle to Western understanding of Islam than orientalism ever was or is.

This concern with 'correct' representations of Islamic religion and culture in the Western media and academia is mirrored by a growing movement of cultural fascism in the United States, led by activists known as 'politically correct persons' or PCPs. A major debate has broken out in American universities following attempts by PCPs to purify the curricula of arts faculties by replacing classical texts (the works of 'dead white males') with 'multicultural' material drawn from the writings of blacks, gays, women and others – often without regard to the wider cultural or historical significance of the texts in question. Their opponents have described the PCPs as 'the cultural left' and 'the new fundamentalists', and accused them of operating like 'an unofficial Thought Police'.

The problem here is a simple one of perspective. There is no reason why we should not study or admire the writings of gay poets, black philosophers or female theologians, no reason why we should not encourage the development of any and every form of talent within minority groups, many of whom are not even true minorities. But we cannot undo the past. Certainly, we may reinterpret it, retrieve from it what was undeservedly obscure, give credit where credit was not given at the time. But we cannot take down Plato and Shakespeare from their pedestals without in large measure distorting the cultural realities of an entire civilization.

Nor are there likely to be any real benefits in turning culture on its head. If we were to introduce Islamic or Japanese literature and philosophy as mainstream components of arts courses, feminists would be certain to feel outraged. If, on the other hand, there were to be a heavy gay or feminist bias, Orthodox Jews and fundamentalist Christians would be sure to protest. Too many Jewish thinkers, and the Muslim lobby would be on the march. And so it would go on.

It is all too easy to see the bias – the racism, the phallocentrism, the anti-Islamism – in other people's writing or teaching. The hard thing is to see one's own. If Muslim leaders like the Aqa Khan could use some of their influence to put their own house in order first, their criticisms might be better received in the West.

(This is a much-expanded version of a letter
published in the *Guardian*, 10 August 1991)

A Barbaric Act that Devalues Our Civilization

Last Tuesday night, following the American raid on Tripoli, a US senator, wheeled on to defend his country's action against Libya, appeared on 'Newsnight'. In the course of his interview, he referred more than once to the concept of 'civilized peoples' standing together in order to combat the barbarism of . . . whom? 'Uncivilized peoples'? He didn't quite say that, but that has to be what he meant.

Since the Middle Ages, when Crusaders left these shores in boats, not F1–11s, Western writers and speechmakers have indulged in an endless stream of rhetoric directed against the apparent barbarism of the Islamic World. Terms like 'Saracen', 'Moor' or 'Turk' became synonymous with 'Hun' or 'Vandal' and with all that was most benighted in heathendom. The Venerable Bede writing towards 735 sounds not unlike Ronald Reagan preaching in 1986: 'That most grievous pest, the Saracens, wasted and destroyed the realm of Gaul with grievous and miserable carnage, but they soon after received and suffered from the punishment of their perfidy.'

Muslims were – and still are – the original 'evil empire' breathing down the necks of the West, stirring up trouble in the midst of good Christian folk. Alternately barbaric and exotic, childlike and sensuous, warlike and romantic, and always steeped in the sinfulness of a false creed, for centuries they represented the only alternative culture to march side by side with the borders of Europe. There they were: along the coast of North Africa, round the Levant, in Spain or Sicily, all the way across to India – pagans in possession of much of what had once been the heartlands of Christendom and the Roman Empire, not least the Holy Land itself. In the seventh and eighth centuries, waves of Muslim armies put the Christian West on the defensive; in the fifteenth they captured Constantinople and severed our last link with the ancient world.

Even after the Western powers punched back the threat of Islamdom in the eighteenth and nineteenth centuries, reducing country after country to colonial status, they retained – indeed, increased – their obsession with Islam as a symbol of all that ran counter to Western ideals and Western ambitions. Muslims served wonderfully well as images of the perfidious Oriental, the 'Other' on to whom we could project all our own less desirable traits. We could call them irrational and feel ourselves the embodiments of rationality; we could depict them as lascivious and wanton and regard ourselves as the essences of sexual purity; we could paint them as men of blood ruled by despots and hold ourselves paragons of peacefulness and democratic reasonableness, even as we stole their territories and interfered in their internal affairs. And in all of this we could, of course, forget that they had a civilization with roots as old as our own and a culture as complex. We were civilized; they were (and are) not.

The end of colonial rule did not bring with it the dawn of enlightenment. If anything, the pitying disapproval and paternalism of direct rule has been replaced by a new kind of racism, every bit as dangerous as anti-Semitism, that sees all Muslims as 'mad dogs' bent on the subversion of the brave new world of the modern West. As Edward Said succinctly puts it in his crucial study of media treatment of the Islamic world, *Covering Islam*, 'it is only a slight exaggeration to say that Muslims and Arabs are essentially covered, discussed, apprehended, either as oil suppliers or as potential terrorists'.

From the Musaddeq crisis and Suez through to the Iranian revolution and the growth of Shi'i militancy in Lebanon, the Western media have perpetuated myths and fed prejudices that would in any other context and directed against any other people have been ruled out of court from the word 'go'. For most Westerners – leaders as well as the man and woman in the street – there is something going on 'out there', in a vaguely defined Islamic realm, typified by the stereotypes of fanaticism, fundamentalism, obscurantism, martyrdom-obsession and terrorism.

In a classically racist manner, such traits are seen as peculiarly characteristic of Arabs, Iranians, Pakistanis or other non-white, non-Christian people, while our own fundamentalists and terrorists are conveniently ignored as unrepresentative of our society. Indeed, by one of those ironies that reveal basic contradictions in our affairs, we are forced to witness pompous Christian fundamentalists in the United States using Islamic fundamentalism as a foil to assert their own adherence to 'civilized values' ('Victorian values', perhaps?).

Of course there is much wrong in the Islamic world, just as there is in ours. Islamic fundamentalists are no more endearing than our Moral Majority, and terrorists are terrorists and reprehensible whether they plant bombs in the name of Marx or Muhammad. Ghadhafi's regime, with its brutal treatment of dissidents and its support for terrorist action abroad, is utterly condemnable. But so for that matter are many regimes in sub-Saharan Africa, Latin America and elsewhere, many of whom Mr Reagan sees fit to support as bastions of freedom.

If we really believe we have values to offer people living in countries still struggling to make sense of the post-colonial world, we shall not do so by dropping bombs on their cities, by proclaiming yet again (as we did in the Falklands) that might is right, or by invoking the obscene image of Rambo as the guardian of civilization. Have several decades of intervention in the Islamic world taught the Americans nothing? Did Iran not show them how difficult it is to cow people who have faith and a sense of purpose on their side?

A few weeks ago, Paul Johnson wrote in the *Daily Telegraph* that the Americans are 'morally our superiors'. Perhaps this latest adventure in the worship of brute force will serve to show how very far from the truth that is. Ronald Reagan may be unaware of it, but there are those in the Islamic world who know very well what counts as civilized behaviour and what sort of actions confer moral superiority. It is now time the new barbarism was stopped in its tracks, time to show an increasingly scornful Muslim world that we too are civilized people with values worth emulating.

(First published in the *Guardian*, 15 December 1986. Reprinted in *Arab Affairs* 1:1 (1986), pp. 46–7)

An Eye for an Eye

Maryam Nazari is a young Iranian woman now in her late twenties. She was married at the age of twelve to Taqi Zavara'i, two years her senior, by whom she had three children. With only six years of schooling, in a society that favours male dominance and female submissiveness, she endured a life of drudgery and anonymity made all the more difficult by her husband's suspicious and ill-tempered nature. He would lock her in the house whenever he went out; grow angry if he found her cleaning the windows, believing she did so merely in order to show herself to the street; forbid her to go on to the roof to hang out clothes to dry. When she did go out, it was always under a *chador* or a headscarf.

In the end, about 1982, Maryam went to the Family Protection Court and told them she wanted a divorce. They agreed that her case merited it, but ruled that, as is normal under Islamic law, her husband himself would have to initiate the divorce. She subsequently left him in order to force his hand, in the hope that he would either seek a divorce or agree to reform his behaviour towards her. Their three children remained in his custody.

In late March of 1984, during the period of the Iranian New Year festival, Maryam set off with her brother Mahmud to visit their sister. On the way, she encountered her husband, who asked her to come with him to see the children. She and her brother accepted a ride in Taqi's car, in which her son Reza was already seated. They drove out towards Varamin, a Tehran suburb, where Taqi claimed he had left the other children, but he changed direction en route and stopped off the road at a deserted spot.

It seems that he had concealed two friends in the boot of the car, and now, with their help, he pulled Maryam outside, threw her to the ground and – grotesque as it sounds – proceeded to gouge out her eyes with a knife. His friends, who do not appear to have expected this, ran off, while Maryam's brother fled for help. Before bundling her into the boot, Taqi told his wife that he had blinded her because she had asked for a divorce.

Driving on towards Varamin, they ran into what was then a daily sight on the streets of Tehran and other Iranian cities – a funeral procession for a soldier 'martyred' in the war against Iraq. Maryam screamed and banged on the lid of the boot, people's attention was drawn, and she was discovered. While she was rushed to hospital, her husband was arrested and taken to the Ni'matabad police station.

After some time, a formal complaint was lodged against Taqi by his father-in-law. The court – a *shar'* court administering Islamic religious law – decreed that Maryam had the right to exact revenge under a ruling known as *qisas*, the *lex talionis* that prescribes 'an eye for an eye and a tooth for a tooth'.

There was, however, one complication. Maryam might only blind her husband in one eye, since a woman is deemed to possess precisely half the value of a man in such matters. If she wanted to blind both his eyes, she had to pay the difference (a system allowed in Shi'ite law and brought back into force under the revolutionary regime), a matter of 5,000 dirhams in traditional currency. She collected the money and waited for the court to fix a date when she could go to Qasr prison and exact revenge on her husband. That is all I know. There were no later reports, but I must assume that all went as Maryam and her family expected and demanded.

There was, however, a further twist to this gruesome tale. Maryam also received permission for her act of vengeance to be carried out before television cameras – whether live or on film was not made clear. This appears to have been the latest of a series of techniques used to impress terror of the regime on the Iranian public. Television has been used there as elsewhere to broadcast confessions by former political opponents prior to their execution, and there have been reports of mobile cranes being used as gallows, so that the bodies of the dead could be carried through the streets afterwards.

How can the mind dwell adequately on events such as these? Exclamations of 'barbaric', 'brutal', 'inhuman' or whatever really take us nowhere as responses to the renewed application of Islamic law in modern times. Floggings, amputations, stonings, beheadings and now blindings in front of TV cameras are bound to shock us. There are already public executions, and I suppose it may not be long before those are televised as well: Western technology is bringing the effects of fundamentalism into people's living rooms.

We cannot ignore these developments, nor do I think it does much good simply to apply to them sweeping notions of cultural relativism, arguing that Western standards of human rights are somehow meaningless in an Islamic context, as Ayatollah Khomeini used to insist.

If human rights are to mean anything at all, then the term 'human' must be applied without reservation to anyone threatened by anti-human practices. It makes as much sense to ignore the excesses of Islamic criminal law as it does to turn a blind eye to apartheid simply on the grounds that other people have some God-given right to do things their own way and that we should not interfere in their societies or their means of cultural expression.

In which case, is it not time we looked again at the whole question of trade relations with countries that make use of barbaric laws in the name of a vengeful deity? Our own judicial and penal systems leave a great deal to be desired, but that is no reason to remain silent about other systems if they seem to have more serious faults. In the long term, changes in Islamic criminal law might lead to more far-reaching legislative reforms, such as giving women the same rights as men in matters of compensation or divorce. Perhaps even an end to the religiously sanctioned system of child marriage.

How the West Gave Islamic Fundamentalism a New Lease of Life

When an Iranian diplomat slaughtered a sheep in a London suburb a few years ago and sparked off protests from outraged neighbours, more was involved than a simple clash of cultures. He was obeying the dictates of what he saw as religious absolutes, which demanded the sacrifice of the sheep in gratitude for a safely completed pilgrimage to Mecca; his neighbours, if they were religious at all, clearly preferred matters of faith to be kept in the private domain (much like the slaughter of the sheep some of them possibly ate later that same day) and regarded religious observances in more relative terms. (In this case: 'All very well in a suburb of Tehran, unseemly in London.')

Whatever the rights and wrongs of that particular incident – I find myself on the side of the sheep – it illustrates fairly well the continuing tension between the ideals of Islamic life and the blunt realities of a largely secular world.

On the Adha festival, millions of sheep are sacrificed throughout the length and breadth of the Islamic world. Like the daily prayers, the *hajj* pilgrimage itself, and the Ramadan fast, it is an extraordinary symbol of the seemingly monolithic quality of Islam. Yet beneath the surface there are differences and internal tensions that threaten to become critical as the implications of the modern context grow clearer to Muslims.

Islam is postulated on an ideal vision of the world that embraces all aspects of human society and pervades every corner of man's everyday life. It is not only a religion in the popular Western sense, it is also a fully-fledged political, social and economic ideology, complete with intricate rules and regulations for the ordering of all human affairs – not only those of the public en masse, but also those of each man and woman in all waking activities.

There is an Islamic way to dress, an Islamic way to eat, an Islamic way to wash and to use the toilet, an Islamic way to make love. It is an essentially totalitarian vision, drawing inspiration from the belief that God has revealed His will to men in the Qur'an and in the sayings and actions of His Prophet Muhammad. God wishes men and their affairs to be ordered after a certain fashion, and the model given is the original Islamic society created by the Prophet himself, its outline forming the *sunna* or path each generation must follow. All else is *bid'a* or innovation – the nearest Islamic equivalent to heresy.

So much, at least, for the theory. But by the time that theory had been formulated, the books of tradition collected and canonized, the law texts written and glossed, and the schools of jurisprudence given their final form, Islam had long become the religion of an empire within which men as often as not continued to do things according to local custom, not Islamic religious law. Hence, there grew up side by side two legal systems – the *shari'a*, embodying the strict and universally valid letter of Islamic orthopraxy as interpreted by four main law schools; and customary law (*'ada* or *'urf*) as developed in each locality. Thus, it is not enough to define someone as a Muslim (or even as a Sunnite or Shi'ite) – you must also ask if he is a Moroccan or a Syrian, an Iranian or an Indonesian.

All of this was, of course, very much complicated by contact with the West, which reached its height in the last century. In country after country, many central areas of society – government, education, law, even family life – became Westernized and secularized, a phenomenon paralleling developments in the West itself following the Industrial Revolution.

For the idealists, this was a savage blow and one from which they are still smarting. Even to modify the sort of headgear a man should wear could be seen as an act undermining the essential Islamicity of the social fabric (hence the dress codes of Atatürk and Reza Shah, designed to help dissolve religious resistance to modernization). Within the religious establishment, a few individuals attempted to regain control of events by arguing in favour of fresh legislation or the reinterpretation of the Qur'an and Traditions in the light of modern conditions, but their influence has been negligible and has waned considerably in recent years.

It is not, ironically, the Islamic modernists but their conservative rivals who have, in the end, succeeded in transforming the post-colonial rejection of Western values into the genesis of a religious revival. Whatever their individual motivations, men like Khomeini, Zia al-Haqq or Nimeiri all had the common goal of reintroducing (or, as often as not, simply introducing) the laws of the *shari'a* to their societies.

There has been and will be resistance to such trends, but there are reasons today for thinking that it may take little to swing the balance in favour of the revivalists. I am thinking particularly of two ways in which, ironically, the techniques of the secular West may now be assisting the renaissance of Islamic fundamentalism. The first of these is the spread of reactionary ideas and symbols throughout the Islamic world thanks to modern communications. The use of recorded cassettes to disseminate the speeches of Khomeini throughout Iran before the revolution and the subsequent control of the media there by the Islamic government are the most obvious examples.

In McLuhan's global village, the encounter of conservative Muslims with Western ideals and behaviour (both good and bad) is commonplace; but easy travel, international education and the trans-global business network also bring like-minded Muslims together more frequently and spread their ideas more easily than ever in the past. In much the same way that these factors have reduced the differences between peoples in the West, so they are now encouraging a process of homogenization in the Islamic world, whereby the local practices of West Africa or Pakistan are under pressure from the universalizing tendencies of the orthodox *shari'a*. Given time and the natural operation of homogenizing influences, Islamic orthodoxy could at last succeed in becoming normative to a degree unprecedented at any time in the past.

A second contribution of Western methods to the success of the Islamic revival lies in the provision of the means of ensuring much broader social control than was possible in the past. Formerly, orthodoxy tended to be restricted to the towns: peasants in their villages and nomads in the desert or mountains were lax in their Islamic observance, but the central religious authorities could seldom coerce them into conformity.

Today, the existence of instant communications, rapid land

and air transport, and facilities for the long-term storage of goods make all but the remotest areas readily and permanently accessible. The coercive powers of state police and the ubiquitous military have been increased to an often frightening degree, while techniques of propaganda, organized mass education, and economic control all provide effective alternatives to or supports for brute force. Even during the war with Iraq, the Iranian authorities were able to ensure widespread acquiescence to their version of orthodox practice.

Prayer and pious instruction are never enough by themselves to accomplish the social transformations of religious totalitarianism. Muslim fundamentalists have already turned to the bomb and the bullet. Fundamentalists in power will not be averse to the use of any other means at their disposal to remake society in their own image, as, indeed, has been and is the case in Iran. We in the West, having supplied the means to such ends, must now consider again whether it is not time to discover ways to export those values of individual liberty and freedom of conscience that are our own uncertain defence against ideological control. It is not the lives of sheep alone that are at stake.

According to a report in this morning's *Guardian*, four Germans – a lawyer and three students – have been put on trial for designing and displaying a poster in which a Catholic priest is caricatured holding up a puppet figure of God. A district court accepted complaints that the poster was an insult to religious feelings, in portraying God as a helpless creature, 'like a hippie from the sixties'. The Germans, it seems, take God, like so much else in life, very seriously. Or perhaps the complainants were more upset by the fact that the priest in the cartoon sported a badge referring to the 1933 Concordat between the Vatican and the Third Reich.

The Italians, if Jean Luc Godard's recent experience is any indication, get upset only by portrayals of the Virgin Mary. In the spring of 1980, just after the abortive attempt by President Carter to rescue the US hostages held in Tehran, a cartoon appeared in the Roman journal *Il Male*. It showed the figures of two deities, one wearing a sort of turban, stern-faced and bearded like an ayatollah, the other a little Pope, much smaller and much less threatening. Underneath, a caption read: *'Allah e Grande, Dio un po' meno'*: 'Allah is Great, God is a little smaller.' '

It bears pondering on, that cartoon. Like much Western comment of the type, it relies heavily on stereotyping to achieve its effect. Muslims – and, hence, the Muslim deity – are perceived as grim, forbidding creatures dredged up from a Gothic nightmare of our own Middle Ages. We and our once-protecting God have shrunk to human dimensions, while they and Allah have grown fat and fierce on oil, terrorism and fanaticism.

The Christian God is love personified, divinity on a human scale, sweetness, light and reason, with Crusades, Inquisitions and missionary fervour the mere embarrassments of a misspent youth. The Muslim Nobodaddy, on the other hand, is an angry, jealous, mean-minded god who could have shown his twin of the Old Testament a thing or two, and who, in the very heart of our modern, rational world, cries out for his tribute of blood revenge and amputated hands and stoned adulterers.

The astonishing thing is how little that Italian cartoon differs in mood or prejudice from any of its medieval predecessors, in which the prophet Muhammad was portrayed as the idol Baphomet, a fetish of enormous size and consummate ugliness, joined at times by the lesser gods Tergavant and Apollo (yes, Apollo), and worshipped by his Saracen devotees in dark temples known as 'mahomeries'.

There may be few today who imagine that Muslims worship Muhammad, but there are many – and those not the most ignorant among us – who believe they venerate a god known as Allah, whose name is invoked by sundry hijackers, car-bombers, and boy soldiers in fervent cries of '*Allahu akbar*.' Allah is a sort of Moloch, an unappeasable god of battle demanding self-sacrifice of His worshippers and the immolation of the rest of mankind on His bloodstained altar.

Not even Nancy Mitford's lovable Uncle Matthew, who called a Hun a Hun and a Frenchman a sewer and who worried incessantly about Catholics, would, I think, have imagined that the French worship a tribal god called Dieu or the Italians a little man with a beard called Dio. Nor are there, I imagine, many today who would argue that the Jews pray to separate creators known variously as Yahweh, Elohim or Adonai. But even in 1985 many writers appear unable to grasp the simple fact that the word 'Allah' is no more than the Arabic for 'God', that it is for Muslims the name of the only god in existence, the creator of all things, supreme, transcendent and beyond all multiplicity. The point becomes crystal-clear if we observe that Iranian Muslims, when speaking in Persian, refer to God by the vernacular terms *Khoda* or *Khodavand*.

The singularity of God is the very fibre of Islam, a simple substance out of which all things Islamic are woven and stitched and embroidered. The essence of faith is the recitation of the *shahada*, 'the witnessing', the testimony that begins with the words *la ilaha illa 'llah*, no god exists but God: a plangent echo of the Jewish *shema*, 'Hear, O Israel, the Lord our God, the Lord is One.'

Islam, by an irony that mocks its Western images as though they were mere reflections in a game of twisted mirrors, is the most stringently monotheistic of all the great faiths, the most uncompromising of creeds professing a belief in one supreme deity. Christianity with its doctrines of the Incarnation and the Trinity, Judaism with its involved, personal God who spoke directly with Moses and the prophets, Baha'ism with its endlessly proliferating manifestations of a coy divinity, are all, in the eyes of Islam, idolatrous deviations from the severe simplicity of a genuine monotheistic faith. For Muslims, the greatest of sins, the one unforgivable transgression, is *shirk*, the joining of partners with God, whether by postulating the existence of another god beside Him or even by depending on one's own efforts rather than on His help.

The central doctrine of divine transcendence in Islam is that of *tanzih*, the unequivocal assertion that God, in His hidden and unapproachable Essence, remains utterly unlike any other thing: aloof, remote, inaccessible. In the early centuries of Islam, a gulf opened up between God and man, a black, yawning abyss that threatened to swallow the love and devotion of ordinary people in their need for a God responsive to their prayers. When the theologians asserted God's sublime detachment in the formula 'these to heaven, and I care not; these to hell, and I care not', the pious fell back on the words of the Qur'an that told them God was nearer to man 'than his jugular vein'. The gulf could be bridged. Or it was, at least, possible for the spiritually adventurous to undertake a journey over the face of the blackness.

In spite of the disapproval of orthodoxy – a disapproval that continues in many quarters to the present day – groups of Sufi mystics embarked on their voyages of discovery, returning to proclaim, not a mere resemblance between Creator and created, but a fundamental identity that threatened to undermine the entire edifice of transcendence so laboriously erected by the exponents of monotheistic absolutism.

In its early years, between the ninth and twelfth centuries, Sufism was a movement of the spiritual elite, Wilsonian outsiders brave enough to risk the perils of the mystical path or the wrath of enraged orthodoxy. But by the twelfth century, the tide of Islam itself had turned, and thousands now entered the burgeoning ranks of the many Sufi brotherhoods that had started to spring up everywhere from North Africa to India. In the succeeding centuries, the Sufi orders were to play a leading role in the further spread and consolidation of Islam, a role that was to be curtailed only in this century with the rapid rise of secularism and industrialization.

There was a price to be paid, of course. Popular Sufism filled the gulf between God and man, not with rigours of mystical experience, but with a tribe of holy men, a vast pleroma of heavenly and earthly intermediaries, whose bodies were vehicles of divine grace and whose white-domed shrines became the centres of a worship far removed from the formal rites of the orthodox mosque. The pendulum of devotion, raised to the extremity of divine remoteness, had swung once more to the opposite pole of its arc, drawing in its train a cult of saint worship that became for millions the authentic experience of Islamic faith and practice. In the course of time, the pendulum swung again, in accordance with David Hume's theory of flux and reflux in religion, as Wahhabis and other neo-orthodox movements strove to restore the uncompromising faith of the earliest theologians.

And yet it was the Sufism of the moderate, urban orders that preserved and fostered religion in the hearts of ordinary people, treading a middle path between the extremes of saint worship, on the one hand, with its attendant temptations of occultism, magic and spirit possession, and the cool sterility and staid legalism of official Islam on the other. It was in the *hadra*, the regular weekly meeting of the orders, with its hymns, its ritual incantations and, in some cases, its music and dancing that large numbers found a warmth, colour and spontaneity lacking in the restrained devotions of the mosque.

At the heart of the *hadra*, infusing and regulating it, was the practice known as *dhikr*, the outward and inward repetition of the names of God. *Dhikr* means remembrance or recollection, the process whereby man is brought back to his origins, centring himself in God as the focus for his devotion. The Qur'an itself had instructed believers to 'make frequent recollection of God', assuring them that in such remembrance their hearts would find rest. Margaret Smith describes *dhikr* as 'the practice of the presence of God at all times . . . an attitude of unceasing prayer, so that the soul can at all times turn to its Lord and find itself alone with Him, for the recollected soul can find God in all things and all things in God'. In the words of an early Baghdadi mystic, al-Harith al-Muhasibi, 'the chief part of the recollection of God is keeping close to Him'.

An undisciplined and irregular exercise among the earliest Muslim mystics, *dhikr* developed by stages to become the centre of the Sufi enterprise, an ecstatic ritual performed in unison by the initiated under the direction of their spiritual director, the *shaykh* of the order. Each brotherhood has its own pattern for the *dhikr*, but all are based on the rhythmical repetition of various titles and epithets of the Divinity. Those present at the ceremony normally stand with hands joined in a circle or square at whose centre is the *shaykh*. The circle forms a sacred enclosure from which all outside influences are rigorously excluded: the world and its distractions, evil spirits, *jinn*. All eyes and thoughts are turned inwards and focused on the act of recollection.

After a prolonged period of liturgical recital, the *dhikr* proper begins with the quiet recitation of the phrase *la ilaha illa 'llah*, 'no god exists but God'. This affirmation of God's existence is intensified in the next phase, as the adepts repeat the word 'Allah' with increasing rapidity, their breath coming in controlled bursts, their bodies moving in unison in a rocking motion. As they continue to repeat the divine name, another group begins to chant hymns in Arabic. The ceremony continues with the recital of other names of God, moving from climax to climax, weaving the names with prayers and invocations and hymns, inducing a trance-state in the adepts by a combination of physical movements and controlled breathing.

From the shared ecstasies of the *hadra*, the Sufi adept moves on to the more advanced raptures of the *dhikr* performed in solitude. Though certain basic Names are still used, the mystic will proceed, under the direction of his *shaykh*, to recite others that are more appropriate to the stage he has reached in the spiritual path. In the Qur'an, the believers are told: 'Call upon God or call upon the Merciful. Whichever you call upon, His are the Most Beautiful Names.' Traditionally, these names are said to be ninety-nine in number, with yet another name, the Greatest Name, concealed from all but the holiest of men.

In the solitary *dhikr*, these names are repeated endlessly, at first with the tongue and then, as the mystic advances yet further on the path, his tongue falls silent and his heart takes up the refrain. Abu Bakr al-Kharraz speaks of 'a recollection with the tongue not felt by the heart . . . a recollection with the tongue in which the heart is present . . . and a recollection when the heart is wandering in recollection and lets the tongue be silent: the worth of such a recollection is known only to God'. Eventually, the mystic will become entirely heart, his every limb engaged in the recollection of God, his whole being immersed in the Divine Names. Finally, the very consciousness of self is lost in the silence of recollection. 'True *dhikr*,' says Shibli, 'is that you forget your *dhikr*.'

The *dhikr* may, then, be said to stand at the very heart of Islam. In one direction, it extends out through the *hadra* into the Muslim community at large. In the convocations of the extreme orders, the *hadras* of the Rifa'iyya or 'howling' dervishes, in the public celebrations of the birth of the Prophet or a local saint, the *dhikr* explodes in motion, in music, in the inarticulate cries of the poor finding forgetfulness in the trance of recollection. At the other extreme, the *dhikr* enables the mystic to explore the inner spaces of his soul, merging in the end with an all-embracing silence in which the oneness of the worshipper and worshipped becomes a reality transcending words and names.

The Divine Names pervade Islam at all levels. In salutations and farewells, in exclamations of praise and wonder, in formulae of gratitude and congratulation, they invade the languages of the Islamic world at every juncture. Personal names are regularly formed around them: 'Abd Allah, 'the Servant of God', 'Abd al-Rahman, 'the Servant of the Merciful', 'Abd al-Latif, 'the Servant of the Beneficent', Fadl Allah, 'the Bounty of God' – the permutations are almost endless.

Above all, the names fill the eye on the walls of mosques and other public buildings, elaborately carved in the graceful lines of Arabic calligraphy that assert the doctrine of the divine oneness on almost every corner. Islam permits no depiction of the divinity, not even the reproduction of any living form. A cartoon like the Italian one we have just mentioned would be inconceivable in the Islamic world. Instead, Islam enjoys an iconography of the Word. The Word of God is everywhere: sometimes simple, sometimes so ornate it cannot be read, always remote and abstract. If the story windows of medieval cathedrals were books in glass for the benefit of the unlettered, the friezes of the mosque confronted the ordinary man and woman with the Word itself, uncompromised and uncompromising.

Not surprisingly, the Word of God and the names of God came to play a major part in the rites and symbols of popular Islam, most notably in the various forms of magic that found widespread acceptance, often in conjunction with the more heretical varieties of Sufism. From the circle or square of the *hadra*, it was but a short step to the magic square as a talisman, a vehicle for the Names of God, angels and *jinn*.

The orthodox Sufi *dhikr* was not an act of communal prayer. As Michael Gilsenen once put it, 'No plea is addressed to the Almighty; there is no supplication, no imploring of His grace . . . No action by God is requested, or expected, in the *dhikr*. No material blessings will follow.'

Far otherwise the talisman. It served as a short cut to influence spiritual powers and principalities, a shield to defend men from the satanic forces that besiege him daily on all sides. Islamic magic is a magic of names: the names of angels, the names of the kings of the *jinn* (or 'genies'), the names of the planets and, above all, the Names of God.

At the most popular level, talismanic magic is little more than a device for the gratification of earthly wishes. Just as the magician seeks to control the demons and *jinn* by pronouncing their names, so by writing down and speaking the various names of the divinity, he seeks to make God a 'servant of the name' who will automatically accede to whatever request is made of Him. The talisman becomes a magic lamp, with God the genie trapped inside for the benefit of anyone who becomes its owner. Just as the *dhikr* is made an instrument for the attainment of immediate rapture in the bliss of a hypnotic trance, so the names are tools for the achievement of even more dubious ends.

But talismanic magic was never restricted to the level of the street magician. In the hands of the intelligentsia, it could become a symbolic system of great subtlety, in which elaborate correspondences were made between the letters of the alphabet, numbers, the divine names, the spheres, the planets, the elements and the zodiacal signs. Nothing was chance, everything in creation could be interpreted as an integral part of an interlocking system, the key to which lay in the twenty-eight letters of the Arabic alphabet, interpreted by means of a complex numerology.

Such speculative systems reached their apogee in the theories of several Shi'ite sects. In the last century, the Bab, the founder of the Babi sect, made the writing and wearing of talismans and inscribed rings an essential element of faith. The divine names were crucial to his thought. In his later writings, most notably in a vast two-volume work entitled the *Kitab al-asma'* or *Book of Names*, he plunged into seemingly endless permutations of the names of God, weaving them into prayers and sermons, bending and twisting the rules of Arabic grammar in order to generate lists of impossible epithets that build into page after page of rhythmical incantations. Nowhere in the whole of Islamic literature can one find such single-minded concern with the names of God or such an elaborate attempt to exhaust the permutations of the Arabic roots from which they are painstakingly derived. The mind boggles at the thought of what the Bab would have done with a modern computer.

The Bab's obsession with talismanic devices and exhaustive catalogues of God's names derived, not from a simplistic belief in their instrumental efficacy, but out of a theological perspective in which the very pattern of the cosmos was ordered according to the correspondences between the letters of the alphabet and the names created from them. For the Bab, as for earlier Muslim gnostics, all things originated in the creative activity of the Universal Will, a Point that first manifests itself in the form of nineteen letters, the numerical equivalent of the divine name *al-wahid*, 'the Single'.

In some of his writings, the Bab describes the Primal Will as a talisman or temple in which all things have their origin and to which they will ultimately return. This truth underlying all existence is made known to men in two ways: first actual talismans are constructed according to instructions given by the Prophet, in which divine names are created on a complex mathematical basis, revealing the many levels on which the divinity manifests itself. Secondly, each of the divine names finds its place of manifestation in an individual. To many of his followers, the Bab gave divine names that corresponded numerically to their personal names, making them living representatives of the epithets they bore.

This is not mysticism, of course; but it is hard to believe that the Bab was not influenced in his theory of human bearers of the divine names by the mystical philosophy of the great Andalusian

Sufi Muhyi' 1-Din Ibn al-'Arabi (1164–1240). For Ibn al-'Arabi, possibly the greatest thinker Islam has ever produced, the Names of God are hypostatic emanations from the Absolute, the One that stands above and apart from all multiplicity. All things, when viewed from the perspective of Ultimate Reality, are existentially one. The world is nothing other than the Absolute in a state of manifestation.

Viewed from the perspective of multiplicity, the process whereby the Absolute externalizes itself occurs through a series of descending levels. The first of these levels is the plane of the Names of God. These names are, for Ibn al-'Arabi, nothing more than expressions of the infinite relationships of the One with the manifested universe. 'Allah', for example, is not the title of the Absolute, but of the concept worshipped by men. Without the act of worship, this 'God' would have no reality. Allah is 'a god created in beliefs', nothing more than a mental construct circumscribed by the limitations of human minds. As such, he stands as much in need of creation as creation stands in need of Him. Both Allah and His creation are, in the end, a single reality in different modes.

In the doctrines of advanced Sufism, the gulf between God and man, Creator and created is not so much bridged as eradicated. The abyss is a fantasy, a mirage engendered by the false consciousness of scholastic theology. By contemplation of the divine names, man is awakened to true understanding. He does not become the Absolute: he realizes that he and the Absolute have never been anything but one. From the names, the mystic passes to the one, comprehensive name Allah, in which all the names and attributes are combined.

We began with an image of God that had its origins in the cheap anthropomorphism of popular imagination and have uncovered an Islamic conception of the divinity that joins God and man in an inseparable unity. Ibn al-'Arabi would have known what to make of our cartoon. For him, even idolatry was a path to the worship of the single God, for if monotheists have laid stress on God's transcendence, idolaters have revealed the immanence of the One in the Many. The ignorant name their idols trees or stones or stars, but those endowed with knowledge recognize that 'the object of worship is the vehicle of divine manifestation' and that 'in every object of worship it is God who is worshipped'.

Thus, the gods that men worship and the names they give them are, for Ibn al-'Arabi, nothing but special forms in which the Absolute has manifested itself to different people in different places. It is, to use his phrase, 'God created in various religious beliefs'. In his system, we have moved from the notion that 'there is no god but God' to the proposition that 'there is nothing but God'.

(First delivered in 1985 as part of a public
lecture series at Newcastle University on 'The
Names of God')

Review: *Holy Terror*

Amir Taheri, *Holy Terror: the Inside Story of Islamic Terrorism*, Century Hutchinson/Sphere Books, London, 1987

The author of this, the first detailed study of Islamic terrorism, is a well-known journalist who has since 1982 been a leading figure in Iranian exile circles. He was Editor-in-Chief of Tehran's largest daily newspaper, *Kayhan*, during the last six years of the Shah's rule, and since then he has written extensively for European and American newspapers.

Taheri is a self-admitted opponent of the Iranian regime in Iran and of Islamic fundamentalism in general, and his book must be read with that bias in mind. He is, moreover, a journalist rather than an academic, and at times his lack of rigour shows itself in errors of fact or in a tendency towards generalization that threatens to undermine some of his arguments. For all that, the book is extremely well documented and, I think, wholly accessible to the general reader (who will, however, have to wade through a large number of footnotes in order to follow many of the text references).

Leaving criticism aside for the moment, however, there can be no question that this is a disturbing book about a disturbing subject, and that it deserves to be widely read, not least in those circles where decisions have to be made about relations with Islamic nations and their governments.

Religious fundamentalism in any guise is a thing of excess: excessive rhetoric, excessive conviction of righteousness, excessive zeal, excessive bigotry. It leads almost inexorably to a love of absolutism and an unwillingness to compromise with the complexities of life in the real world. But when the fundamentalist spirit joins forces with secular power or itself takes up arms to impose its vision of a holy society on others, it erupts in a particularly nasty kind of violence.

That tendency to violence is not uniquely Islamic; but it lies very close to the origins and spread of the faith: to the military campaigns of the Prophet, the spread of the Islamic empire by armed force, the continuing law of *jihad* or holy war, the conceptual division of the world into realms of belief and unbelief, the 'realm of Islam' and the 'realm of war'.

The compulsion to violence is frighteningly clear in the quotations from books, pamphlets and speeches that thunder at us out of every other page of Taheri's book: 'A believer who sees Islam trampled underfoot and who does nothing to stop it will end up in the seventh layer of Hell. But he who takes up a gun, a dagger, a kitchen knife or even a pebble with which to harm and kill the enemies of the Faith has his place assured in Heaven.' 'Every single lock of hair that shows from beneath a chador [veil] carelessly worn is like a dagger aimed at the heart of our martyrs.' 'Killing a hypocrite who refuses to reform is more worthy than a thousand prayers.' 'Khomeini says that democracy "leads to prostitution".' 'We say that killing is tantamount to saying a prayer when those who are harmful [to the Faith] need to be put out of the way. Deceit, trickery, conspiracy, cheating, stealing and killing are nothing but means.' 'Those who are against killing have no place in Islam.'

There is an inescapable ugliness about such rhetoric, all the more so because it issues in the bloody and mindless action we are all so familiar with. It is not, perhaps, any uglier than fascist rhetoric or the self-justificatory polemic of any modern terrorist group you care to mention. But at least Nazis, the PLO or the IRA do not invoke divine sanction for their deeds.

There are, of course, many ordinary Muslims who would refute – some angrily, some in sorrow – the extremism here on view. And I think they would be right in saying that, in spite of a rather token effort at making a distinction, Mr Taheri does tend to tar all Muslims with the same brush. Even if he intended otherwise, his book does have something of that effect, particularly, I would guess, for more uninformed readers unable to place much of what they read into a proper context.

That, of course, is not sufficient reason to remain silent about the darker side of resurgent Islam. Moderate Muslims do themselves something of a disservice by insisting on an idealized Islam to which all non-Muslim accounts of the subject must conform. Like all religions, Islam has skeletons in its cupboards. Violence towards non-believers is not an invention of Hasan al-Banna or Nawab-Safavi or other modern fundamentalists: it is enshrined in medieval books of law and the actual practice of more than one Islamic state of the past. The repression of women in Islam is not a fantasy of Western orientalists: it is as much a fact of traditional Islamic life as slavery or anti-Semitism has been of ours.

A more serious criticism of the present work is that the author tends to lump together ideas and movements that are not necessarily coherent with one another. To devote a chapter to Nizari Ismailism as 'background' to modern developments is bizarre, especially when no proper explanation of the origins, social context and political situation of medieval Ismailism (or Shi'ism generally) is provided. To make matters worse, the chapter in question is hopelessly muddled, and the author only succeeds in embarrassing himself, as, for example, when he speaks of Silvestre de Sacy (d. 1838) as a 'recent historian'.

The lengthy twelfth chapter, which provides us with a Cook's tour of modern Islamic fundamentalism, has some interesting information. But Taheri fails to look in sufficient detail at the often important differences between, say, Shi'i and Sunni fundamentalism, or between Sunni fundamentalism in Saudi Arabia and Pakistan. The statement made early in the book, that '. . . there exists today a phenomenon justifiably described as "Islamic" terrorism' (p. 3) is a sweeping one, and Mr Taheri has not succeeded in convincing me of its validity.

But I am, perhaps, too carping. The author's heart is in the right place – or, at least, the same place as my own. He abhors fanaticism, cant and bigotry; and he seeks to uphold the Western values of human rights, liberty, democracy and human dignity against a system that derides and attacks them. I believe, like Mr Taheri, that what has happened in Iran and elsewhere is a tragedy of immense proportions. I try to understand it and, where possible, to help others understand it too. But in the end, I too cannot stomach another vial of acid thrown in the face of an unveiled woman or another child torn to shreds by a landmine for the sake of a bitter, psychopathic God.

(Originally published in the *New Humanist*, 102:4, December 1987)

Review: *Islamic Fundamentalism and Modernity*

W. Montgomery Watt, *Islamic Fundamentalism and Modernity*,
Routledge, London, 1988

Writing about Islamic fundamentalism has been darkly overshad-
owed by the events of the past two months. Whatever the future
holds for Salman Rushdie, relations between the West and the
Islamic world can never be quite the same again.

William Watt's short study, published just on the eve of the
uproar over *The Satanic Verses*, provides a thorough, sympathetic
guide for the general reader seeking to understand the motives
and justifications behind what often seems quite irrational and
inexplicable behaviour. Watt (Emeritus Professor of Arabic at
Edinburgh University) has long enjoyed a reputation as the
leading Western authority on Islam. He has, in particular,
brought to the subject the insights of a modern churchman
and academic engaged in dialogue with the texts and exponents
of a faith with which the West has been in a state of active
or suspended hostility for fourteen centuries. Sometimes, Watt's
eirenic intent has led to a fudging of crucial issues: attempts to
validate Muhammad's prophethood without going so far as to
embrace Islam have, in particular, cut little ice with orthodox
Muslims for whom such subtleties remain incomprehensible.

The present work is somewhat harder-hitting, betraying perhaps a growing unease with the militant form of Islam that has
come to dominate at least the public expression of the faith.
The study revolves around the notion that 'the thinking of the
fundamentalist intellectuals and of the great masses of ordinary
Muslims is still dominated by the standard traditional Islamic
world-view and the corresponding self-image of Islam'.

This world-view is explained in a stimulating first chapter as
a combination of an ideal of unchangingness that makes the idea
of social reform almost unthinkable; a sense of Islam's finality

and self-sufficiency, coupled with suspicion of all that is not Islamic; a notional division of the world between a realm of Islam and a realm of war; and an idealized view of Muhammad and early Islamic society (something sharply relevant to the Rushdie crisis).

This tendency towards idealization is seen by the author as a serious obstacle to meaningful reconstruction, bringing with it a general danger 'that the community becomes so obsessed with recreating something past that it fails to see and deal with the real challenges and problems of the present' (p. 22).

The study continues through historical and contemporary surveys of the role of the religious institution and its imposition of a unitary world-view (including some topical passages on modern heresy hunts); the beginnings of Islamic resurgence, largely in response to the impact of the West on traditional society; the liberal search for a new identity more in accord with Western values; the difficulty of reconstructing the traditional world-view to enable Muslims to tackle contemporary problems; and a competent if sketchy account of the Iranian experience.

The range is considerable, in spite of the book's shortness. Absolute beginners may, perhaps, need less concentrated introductions like Dilip Hiro's recent, more popular study (see review, pp. 85–6). But for anyone who has a passing acquaintance with the field, this provides thoughtful discussion of all the main issues.

Of particular interest is the long fifth chapter on the tension between the traditional self-image and contemporary problems. Watt argues that, although there is awareness of the gulf between Islamic and Western thinking, Muslim leaders have no real understanding of the true nature of the difficulty. The widespread notion that all that is needed is to Islamize knowledge – promoted by men like S.M. Zaman, S.A. Ashraf or the late Ismail al-Faruqi – is dismissed as a naïve proposal that fails to tackle the real problem.

Later in the chapter, Watt examines social issues such as human rights and the position of women, as well as the crucial issue of relations between Islam and other religions. This last section would, I think, have benefited from a wider discussion, bringing in, not only Christianity and Judaism, but Hinduism, Buddhism, African animism and Baha'ism (which would also have been usefully included in the early survey of challenges to traditional concepts of revelation).

This section ends with a brief attempt to provide an outline of the elements that might be used to form a 'truer world-view and self-image' (pp. 123–4). Here, as elsewhere (e.g. pp. 80 ff), Watt tries to engage in the debate about Islamic modernity directly. Tragically, it is unlikely that many Muslim intellectuals will address themselves to his ideas.

If the book has a flaw, it is, I think, too great an emphasis on intellectual problems and too little examination of the grass-roots movement taking place within less articulate fundamentalist groups (such as those running the show in Bradford). Like Gibb and others before him, Watt's involvement is more with texts than the man on the street, but the latter has come to play a vital role in Islamic resurgence.

As far as the intellectuals are concerned, Watt divides modern Muslims into two broad groups: fundamentalists (conservatives, traditionalists) and liberals. There are, I think, certain dangers in such an easy division, but it serves well enough to identify the two most constant strands in modern Islam. Watt, like many Western writers before him, pins his hopes on the liberals or, more precisely, the emergence of a great liberal thinker who will revolutionize the Islamic vision:

'The right man at the right time with the right form of words might quickly gain a very extensive following among the religiously-minded Muslims of Western outlook. This would be particularly likely to happen if some failure of their programmes discredited the traditionalists, whose voices alone are being heard at the moment' (pp. 69–70). Later, he calls for the appearance of 'a renewer or *mujaddid* with the poetic gifts of an Iqbal'.

This seems to me little more than intellectual Mahdism. Events of the past few weeks have shown dramatically how unlikely such a *parousia* has become. A swing towards rational debate and compromise with the West grows more remote with every day that passes. That must seem a terrible tragedy to someone like Professor Watt, who has spent a lifetime encouraging balance and mutual respect between Christians and Muslims. If his book helps demonstrate to some Muslims that there are Westerners deeply concerned about the fate of modern Islam, it may do something to hasten the inevitable day when confrontation is replaced by common sense.

(Originally published in *The Times Higher Education Supplement*, 28 April 1989)

Review: *Discovering Islam: Today's Problems, Tomorrow's Solutions*

Akbar S. Ahmed, *Discovering Islam: Making Sense of Muslim History and Society*, Routledge and Kegan Paul, London and New York, 1988; Abdullah Omar Naseef (ed.), *Today's Problems, Tomorrow's Solutions: The Future Structure of Muslim Societies*, Mansell, London and New York, 1988

The year 1989 has become a crucial one for both the external and internal evaluation of Islam. The Salman Rushdie affair has moved us from familiar issues of politics – oil, conflict, terrorism, revolution – to those of faith itself, leaving non-believers and many Muslims puzzled, pained and uncomprehending. As a novelist and academic, I find myself suddenly bound by constraints that would have been unimaginable a few months ago – not least the fear of physical danger should my writing be deemed 'blasphemous' by some group of self-appointed guardians of Islamic purity.

Akbar Ahmed writes as a believing Muslim, without the doubts or reservations that I and other non-believers might bring to the subject; and yet, for all his idealism, he is at times critical of one or another feature of contemporary Islam: the plight of women, the state of education, ethnic squabbles. Muslim writers in the East have long been subject to fairly rigid controls over what they may write on religious topics; in the new climate of fear and uncertainty generated by the outcry over *The Satanic Verses*, will they now face less direct but similar restrictions when writing in the West? If so, Dr Ahmed's book may mark, not the beginning of a new process of self-appraisal, but its end.

The book itself is rather a hodge-podge. I found myself enjoying parts of it immensely – it is well written, moderate in tone, intelligent, perceptive – while being hugely irritated by others. In spite of an overriding intention to bring together a disparity of strands within the compass of a unifying theme – or set of themes – the strands remain stubbornly disparate: set pieces from Islamic history jostle with detailed discussions of contemporary Muslim scholarship and social sciences; Sufis bang into Pakistani migrant

workers in Dubai; biographies of al-Biruni and Ibn Khaldun
nestle uneasily beside lengthy accounts of Hyderabadi history,
Pukhtun ethics, or even a poem for the author's father.

In theory, of course, this should be the work of scholarship: to
forge links between the formerly unconnected, to make sense of
what has become muddled, to impose a modicum of order on the
natural chaos of human ideas and institutions. Indeed, Dr Ahmed
is acutely aware of this ideal: his book is subtitled 'Making Sense
of Muslim History and Society', and his final chapter takes its title
from Forster's much-quoted dictum, 'Only connect'. And yet, for
me at least, he does not connect. This is really a collection of
essays, some trite, some fascinating, upon which our author has
attempted to paint a veneer of coherence and underlying unity
of purpose. Better to have called the thing 'Collected Essays' and
left it at that.

The book is consecrated to the exploration of a series of related
questions. How are we to understand, or discover, simply yet intel-
ligently the history of a major world religion and its relationship
with its society? What are the keys to Muslim society – those
which will allow us to make sense of how Muslims behave, what
motivates them, what are their concepts of right and wrong? How
are we to explain the turbulence in contemporary Muslim society
which has helped create the negative images of Islam?

This is a massive undertaking. To make it all knit together, the
author has constructed what he describes as his 'main argument':
'The ideal is eternal and consistent; Muslim society is neither,
as we shall see.' Is this not rather stating the obvious? I fear
that the notion of a rift between ideals and realities is of little
service in the task of making sense of such a congeries of social,
political, cultural and religious themes. The argument is largely
redundant: what society, after all, does not know the same
tension, albeit expressed in the language of a different conceptual
universe? Is the failure of the ideal more of a problem for Muslims
than for Christians, say, or Buddhists? If that could be argued
(and I admit there are ways in which it could), that would be
the most useful context for the argument's initial construction,
rather than that of simple internal evaluation.

For me, however, the book's greatest flaw lies precisely in
Dr Ahmed's own failure to disengage the ideal from reality, in
historical terms at least. The first part of the book, 'The Pattern

of Islamic History', provides us with an overview of historical events, beginning with the Prophet, going on to the Ottoman, Safavid and Mughal empires, passing by Islam in peripheral regions such as China and Russia, and concluding with the period of European rule. Much of this – notably the portions on early Islam – is apologetic in tone and derivative in content. The approach is historicist in the Popperian sense, with an uncritical acceptance of the notion of a natal golden age followed by decay: 'The Prophet and the cluster of his companions provided the highest and best form of Muslim behaviour. After them a decline was inevitable.' Not a word here about the way in which later generations of Muslims constructed (and continue to construct) an ideal around those early figures that makes the sense of decline more a property of contemporary back-projection than the result of any actual falling away.

The six 'socio-historical categories' that Dr Ahmed suggests as a framework for Islamic history (1. The time of the Prophet and ideal caliphs; 2. The Arab dynasties; 3. The three Muslim empires; 4. Islam of the periphery [a geographical rather than historical category]; 5. Islam under European rule; and 6. Contemporary Islam) are, like all such periodizations, arbitrary and of little real help in understanding actual historical trends. Their usefulness is further marred by careless editing, which throws the numbering of these categories badly out of line.

At times, the historical analysis offered here is plainly banal. In one paragraph (p. 87), for example, we are told that the Ottomans, Safavids and Mughals all produced art, architecture and poetry; allowed women to participate in elite culture; created new capitals; had, at their peaks, contented peasantries and impartial administrations; and had stable and contented populations. Since all of the foregoing would be true of any large and stable imperial civilization, it tells us almost nothing about the three empires referred to. The idealizing evident in the last two statements sets us even further from Ottoman, Safavid or Mughal reality. What we want to know – and what we are not really told – is in what ways their Islamicity gave to each of these systems peculiar and significant features.

Dr Ahmed is at his best when he stops trying to be an historian and writes about matters on which he is better informed or with which he has been directly involved. The last of the historical chapters, dealing with colonial rule and, in particular, the fate of Muslim tribespeople during the modern period, is vivid, intelligent, and would be well worth expanding into a full-length study.

Several of the later sections share this liveliness, particularly those which concern themselves with the sub-continent. Here, the author is on home ground and in command of his material for once. Even the poem for his father reads well in this context, as an expression of personal feeling about the dilemmas facing a modern Muslim. The chapter devoted to the reconstruction of Muslim thought raises several important issues in a critical and intelligent manner, with several pertinent remarks about the difficulties involved in creating Islamic social sciences. Perhaps there could have been more discussion of the basic question of whether the concept of Islamic sciences is, in itself, a healthy thing; but, that apart, I found much to ponder on in this section.

Dr Ahmed's discussion of contemporary Islamic sciences would have formed an excellent contribution to Abdullah Omar Naseef's edited volume of essays on Islamization. The volume is based on papers delivered at an international conference on 'Dawa and Development in the Muslim World: The Future Perspective', held at Mecca from 11 to 15 October 1987. The papers presented here are, according to Parvez Manzoor's intelligent introduction, 'firmly committed to solving the problems of Muslim societies from a reformist perspective'.

For me, the greatest stumbling block in these presentations lay in the faintly beleaguered air of confrontation with the West that so many writers expressed. As Professor Manzoor puts it: 'The most serious moral problem connected with the implementation of the Shariah and the creation of an Islamically authentic socio-political order ... may not be situated in any crisis of Islamic thought and conscience but may lie with the non-Muslims' perception of it and their obduracy against the acceptance of its sovereignty.' To ignore the real crises that exist in modern Islamic thought (many of them admirably related in Akbar Ahmed's volume), while placing blame for problems on the ever-available scapegoat of the West (which has now become as much a creation of Muslim imagination as the East was ever a child of orientalism), is itself to generate problems of real seriousness and intractability. The West is not there just to be ignored or defied: it will not simply go away in the face of increased '*shari'a*-mindedness'. To understand that fact and act upon it must, I am the more convinced after reading this collection, be the first responsibility of any Muslim thinker today.

The book is divided into two roughly equal parts, the first dealing with 'The Shariah and Islamization', the second with 'Economy and Family Life'. Part one begins with an essay by Ibraheem Sulaiman, Director of the Centre of Islamic Legal Studies at Ahmadu Bello University, Nigeria. Entitled, 'The Shariah and the Challenge of Our Time', this paper views Muslim problems as global problems and the *shari'a* as 'not only . . . a panacea for Muslims, but . . . a panacea for all mankind, and not only for the problems and crises of today, but of tomorrow as well'. This is all very well, but Dr Sulaiman does not go on to tell us exactly how the *shari'a* is to become a panacea for all mankind. Does he intend a global extension of *Dar al-Islam*, coupled with universal implementation of the *shari'a* (which amounts to no more than the traditionalist solution)? Or does he envisage ways in which non-Muslim societies may borrow from *shari'a* rulings? If so, how? And why? It is a failure to answer simple questions like these that turns statements like the foregoing into mere rhetoric. Not for the first time in this volume did I sense that the 'reformist perspective' is little more than the traditionalist perspective dressed up in borrowed clothes.

After an informative and timely digression on the Sudan experiment, Dr Sulaiman concludes by asking 'What Should be Done?' Here again, rhetoric dominates rational argument. He begins by saying that 'in almost every country in the Muslim world one encounters heartfelt and genuine desire of Muslims to have an Islamic order', but does not go on to say how many express such a desire, how many would oppose such an order, how many would be indifferent, what types of 'Islamic order' different groups might want, or how rigorous an order may be desirable.

Dr Sulaiman's second contribution, 'The Future of the Shariah', is devoted to a largely historical account of the Sokoto Caliphate under Shehu Usman dan Fodio. Certainly, any detailed examination of a self-consciously Islamic state must prove illuminating;

but one must, I think, be cautious about what lessons can really be learned by modern society from a nineteenth-century experiment. The author concludes that modern Muslims everywhere have three tasks: 1. to create political and social conditions under which the *shari'a* can be the supreme law; 2. to raise a body of scholars and jurists charged with the task of developing laws based on the Qur'an and *sunna*,[1] which will meet the needs of modern society; and 3. a reconceptualization of Islamic law for the modern age, disengaging itself from the confines of the traditional law schools.

Ibrahim Ahmad, Shaykh of the Faculty of Shariah at the International Islamic University of Malaysia, contributes a short piece entitled 'Some Thoughts on the Future of the Shariah'. This paper deals with three topics: the study of the *shari'a*, its application to Muslims, and the possibility of its application to non-Muslims. In the last section, Dr Ahmad argues for the superiority of the *shari'a* over other legal systems and its acceptance as a single code for everyone. Such a dogmatic approach raises several thorny questions, all of which are passed over here in silence. More than at any other point in the book, I was here conscious of how much this debate is being carried on in a vacuum: without the opinions of non-Muslims, how can there be intelligent discussion of the issue of applying *shari'a* law to them?

The final chapter in the first part is S.M. Zaman's paper on 'Islamization and Strategies for Change: The Educational Perspective'. This deserves to be read alongside the section on scholarship in Akbar Ahmed's book, where the problems are, I feel, addressed more critically. Dr Zaman discusses the emergence of 'Islamic universities' throughout the Muslim world, concluding that these 'have failed to achieve the purpose of modernizing Muslim education'. In his view, a new model would aim at 'teaching all the modern sciences within an Islamic perspective', unlike the older Aligarh model, 'where religious sciences were peripheral to the modern sciences'. He rightly draws particular attention to the social sciences, for it is here 'that modern scholarship has succeeded in making the furthest inroads into the Muslim mind'.

---

[1] Broadly speaking, the body of sacred literature known as Hadith, which relates the sayings and doings of the Prophet as a basis for legal and moral rulings.

The author's use of the phrase 'Muslim mind' is illuminating, revealing a kind of stereotyping that we have come to censure in the work of some Western writers, such as Charles Waddy. Modern science may have its flaws, but one of its truer characteristics is the rejection of any notion that real knowledge can be determined by incidental factors such as race or creed. Of course, determination is there, as studies in the sociology of knowledge amply demonstrate; but the impetus of scientific method is against such biases, for Muslims as much as for Westerners or anyone else.

I find myself extremely uneasy about the sort of ghettoizing of knowledge that writers like Dr Zaman engage in. What will be the end result of such an approach? A congeries of different knowledge systems, each self-consistent within its own universe of discourse and immune to outside comment or criticism? Western sociology side by side with Muslim, Jewish, Hindu, Buddhist, Baha'i, Marxist and other sociologies? Ditto for economics, history, anthropology, what you will? Sunni science versus Shi'i science? Zaidi anthropology versus Ismaili? Sufi physics against Hanbali? The whole concept of ideologically predetermined sciences is, at heart, a nonsense, and I cannot see that any good is served, for Muslims or anyone else, by its perpetuation.

The next set of papers deal in a fairly straightforward fashion with Islamic economics. Muhammad Arif, Ziauddin Ahmad and Muhammad Nejatullah Siddiqui all contribute surveys of the general area of interest-free banking, and of the problem of shifting from modern economics to an Islamic version. I found Siddiqui's paper the weakest of the three, relying as it does on a heavy dose of Quranic quotations and appeals to 'how Muslims should live'. It would be pleasant if it were otherwise, but economics is a science about how people do live.

This same problem of idealism also mars Kamal Hassan's paper on 'Family Life and Responsible Parenthood in Islam'. We are nowhere offered any solid information (statistics, official reports) about how Muslim families really live, and are instead treated to what is less an academic survey than a moralistic tract on the family life of saints.

Alia Nasreen Athar's contribution on 'The Future of the Muslim Family' is much better attuned to the sociological study of real family situations. Her conclusion that 'the Islamic system aims at creating a kind of semi-nuclear family' is well reasoned and supported by both sound evidence and well-assimilated theory. The only part about which I had serious reservations was the highly naïve and parodic version of modern feminism, based on a polemic by a Muslim writer. The following discussion of the role of women contrasts badly with that in Akbar Ahmed's book (although his section on the women's movement is also grotesquely distorted), turning dogmatic and inconsistent. Professor Athar needs to do some basic reading about the subject.

Finally, Ziauddin Sardar's epilogue entitled 'Reformist Ideas and Muslim Intellectuals: The Demands of the Real World' proved, for me, the book's redemption. This is a highly articulate, illuminating essay that deserves to be reprinted and widely distributed. 'All reformist work,' it begins, 'must start with recognition of the world as it is . . . We must see and understand the world as it exists and not as we would like it to be. Only when we appreciate the true dimensions of contemporary reality, can we contemplate reforms that will create the world we want.' If only most of the other contributors to this volume had taken these observations to heart, the final product would have been infinitely more useful.

Dr Sardar's observations on the dangers of a monolithic approach to reform, the dearth of intellectuals in the Islamic world, and the need for the re-emergence of 'the classical polymath' to reshape contemporary civilization all deserve study and comment. The only features of this article that seemed to me less well thought out were the belief that the *umma* can 'halt the advance of western civilization at its boundaries' (just how meaningful are 'boundaries' in the modern age?); and the tendency to stereotype Western logic and social grammar as 'jingoist and chauvinist' (has Islamic thought never been, is it not often now, any of these things?). For all that, this final paper does point the way, as critically as does Akbar Ahmed's book, to the direction which Islamic thinking must take in the next few decades.

(First published in *Arab Affairs*, 1:9, Spring/Summer 1989)

Review: *Islamic Fundamentalism*

Dilip Hiro, *Islamic Fundamentalism*, Paladin Books (Paladin Movements and Ideas), London, 1988

Christian fundamentalism attracts sociologists and psychologists, Islamic fundamentalism political commentators. If nothing else, this helps point up the often-ignored fact that the two phenomena have remarkably little in common. The myth of a universal phenomenon known as 'religious fundamentalism' obscures major distinctions between ostensibly similar movements within Christianity, Islam, Judaism, Sikhism or whatever.

Equally, terms like Islamic 'fundamentalism', 'revivalism' or 'renewal' obscure a wide range of religious and political options that often make awkward bedfellows. The differences range from the purely theological (notably between Sunnism and Shi'ism) to the overtly political (as between royalist Saudi Wahhabism and the consensualist Muslim Brotherhood).

Hiro makes a brave attempt to take us through this minefield: geographically, ideologically and even historically. He is least at ease with the last. His history is second-hand and shows it. There is a rawness in the first three chapters, reminiscent of a student essay still bristling with partly-digested information.

This is reinforced by Hiro's patent uneasiness with Arabic and Persian words and names. It is not pedantic to grumble that he appears to know neither language well, if at all: an ability to read texts in at least one major Islamic language is surely a *sine qua non* of one seeking to explain Islamic phenomena to the uninformed.

To be fair, the rest of the book amply makes up for the early chapters. Once Hiro moves on to the modern period one can almost hear him sigh with relief. Here are situations with which he is more familiar, and he weaves his way in and out of them with ease.

Hiro's problem was to convey something of the diversity of

Islamic fundamentalism in a short volume aimed at a mass readership. His solution is to limit himself to four detailed chapters on selected regional developments: the Muslim Brotherhood in Egypt and Syria; Saudi Arabia as the oldest fundamentalist state; Iran as the prime example of revolutionary fundamentalism in power; and the changing fortunes of fundamentalism in Afghanistan.

These are all clearly presented, and the reader looking for a broad survey of the major themes in the modern history of these regions will not be disappointed. In other respects, however, the solution backfires. At times I was unsure how much I was reading a study of Islamic fundamentalism and how much a simple history of modern Egypt, Iran *et al* with an emphasis on religion. Less detail here might have freed some space for a few pages on developments outside the Islamic heartlands.

Perhaps this is unfair. Just how does one disentangle the development of the Muslim Brotherhood from broad currents in twentieth-century Egyptian history? But many readers will remain uncertain how to distinguish 'fundamentalism' from 'reformism' or 'traditionalism' or even plain, unadorned Islam. It is a problem inherent in trying to cover all developments, and I would not claim to be able to make those distinctions with ease myself. A chapter on definitions might have helped, not least for tackling the essential question of whether such distinctions are actually useful in an Islamic context at all.

(Originally published in *The Times Higher Education Supplement*, 22 July 1988)

II

GOD, THE DEVIL AND
SALMAN RUSHDIE

Satanic Farces

On 14 January 1989, a crowd of about one thousand Muslims demonstrated in the northern English town of Bradford against the sale of Salman Rushdie's latest novel, *The Satanic Verses*, shortlisted earlier this year for the Booker Prize. While inflammatory speeches were made by Muslim leaders, a copy of the book was hoist on a sort of gallows and ceremonially burned.

The mob's chief target was the local branch of W.H. Smith, Britain's largest bookstore chain. On the advice of the local police chief, who argued that his men were powerless to prevent damage to property or staff, the store's manager ordered all copies of the offending book removed from the shelves. On the Monday, it was announced that the book would be withdrawn from W.H. Smith branches throughout the country, on the grounds that it was no longer selling enough copies to be worth carrying. A demand has now been made that public libraries also remove copies from their shelves. Elsewhere, bookstore staff have been threatened at knife-point and told to remove copies from sale. Bomb threats have been made.

This is not the first time Rushdie's book has been the subject of controversy. It has previously been banned in India, Saudi Arabia and other Muslim countries, as well as South Africa. It is argued that the book presents a derogatory picture of the prophet Muhammad, who features in it as the prophet of Jahilia, a city of sand. In *The Satanic Verses*, he takes the name 'Mahound', a medieval European corruption of Muhammad, 'the demon-tag the farangis hung around his neck', of which Rushdie writes ironically: 'To turn insults into strengths whigs, tories, Blacks all chose to wear with pride the names they were given in scorn; likewise, our mountain-climbing, prophet-motivated solitary is to be the medieval baby-frightener, the Devil's synonym: Mahound.'

The crime of insulting the Prophet (*sabb al-nabi*), is one of the most unforgivable in Islamic law. It is technically punishable by death. Even as recently as 1986, a law was passed in Pakistan prescribing severe penalties for anyone writing or speaking disrespectfully about Muhammad. In a strict Islamic state, Salman Rushdie would be on trial for his life. In Britain, only his books have so far fallen victim to the wrath of believers convinced that *The Satanic Verses* defames Muhammad and dishonours Islam.

The conviction that Western writers have engaged in both witting and unwitting misrepresentation of Islam is one that has taken firm hold of the modern Muslim consciousness. It has found its finest and most articulate expression in the books of Edward Said (notably *Orientalism* and *Covering Islam*); and it receives confirmation every time a journalist offers sweeping statements about fanaticism or a politician equates the whole of Islamic life and culture with terrorism or backwardness.

There is a long history to Western prejudice about Islam (and as long a pedigree to Islamic prejudice about the West). It began with the Arab invasions of the seventh century, made strides during the Crusades, was up and running once more during the years of confrontation between Europe and the Ottoman Empire (the 'Evil Empire' of its day), and galloped into the home straight throughout the long years of Western imperialism. The recent resurgence of Islam has only served to provide fresh substance to the bogey of a Muslim peril.

Writers, academics, painters all contributed to a potent and enduring image of Islamic decadence, brutality, sensuality, exoticism and irrationality. Orientalism became the intellectual handmaid of the imperial enterprise, creating an Orient of the mind, controlling, encapsulating and above all stereotyping Muslims in order to justify their subjection to Western physical and mental superiority.

Why then do I feel such unease at the ban on Rushdie's book? Should I not feel a certain exhilaration that the East is fighting back, that the stereotype is drawing blood from the hand that moulded it? Surely *The Satanic Verses* is no more than the progeny of *Vathek* or *Lalla Rookh*, not worth the paper to defend. I think not.

I will, in Voltairean fashion, defend the right of Muslims everywhere to protest against the often careless and frequently ignorant portrayals of their faith and culture that abound in our media. I will not, however, applaud their action in seeking and obtaining a ban on the sale and possibly the loan from libraries of one book thus singled out by them for censure. And I certainly will not condone the symbolic burning of *The Satanic Verses* on the streets of Bradford.

Islam is no exception to the rule that all religions create and foster idealized – Toynbee would have said idolized – images of themselves. The lives of founders, the origin of scriptures, the miracles ascribed to saints, and the purity of doctrines all receive cosmetic treatment at the hands of historians and theologians. It is axiomatic that outsiders must give offence to such idealized images, if only because they implicitly reject their truth by remaining outsiders. If censorship were to become the standard response to any remark about a faith that failed to find favour with the most sensitive of its adherents, all meaningful comment about religion would cease.

The Bradford controversy has led several politicians from both right and left to issue renewed calls for the extension of Britain's law of blasphemy to cover non-Christian religions. If a law of that sort were in existence today, no doubt Salman Rushdie would actually face trial and possible imprisonment.

On the face of it, such legislation seems wholly in keeping with modern trends in the field of race relations and the encouragement of a multi-cultural society. That is why sections of the British left have favoured it. But it seems self-evident that, were such a law to be passed, it would quickly devour its own parents and grow up rapidly into a charter for bigotry.

The reason is not difficult to find. It would clearly be outside the capabilities of any Western legislature or individual courts to define precisely what may constitute blasphemy against, for example, Islam. Only Muslim authorities could decide that, and clearly their criteria would be very different to those of our own society.

For pious Muslims (and we can be sure that only the pious would bother themselves with the minutiae of a blasphemy law), much would be anathema that might seem to you or me no more than fair comment. To suggest that Muhammad in some sense wrote the Qur'an (and not that God revealed it to him by means of the angel Gabriel), or that the sacred Traditions ascribed to the Prophet are really the product of later generations, or that Muhammad may indeed have uttered what are known as the Satanic Verses – all of this would be wholly unacceptable to any orthodox Muslim. And yet such views, far from being deliberate insults devised by ignorant or perverse minds, are common ideas in modern Western academic writing about Islam.

If Muslims are allowed to have books withdrawn from circulation simply because they do not meet with pious approval, we could rapidly find ourselves in a situation where legitimate scholarship or fair comment, quite as much as careless journalism, would be pilloried. We should not be complacent about this. Much Muslim writing in recent years has concentrated on the 'insults' offered by Western scholars to Islam. Not all such writing has the intelligence or sensitivity of Said (who is, in any case, not himself a Muslim).

The ban on Rushdie's novel could prove a precedent with horrendous consequences. We have all seen the results when religious fundamentalism succeeds in intimidating courts and shops, coercing them into banning certain books or records as offensive: in some parts of the United States, battles still rage over textbooks in schools or public libraries.

The use of liberal principles to gain victories for illiberal causes has become widespread. Bigots will readily go to courts to argue that their liberties are infringed by the presence of offensive literature in the schoolroom or on the library shelf. Yet, as always in such matters, there is much hypocrisy very near the surface. Muslim writers are not innocent of offensive behaviour – far from it. Muslim writing about the religious minority of Baha'ism, for example, is often extremely coarse, grossly unfair and deliberately offensive. There has seldom been anything in Indian Islam but open contempt for the polytheism of Hindu belief. Christian and Jewish beliefs are repeatedly derided in the Qur'an itself. What if British or American Jews were to call for a ban on the Qur'an tomorrow?

Should the present process be allowed to go unchecked, calls for censorship will grow more strident, and Salman Rushdie will become the first in a long line of literary and academic martyrs. I myself lost a British university post two years ago because the Saudi Ministry of Education (who funded it) decided it did not

like the way I was teaching Islam. Who will be next? Dante?
Morier? Voltaire?

Serious literature, like exciting scholarship, is, almost by
definition, controversial. Without controversy, nothing thrives.
Should there be a sustained ban on *The Satanic Verses*, its
effects on literature and scholarship could prove devastating. The
repercussions will touch not only Western scholarship on Islam or
reportage about the Muslim world, but a host of other, unrelated
areas. Other religions have their sensitivities, other believers are
easily offended by what they see as misrepresentations, lies
or insults. Sikhs, Jews, fundamentalist Christians, Mormons,
Baha'is, Moonies – the list is inexhaustible. Already the publication of an academic book of mine has been delayed for over
two years because of pressure brought to bear on its American
publishers by a religious body.

Writers must offend. It is, in a manner of speaking, their trade.
The inoffensive is also the bland. It is all too easy to make a close
comparison between racism and the giving of offence on religious
grounds. But there is, in fact, a vast difference. Race is a matter
of skin, religion one of perception. If I call a man a fool because
he is black, I am clearly talking nonsense, even if he happens to
be both a fool and black. But if I say a man is a fool to believe
that creation took six days or that Muhammad split the moon in
two, or that the dead will be resurrected, surely I am expressing
a valid opinion. And if I want to say that polygamy or holy war
or the doctrine that only those washed in the blood of Christ are
heaven-bound offends me, am I to be denied that freedom?

(First published in *The Times Higher Education
Supplement*, 27 January 1989)

The Law of Blasphemy and Civil Liberties

What will happen if *The Satanic Verses* is withdrawn from circulation? Very little, in any obvious sense. Muslims in Britain and elsewhere will celebrate a victory. Salman Rushdie and his publishers will breathe a collective – and undoubtedly premature – sigh of relief. Viking Penguin shares will go up a few points. The literary world will feel a sense of impoverishment or weakness for a while. Articles will be written and interviews given deploring the decision. But for the rest, the world at large will go on much as ever, and in a matter of months, it will be as though the fever that has gripped us all in these past weeks had been no more than a bad dream.

There will, of course, be negative results that no one will ever be aware of. Some novelists – myself included – who might very well have written on Islamic themes will think twice and turn their energies to other subjects. And if they do not, their agents and editors will quickly put them right. Journalists filing copy on events in the Muslim world will modify their articles or see them amended by nervous editors. Television documentaries on Islamic fundamentalism or Iran after Khomeini or the plight of Muslim women will be filmed and edited with an eye on the bearded faces on the other side of the screen. There will be no more cartoons of turbaned prelates wielding scimitars. 'Spitting Image' will have lost a beloved character or two.

Then, a year later, maybe two, it will happen again. It will not be a novel next time. In all likelihood, it will be an academic work, something scholarly but not too obscure. The theme will be early Islamic history, the Qur'an or the sacred Traditions. The argument may not be very original, merely a restatement of standard Western views, but someone somewhere will be sure to find it offensive, someone with like-minded friends who do not need to read books before burning them. This time, they will have the force of precedent, perhaps even the law, on their side.

It may not be an academic work, of course. It could just as easily be something more classical: Dante's *Divine Comedy*, Voltaire's *Mahomet*, Carlyle's essay on the Prophet from *Heroes and Hero-Worship*, Beckford's *Vathek*, Morier's *Hajji Baba* – who knows what the hardline fancy may light upon? Someone has already threatened to blow up Dante's tomb in Ravenna.

To make matters worse, next time it may not even be a book about Islam. All religions and sects have their fundamentalists, their no-compromisers – and fundamentalists are by nature ready to take offence. Offence is built into the system: without it, where would be the 'militant wrathfulness' that one British Muslim intellectual has insisted is religion's only defence against the onslaughts of a secular society?

A year from now, Sikhs may take to the streets because a Hindu has insulted Guru Nanak, or Mormons because Brigham Young has been portrayed in a new biography as a womanizer; or Jews because someone has written an anti-Zionist novel; or Moonies because Sun Myung Moon has popped up in an unfavourable light in yet another anti-cultist publication. Extend this list at your own discretion. A ban on *The Satanic Verses* would be the golden key to unlock a Pandora's box most of us did not even suspect was lying in the cellar.

The foregoing is the best scenario. Actually, things may be a lot worse. I refer in particular to the attempts of the Muslim community, aided and abetted by MPs on both sides of the House (not to mention sundry clerics and community leaders muddled into thinking they are dealing here with a race-relations issue), to have our antiquated law of blasphemy extended to non-Christian religions. And what a mess that will be, if it comes off. That may seem a harsh verdict on what is, after all, a proposal prompted by the best of liberal intentions. But I firmly believe that the net result of such a change in the law would be greater, not less, intolerance.

In order to understand this seeming paradox better, it may be instructive to glance at the experience of the United States, where the issue of religious toleration has a long and complex history. At the root of American legal attitudes is the opening clause of the Bill of Rights: 'Congress shall make no law respecting an establishment of religion.' This view seemed to be challenged by the judgment of a New York court in 1811, which upheld a charge of blasphemy against a man who had asserted that 'Jesus Christ was a bastard and his mother was a whore', while explicitly denying similar protection to Muslims and others on the grounds that the United States was a Christian country.

Later American practice, however, has favoured almost unrestricted freedom of conscience, as summarized in a famous ruling of the Supreme Court from 1872:

> In this country the full and free right to entertain any religious belief, to practice any religious principle, and to teach any religious doctrine which does not violate the laws of morality and property, and which does not infringe personal rights, is conceded to all. The law knows no heresy, and is committed to the support of no dogma, the establishment of no sect.

Over the years, in numerous cases involving marginal groups, such as Mormons, Jehovah's Witnesses or Black Muslims, American courts have adopted a non-interventionist approach. One court declared in 1944 that heresy trials are foreign to the Constitution, arguing that no jury could be competent to decide on the truth or falsity of a given set of beliefs.

Such principles are subject to severe challenges. In the States in recent years, courts have on several occasions passed judgment in favour of 'deprogrammers' and other anti-cultists, thereby involving the state directly in decisions as to what is and what is not acceptable religious belief or behaviour. Such cases have usually involved controversial new religions like the Moonies or Scientologists; but the dangers of legal meddling in religious controversy are shown most vividly in a case involving a religious group of very little notoriety. The incident is not well known, even in American legal circles, but it illustrates dramatically the hazards involved when a secular court tries to intervene in a doctrinal dispute.

The case was the second in which the orthodox leadership of the Baha'i movement in the United States tried to suppress the activities of a dissident group. In 1928, the Baha'i authorities had successfully registered the religious name 'Baha'i' as a trademark with the US Patent Office. Some years later, in

1939, they brought a suit against a breakaway group that had opened a 'Baha'i Bookshop' in New York. Supreme Court Justice Louis Valente ruled against the orthodox authorities on several grounds, including the principle that they 'have no right to monopoly on the name of a religion'. The old, non-interventionist liberalism of American justice was still firmly in the saddle.

In 1964, however, the central Baha'i organization filed a claim against another heretical group, based on trademark infringement, and in 1966 they actually succeeded in winning an injunction against the dissidents, who were prohibited the use of the name 'Baha'i' or any symbols of the religion. In other words, the court (in this case, an Illinois district court) had actively supported the right of a particular religious body to exclusive use of a religious name and symbols. The law had recognized heresy and made its promotion illegal.

In several other countries, attempts have been made to frame legislation aimed at state control over unconventional religious groups. In 1984, Richard Cottrell, then Tory MEP for Bristol, presented a 'Motion for a Resolution on the activity of certain new religious movements within the European Community', which received the approval of the European Parliament. Cottrell has been supported by a loose grouping of churches and anti-cult groups, all eager to restrict the activities of deviant sects on the flimsy grounds that they may prove injurious to vulnerable individuals.

It is these instances of actual or intended state interference in religious liberty which make me particularly nervous about the passing of an extended law of blasphemy in this country. Manifestly, no British parliament and no British court could be expected to rule on what actually constituted blasphemy in any given instance. A jury would be irrelevant, since no average group of British citizens could be deemed capable of weighing a body, not of facts, but of opinion rooted in alien beliefs and traditions. As in the Illinois ruling based on trademark law, judgments would veer towards technicalities.

If, for example, a succession of expert witnesses testified that, in the opinion of Muslim religious authorities in Egypt or Saudi Arabia, a given statement constituted blasphemy, the court could in no circumstances find that it did not. Leaving aside obvious insults or gross distortions, this would leave the field wide open to suits against dissident Muslim groups (Ahmadis, for example, or even Shi'ites, whose literature is often insulting to the early Caliphs of the Sunnis).

Similarly, Muslim academics attempting to develop modernist interpretations of, say, the life of the Prophet, the Qur'an, or the sacred Traditions, could suddenly find their works as easily banned in Britain as in Saudi Arabia or Iran. By the same token, non-Muslim academics writing on similar topics might find their books or articles the subject of court cases: much modern Islamic writing is already scathing about orientalists and their role in a broad imperialist plot to destroy Islam.

There are fundamental differences between British and Islamic (or Islamic-based) law which cannot, I think, be readily resolved by the introduction of a broader law of blasphemy in this country. Let me, as before, but in a very different spirit, take the case of the Baha'is and, in particular, an instance of legislation directed against them in a Muslim country. In 1947, an Egyptian Baha'i, Mustafa Kamil 'Ali 'Abd Allah, sought official recognition for his marriage, which had been refused on the grounds that Baha'is, as renegades from Islam, could not legally marry. His case was eventually taken before the Egyptian Supreme Administrative Court by two of the country's leading lawyers, Saba Habashi Pasha and Professor Sa'd al-Fishawi, who rested their plea on the provisions of article 12 of the constitution, which provided explicitly for absolute freedom of religious belief.

After two years of deliberations, the court argued that the framers of the constitution had not intended by this article that there should be 'freedom to believe in apostasy or to change one's religion'. Subsequently, Shaykh Bakhit, the Mufti of Egypt, demanded that the article be modified, in consequence of which the term 'religious' was removed from the clause permitting freedom of thought. In 1960, following another incident, law no. 262 was passed, outlawing Baha'ism in Egypt.

Such measures – which can be duplicated in many other Muslim states, including Iran, Iraq and even supposedly secularist Turkey – are manifestly prejudiced. Yet they have the force of law and express something basic in the Islamic view of the world. For Muslims, the very stability of society rests on the maintenance of proper religious belief and practice.

According to Islamic belief, some religions – Christianity and

Judaism – have been divinely revealed, and their followers may, subject to certain restrictions, exercise their right to believe in them and observe their rituals and their laws of personal conduct within the framework of an Islamic state. Others, such as Hinduism or Buddhism or animism, are, by their very nature, false, but prudence dictates that Muslims should not engage in any outright onslaught on them. And yet others, such as Baha'ism or other minority sects, are not only false but must be removed from the body politic, by force if necessary.

Such attitudes will, of necessity, dictate how Muslims will approach issues of blasphemy. But no Western court or constitution could possibly give them satisfaction without betraying its own principles and creating just the sort of anarchy that Muslims themselves claim their legislation is intended to prevent.

Blasphemy, like obscenity, is notoriously difficult to define. There is, of course, never any trouble in establishing that someone has been offended, but if taking offence were to become adequate grounds for the banning or bowdlerization of books, films or music, very little would escape unscathed. To the extent that people choose to believe one thing rather than another, it is inevitable that some of the things they do not believe will offend them, sometimes severely.

The problem is that some of the offending statements – some of the blasphemies – may, for other people, be true, or may represent valid comment on specific beliefs or life in general. We are, after all, dealing here with more than private beliefs. Religions are also ideologies, often militant, uncompromising and eager to convert. Radical Muslims seek to win not only hearts, but entire states. If such ideologies cannot be criticized, even mocked, our most basic freedoms are all at risk.

The law should not be used to delegitimize debate, whether it be carried on at an academic level, as in serious articles on Islamic history, or at the level of the imagination, as in *The Satanic Verses*. But that is precisely what a general law of blasphemy would achieve.

Somewhere, a line has to be drawn. If it is to be anywhere, it must be here, at the point where we are threatened with the loss of our most fundamental freedoms in the name of a misguided liberalism that aims to provide a cloak under which the most illiberal motives and actions will be given free rein.

(Based on an article first published in the
Bookseller, April 1989)

The Blasphemy Debate: Reflections on Richard Webster's *Brief History of Blasphemy*

Hard as I tried, I found I could not quite dislike Richard Webster's little book on 'Liberalism, Censorship, and *The Satanic Verses*'. John Hyams, reviewing it in the *Bookseller*, had prepared me to do so. It is, after all, a vehement attack on Rushdie and the liberal establishment which has supported him. As a self-confessed liberal intellectual who has written widely in Rushdie's defence, I had reservations about a tract by a British bookseller who seemed to be 'selling out' to the forces of obscurantism. I expected a half-baked diatribe.

Instead, I found myself reading a well-written, intelligent and reasoned contribution to the debate, a book that I could recommend to friends, not because I agree with its conclusions, but because I think it raises an increasingly sterile argument to new levels, levels that must be entered on if anything positive is ever to emerge from this battle of ideologies.

In spite of this, I still have reservations. John Hyams got it broadly right, in his perception that the book lacks 'a sound centre'. There *is* something missing at its heart, and I think it worth a closer analysis to find what that something is.

Webster is right in saying that liberals can be hypocritical, that they defend Jews, blacks and other minorities against abuse but are seldom outspoken about insults directed at Muslims. He is right in tracing many current prejudices about Islam to a long history of anti-Muslim polemic. Quite properly, he draws attention to increased anti-Asian and anti-Muslim racism in the wake of the Rushdie affair and insists that we should not ignore the very real consequences of this debate for ordinary Muslims in our society. Like others before him (including myself), he argues that anti-Semitic bigotry has become anti-Arab and anti-Muslim bigotry. And his critique of Rushdie's article, 'In Good Faith', is careful, sharp and occasionally insight-ful.

The trouble is that he is as one-sided as some of the writers he criticizes. If *The Satanic Verses* is Salman Rushdie's attempt to dis-sociate himself from his early religious and cultural background, *A Brief History of Blasphemy* is Richard Webster's rejection of the liberal tradition in which he was brought up. He has eyes only for the abuses of Western thought and practice. 'The church,' he says, 'has at times actively encouraged Christians to engage in blasphemy, sometimes of a scurrilous and obscene kind, against rival faiths.' That is true, but it is also true, and needs to be said, that Islamic and other religious leaders have done exactly the same thing. It also needs to be said that, with the exception of some fundamentalist groups, most Christian churches have abandoned such practices. That does not hold true for many other faiths (including, significantly, Islam) which have benefited less from the impact of secular liberalism. The fact that we have been wrong does not make them right.

Webster's problem is that he knows his European culture and history, and is well placed to criticize them, but is clearly much less familiar with Islam or with authoritarian religion in general. This leads to a degree of naïveté surprising in an otherwise critical thinker. It is disturbing, for example, to see how often he tries to play down the enormity of the Muslim challenge to free speech by emphasizing the extremism of those who have pronounced and supported the *fatwa* for Rushdie's death. In doing so, he overlooks the fact that it is a fundamental enactment of Islamic law that renders apostasy punishable by death and that it is as much for apostasy as for blasphemy that Rushdie has been indicted.

Not only that, but he forgets that, in the Islamic world as a whole, there is widespread governmental and public support for the suppression of books and articles deemed derogatory of the faith. This includes texts that would seem innocuous by most standards, as well as the writings of heretics and followers of other religions. He should open a bookshop in Riyadh and try selling Christian or Jewish books.

He writes that 'most Muslims have gone out of their way to distinguish between criticism and abuse, and to make it clear that they are campaigning only against the latter and against the use of obscene and violent language in relation to their religious tradition'. That is true only with respect to *The Satanic Verses*. Numerous critical works have been banned in Muslim countries, works whose only obscenity is to challenge the assumptions of a triumphalist faith. Webster passes over that fact in silence.

This naïveté encourages him to call for the replacement of the present blasphemy law by one that would embrace all faiths. Although he discusses at length the booklet of the International Committee for the Defence of Salman Rushdie, *The Crime of Blasphemy – Why It Should be Abolished*, he nowhere tackles the real problems that an extension of the law would entail, remarking only that 'a number of extremely important questions have yet to be resolved'. Let me try to summarize some of the problems.

We have laws, argues Webster, that restrict libellous, obscene or racist publications, and so we should have others to control blasphemy. But who will frame those laws? Could a British parliament define the limits of blasphemy for Islam? Would Muslims allow it? Could it, conversely, introduce into British law the rulings of medieval Islamic jurisprudents? Since, as I have noted, Rushdie's technical crime is that of apostasy, are we to see a man jailed for loss of faith?

Imagine that Salman Rushdie is brought to trial under new legislation, and suppose that he has been found innocent. Will Muslims, who have brought the case and unitedly deem his book blasphemous, accept that verdict? Their own tribunals will have found him guilty. The judgment of a British court cannot change what is blasphemous to what is not, cannot challenge the rulings of God's law. What, then, is the point of passing legislation that would force courts to adjudicate on such matters? The alternative is to find anyone accused of blasphemy automatically guilty on the principle that, if a religious community says its beliefs have been blasphemed, the accused must be, *ipso facto*, guilty. And why stop there? If Muslims can decide who is guilty and who is not, why not allow them to carry out punishments as well? Since the flouting of religious law is offensive to sincere believers, will our police forces and courts be called on to enforce *purdah* or abstinence from alcohol and pork?

The concept of blasphemy is a double-edged sword. Offence comes from all sides, but the followers of most religions act as though they are in a one-way street. Like beauty, blasphemy is in the eye of the beholder. Or the believer. One man's declaration of faith is another's insult. The line between criticism and offence is hard to draw, and in religious situations seldom if ever drawn.

Webster is painfully conscious of the ways in which liberals may grow strident and even bigoted. That is true and to be regretted. What he seems unaware of is how even the most liberal religions may harbour fundamentalist tendencies. Take the example of Baha'ism, a widespread religion originating in Islam in the last century. In the West, it has a reputation as an ultra-liberal faith, preaching the abolition of all prejudice, the independent investigation of truth, and religious harmony. And yet the Baha'i authorities have several times suppressed publications and exercise a total veto over everything followers write. This year, in the United States, a Baha'i publishing house was forced to restrict its activities because many of its books had been put on a blacklist. That is a religion generations ahead of Islam in its liberalism. Think what use they might make of a law of blasphemy, then imagine what less liberal faiths might do.

At the recent Liberal Democrat conference, a number of delegates called, like Webster, for an extension of the blasphemy law. One woman said it would be dangerous to abolish the law of blasphemy altogether, since its removal would leave a vacuum. What sort of vacuum did she imagine that would be? Room for doubt, for the mocking of pretension and dogmatism, for freedom to call in question even the most sacred things? Room for Muslim women to discard the veil, for non-Muslims to receive full citizenship in orthodox Muslim states, for anyone to convert from Islam without the fear of being put to death? A society without blasphemy laws holds dangers only for religious dogmatism, the suppression of dissent, and the longing some men have to strap their moral straitjackets on the rest of us.

Richard Webster is right. There are problems with secular liberal democracies: arrogance, self-righteousness, hypocrisy and blindness. And he is correct when he writes that 'if the West continues to refine and develop the forms of demonological anti-Islamic prejudice which have emerged since 1945, and if it continues on a course of confrontation with Islam in general, or with Iran in particular, then the kind of conflict which might ultimately arise would be on a huge scale' – words more pertinent today than when they were first written earlier this year.

But he is wrong if he imagines that the solution lies in an

abandonment of liberal principles or capitulation to the forces of obscurantism, whether external or internal. Freedom is fragile, and we have trouble keeping it intact. We make mistakes. But we learn from them.

Liberalism is not, as Webster alleges, a fundamentalist faith embarked on a holy war. Nor is there, as Kalim Siddiqui claims, 'a crusade of fundamentalist liberal inquisition against Islam and Muslims'. We liberals have no priests, no unchallengeable texts, no unchangeable laws, no hardened dogmas. The achievements of modern Western civilization in respect of human rights, civil liberties and personal freedom are greater than those of any past society. Richard Webster would not have the freedom to declare himself an atheist in an Islamic state. I would not be free to write, or the *Bookseller* to publish, this article. That is the bottom line. And that is where I and other liberals stand.

(First published in the *Bookseller*, 9 November 1990)

A Sense of Proportion

During a recent debate on the rights and wrongs of *The Satanic Verses*, the following letter by Brian Anson appeared in the columns of the *Guardian*:

> The tidal wave of letters on the Rushdie affair has little meaning when seen against the hypocrisy of our society. Most writers seem inspired with the great ideals of freedom and it is assumed that we must not let up in our defence of Rushdie lest we lose something precious: despite the fact that we have already lost those freedoms. Daniel Easterman wonders '... how many articles, films or TV documentaries have been abandoned, rejected, not commissioned ...' On Northern Ireland alone, dozens, hundreds?
>
> Rushdie should be supported because it is right to support him but let's not pretend that his is a test case of our 'beloved freedoms'. Free comment in our society was taken away long before his book was published. Let those who support Rushdie do it with integrity if they do it at all. Double standards can be left to the politicians and the media.
>
> As a writer I supported the Salman Rushdie campaign from the beginning but I did so with a 'heavy heart' because of the unprotested lack of freedoms elsewhere in our society.

If Anson is right, some of us have blown the Rushdie affair out of proportion or mistakenly allowed it to distract us from broader, more important issues. I gave his letter much thought, but in the end concluded that he is mistaken. I sympathize with him, but I think he is wrong. There is, I believe, something special about the Rushdie affair, something that makes it, not only a test case, but a central issue in the debate about what it means to possess freedoms, to be tolerant, to live in a mixed culture.

It is indeed true that many of our basic freedoms have come

under attack in recent years. The reporting of events in Northern Ireland is an excellent example. We can all think of others. But the fact does remain that such attacks can be and have been challenged, often successfully, both in the press and in the courts. The publication of *Spycatcher* was a triumph for the public and a sign that even the most hard-headed government can sometimes be brought to heel.

However tough things get, we have recourse to free elections, we have a press that is relatively unfettered, and we have courts that will stand up for our legal rights. It is a struggle – when has it not been? – but it is a fairly balanced one, perhaps even weighted, if only marginally, in favour of freedom and the public interest.

The Rushdie affair involves a struggle where such balances are not even implied. Islamic law is not democratic: it is a system rooted in a series of supposedly infallible and unchallengeable texts, established by an elite body of scholars long since dead, and today interpreted and implemented by a similar elite. Shi'ite law is, if anything, less democratic than its Sunni equivalent: *mujtahids* achieve their positions, not by election, but by scholastic achievement.

In Shi'ite theory, believers are divided into two groups – *mujtahids* on the one hand and everybody else (*muqallidun* or imitators) on the other. Not even the simplest questions – whether the death sentence is a proper punishment for blasphemy, whether *The Satanic Verses* is actually blasphemous – can be raised by the mass of Muslims. Non-believers do not count at all, of course. Even Jews and Christians, the (sometimes) tolerated People of the Book, have no say whatever in such matters.

In the Western context, the Rushdie controversy has introduced factors previously absent in similar affairs, most notably the threat of violence. I still remember vividly the night they announced that Peter Sissons had been sentenced to die simply because he had interviewed Iranian chargé d'affairs Akhundzadeh-Basti in a vigorous manner. Nothing could distort debate more than this threat that one might be beaten up or killed merely for putting one's views uncompromisingly. It happens in many countries, of course, and we in Britain should think ourselves lucky that we have been spared such threats until now. That, however, is precisely the point: the freedom to speak out without threat of violence is something to be thankful for and something to defend.

Death sentences aside, the broadest Muslim position now seems to centre on toleration, on a supposed inability of Western secular society to tolerate the presence within it of alien values, on what Kalim Siddiqui has called 'the current British crusade of fundamentalist liberal inquisition against Islam and Muslims'.

The long history of Western anti-Islamic prejudice – those medieval diatribes against Mahound, the polemics of Crusader theologians, the orientalist vision of imperialist scholars and administrators, writers and artists – is cited as the context within which current attitudes must be judged. (The equally long history of Islamic anti-Christian or anti-Jewish or plain anti-Western prejudice is, of course, passed over in silence.)

This does, naturally, present a dilemma. It is very hard to convince a Muslim brought up on negative images of the West that our defence of a supposedly blasphemous book is not a continuation of centuries-old intolerance but rather a position postulated on the need for absolute tolerance, including tolerance for Islam. Harder still to make it clear that a properly secular society, precisely because it favours no one religion, is a defender of all religions.

How to get across this crucial point, that victory in the campaign against *The Satanic Verses* would spell defeat in the broader struggle to find tolerance within the secular system? That a widened law of blasphemy would mean less, not more, freedom for religious minorities. That a privileged position for religious ideas would provoke disaster for the free expression of religious opinion.

Let me come to this sideways and by means of anecdote. Some years ago, an American publisher asked me to allow them to issue an old dissertation of mine, dealing with the early textual history of Baha'ism. Last year, a much-rewritten version of the book was ready for publication, but at the last moment the publishing firm, itself run by Baha'is, was instructed not to go ahead. The Baha'i authorities had decided that my text insulted certain key figures of their faith.

The book in question will now be published by a major European academic publishing house, and the issue of freedom of speech does not arise. What is at issue is, I think, subtler. The book is not one of my novels, but an excessively dry, elaborately footnoted study of nineteenth-century

Arabic and Persian manuscripts. For all that, the representatives of a religious community noted for its tolerance saw fit to ban it. More seriously, the publishing house who had tried to issue it has now been forced to limit its activites, apparently because so many of its titles had been placed on an official blacklist.

I use this anecdote very deliberately. Religious tolerance is one of the key teachings of the Baha'i religion. So, for that matter, is the harmony of reason and revelation, religion and science. The Baha'i public image is very different from that of fundamentalist Islam. And yet Baha'is have burned books. Baha'is have launched court cases in the United States against their own heretics. Within the movement, all texts – even music and poetry – are subject to formal approval before publication. And woe betide the author who steps, however marginally, outside the bounds of what orthodoxy deems to be the truth.

Why is it that even a religion that wants to be tolerant, that in many crucial respects is tolerant, will still resort to censorship within and, where possible, suppression without in order to ensure uniformity of thought?

The answer is, I think, quite simple. Religions are wholesale ideologies, they cannot be taken piecemeal, a bit of this, a little of that, as it suits us. If they are not true they must be false, and if they are false they are worse than useless. It is not possible to be ninety-nine per cent God. His Word cannot be ninety-nine per cent true. His prophets cannot be ninety-nine per cent inspired.

This is, of course, Durkheim's absolute dichotomy, that between sacred and profane. The early history of Islam and the text of the Qur'an are case studies in just this sort of dichotomization. It is there in orthodox Judaism, in evangelical Christianity, in Baha'ism: 'This is the truth and all else naught but error.'

This means that even tiny points of fact – mere quibbles from the outsider's viewpoint – can pose severe tests to faith. It may not seem to you or me to matter much whether the Qur'an contains historical or linguistic inaccuracies, as some Western scholars believe. But it does matter to Muslims very much indeed.

If the Qur'an is the unerring word of God, it cannot contain errors. If it does have even tiny errors it may begin to look as though it is not the Word of God at all. The same goes for the

Bible, for the Book of Mormon, for the whole vast canon of Baha'i scripture. It also goes for historical texts on which our knowledge of the lives of Jesus, Muhammad or other religious figures are based: if the authors have got one detail wrong, may they not have got everything wrong? If the Gospel genealogies of Jesus are mutually contradictory, can he have been born at all?

This is why religious orthodoxies are forced to such lengths to preserve their myths intact, why they cannot tolerate anything that may open up doubts. Within religious states, this means the suppression of a wide range of dissident views and, as often as not, the views and writings of those who adhere to other faiths. Other religions, after all, offer the ultimate challenge, the possibility that truth may not be absolute but relative. The forms such suppression takes will vary from time to time and from place to place, but the aim will always be to preserve the world-view of orthodoxy intact.

Among other things, this means that the concept of 'insult' will be very different to religious authorities than to other people. Which in turn means that once such authorities find themselves in a position to do so, they will take action against anyone and everyone who offends against what will always be an exceptionally fine sense of what is proper.

Look, for example, at what happened a few years ago in the United States, when evangelical Christians attempted to have school textbooks banned in some states. The contents of certain books, they argued, offended their beliefs and therefore constituted an infringement of their religious liberties. Darwin was in there, as you might expect. But so was Snow White (fairy tales are deemed works of the occult). So were texts which suggested that woman's place might be other than in the home. And so, significantly, were books dealing with world religions.

What would happen, then, if the law did allow the Muslim case against *The Satanic Verses*, whether under existing legislation or through the extension of the blasphemy laws? Clearly, our starting point should not be Mr Rushdie's book, but rather the many others currently suppressed or proscribed by the *ulama* in Muslim countries. If one book is banned, what reason can there possibly be to spare the rest? Circumstances have given prominence to Rushdie's novel, but fundamentalist zeal could draw up an ever-expanding list of additional titles for the attention of the courts.

Logically, the courts themselves would be forced to relinquish responsibility for such bannings to Muslim authorities in this country or elsewhere. Stop and think. Suppose a British jury or a British judge were to say, 'I do not find such and such a book offensive.' What do you think the Muslim reaction would be? 'Oh, yes, of course, you're perfectly right, why didn't we notice that ourselves? We're sorry to have bothered you'? Of course not. They will say, 'You are wrong. Muslim *ulama* in Cairo/Medina/Qum have declared this book blasphemous. They are experts. Muslims everywhere support them. How can you tell them they should not be offended?'

Now, what does that mean? For one thing, it means that books by Muslim heretics could be cited as blasphemous and banned in Britain. Studies by Muslim scholars challenging received wisdom about the Qur'an, Hadith, Prophet or law would meet the same censorship here as they already do in Iran, Saudi Arabia or Egypt. Books by Baha'is – a group universally hated throughout the Muslim world – could be taken off the shelves in London or Edinburgh. Academic works on Islam would be scrutinized and, where found wanting, removed from university reading lists or libraries or bookshops. Older European texts deemed unflattering to Islam or Muhammad – Dante, Gibbon, Carlyle, Voltaire – could appear in bowdlerized editions.

Remember, this is not paranoia on my part: books like these are already banned in most Muslim countries on the grounds of blasphemy. Why on earth would anyone stop at *The Satanic Verses* if they had the power to regulate anything and everything written about Islam?

In a sense, such regulation has already begun. In the year since the *fatwa*, several publishers have approached me asking whether they should go ahead with the publication of certain titles touching on Islam. In all these cases, I saw no reason why they should not proceed. But for all I know, other publishers have already withdrawn planned publications or turned down scripts or demanded massive editorial changes. The effects of the Rushdie furore have, I suspect, been incalculable. There can no longer be open debate about Islam in our society, and not even a pretence of it in Muslim countries.

This might not matter very much if Islam were a small, quietist cult with no political or social aspirations. The truth is very different. Islam is the fastest-growing religion in the world today. Throughout the Muslim world, there are more and more hardline groups entering the political arena with the aim of creating Islamic states ruled by the *shari'a*. In Africa, the USSR and south-east Asia, the destiny of whole regions is closely linked to that of Islam.

We cannot afford not to debate Islam, as religion and as ideology. The views of Muslims of all varieties must be freely aired. So too must the views of those who oppose them or have reservations about them.

Tolerance exacts a price. The price the Baha'is pay for not having their books banned as offensive to Muslims is to see books and articles by people like myself on sale or in public libraries. The price Muslims pay for complete freedom to publish here even the most vitriolic of attacks on Western society and morals is to be confronted by Baha'i, Sufi, Ahmadi and other texts on the open shelves beside them, or to read newspaper articles by Christian commentators critical of Islamic belief, or to meet Muslim feminists on the streets of Bradford calling for the abolition of the veil.

If there is hypocrisy in this affair, it is, I think – *pace* Mr Anson – not to be found predominantly in our society but among Rushdie's Muslim critics. Religious insult is alive and well in the Muslim world. It is, for example, possible to buy in Iran and the Arab world many books and pamphlets of the most abusive sort attacking the religious beliefs, holy figures and scriptures of the Baha'is. I have several on my shelves. They make *The Satanic Verses* seem like hagiography. Until not that long ago, it was common practice in Shi'ite communities to engage in the ritual cursing of the first three Caliphs of Islam, arch-enemies of the Shi'ite Imam Ali.

In many Muslim countries, the *Protocols of the Elders of Zion* is still freely available. Anti-Ahmadi publications are common in Pakistan. In Africa, animist beliefs are frequently derided by Muslim writers. Hinduism and Sikhism have been vilified by Muslim writers in India.[1] Until Muslims can get their own

---

[1] In 1990, an Iranian government agency banned the publication of the Gospels because the Persian Bible Society would not alter the phrases 'Son of God' and 'Lord' to 'Prophet'.

act together and show a determination to root out their own often severe prejudices, it is asking a great deal for us to turn a sympathetic ear to their demands for protection from other people's.

The shouting must stop before it is too late. Muslims in Britain must not only claim to be tolerant and reasonable, they must demonstrate their reasonableness by entering into a sensible debate about these issues and by showing a little concrete tolerance of other people's beliefs. In particular, it is time for some open discussion about the book itself. It can be argued that *The Satanic Verses* is not, in fact, blasphemous at all, or at least much less so than has been claimed. But the critics have closed their ears so tightly that not even a whisper of a debate can be heard anywhere. Shouts of 'Kill Rushdie' are no substitute for careful analysis of what has become an important literary and religious text. Shows of hands are no replacement for reasoned dialogue.

Muslim leaders must, I believe, face up to some facts. *The Satanic Verses* has been published. It is likely to go on being published by someone somewhere. If Rushdie or others die, secularism will have gained martyrs. If the book is widely banned, there will be an ongoing campaign to have the ban lifted. If all copies of the book are burned, there will be people to memorize it, as in Ray Bradbury's novel, *Fahrenheit 451*. It is time to take the existence of the book as an inescapable fact and to find more constructive ways in which to cope with it as a challenge to faith. The alternative is to perpetuate a struggle in which everyone will emerge a loser.

(First published in *Index on Censorship* 19:4
April 1990)

In Defence of *The Satanic Verses*

A year ago, I turned forty. I could look forward, I thought, to a straightforward future. Two years previously, I had given up my first career as a university lecturer in Islamic Studies, and was now well established in my second as a novelist. Then, out of nowhere, Islam came hurtling back into my life – into all our lives – with a vengeance. Literally, with a vengeance. I had thought that sort of thing behind me – argument, controversy, religious rage; the passionate defence of Islamic values against Western crassness, Western values against Islamic militancy. Overnight everything changed. A novelist became Antichrist (or Anti-Muhammad, Dajjal, what you will), a book the repository of all that is most loathsome in Western culture.

A year later I still find myself deep in paradox. For years, I sat with students or vicars or teachers or journalists, explaining the many ways in which our culture has misapprehended, mis-represented and misjudged the Orient – above all, the Orient of Islam, the Islam of our imagination. I did all I could to dispel misunderstandings and replace stereotypes with realities. But for the past year I have been deeply concerned to defend Salman Rushdie's *The Satanic Verses* against Muslim critics who maintain that it is a replay of orientalist fictions about the Prophet and his followers, that it offends in all the ways the worst Western polemic ever offended.

Have I, then, betrayed my own ideals? I believe not. Like the Smiths in Greene's *The Comedians*, who took so long to accept that the blacks they had spent a lifetime defending could behave as badly as whites, many supporters of inter-religious understanding and dialogue find it hard to speak up for the values on which that understanding is based. Almost all Islamicists, desperate to forge a new, post-orientalist image for themselves, keep silent, hoping the nasty thing will go away.

It is understandable that the liberal conscience should be stricken by this affair, incapable of responding to a situation that tears it so fiercely in two directions. The book is offensive: that is simple fact, for which there is plenty of evidence in the protests of Muslims everywhere. But the burning and banning of books, not to speak of the pronouncement of death sentences against their authors, are equally offensive. The unkindest cut of all for anyone concerned about fostering good community relations in this country is that the Muslims themselves have, in a matter of months, done more damage to their own cause than any number of orientalists could have done in decades. It will take more than an apology from Kalim Siddiqui to repair the damage done to Islam's international image through this sorry affair.

The fundamental error made by Rushdie's Muslim opponents and those who have supported them in the name of inter-religious harmony is to claim that religion should, somehow, be sacrosanct, above criticism, question or ridicule. You can insult my mother, my wife, my sister, they say, and I will swallow it; but insult my prophet or my holy book, and I will be obliged to take action against you. John Le Carré wrote recently in the *Guardian* that 'Nobody has a God-given right to insult a great religion and be published with impunity.'

The error in this is to think that religious belief, however venerable or deeply held, belongs to a special category of ideas, that it can be hermetically sealed from all contagion inside some sort of isolation unit. Ironically, such a view of religion is one explicitly rejected by all modern fundamentalist Islamic writing, not least that of the late Imam Khomeini himself. His best-known work, *Wilayat al-faqih*, opens with a lengthy attack on the notion that Islam, like Christianity, is nothing more than a private affair, with a few regulations for personal ethics and social behaviour. On the contrary, he argues, Islam is a comprehensive socio-religious system with rules and guidelines for every aspect of human affairs, from dress and diet to government and war.

Islam, as we have noted before in these pages, is an all-encompassing ideological system, a blueprint for the ideal society, God's mundane Kingdom. Modern Muslims involved in the worldwide renascence of their faith do not hesitate to urge this view. They are engaged in a summons to truth, social order and divine justice – salvation, not only for the individual, but for cities and nations. The Islamic nations first, then, bit by bit, the whole world.

It is here I begin to grow choleric. We have granted radical Muslims the right (often denied them in secular Muslim countries) to publish, to preach, to disseminate their beliefs. The Islamic missionary effort throughout the world is vast and not unsuccessful in winning converts. Some estimates make Islam the fastest-growing religion in the world today. And yet, should anyone so much as question the beliefs of Islam, or restructure its history, or criticize its legal system, or mock its pretensions to moral supremacy, an outcry is raised.

'Whoever changes his religion, slay him.' That, according to Islamic tradition, was the Prophet's own verdict on the supreme crime of apostasy. As ideologies go, Islam is among the most absolutist. Certain religious minorities (but by no means all) may be tolerated, provided they are kept in an inferior position, offer no threat to Islam, and do not try to convert Muslims. Otherwise, there is no room for manoeuvre. All thoughts, all sentiments, all words that challenge this monopoly of the truth run the risk of being condemned as blasphemy, and those who hold or utter them that of execution for the crime of apostasy. We have already noted the removal of the phrase 'absolute religious freedom' from the Egyptian constitution in order to accommodate an Islamic demand for controls over individuals seeking to convert from Islam to 'false' beliefs such as Baha'ism or atheism.

In practice, of course, Islam has been richer and more varied than the prelates of Qom or the jurists of al-Azhar would have liked. The eccentricities of the vast Sufi tradition, the saint-worship and miracle-working of popular piety, the speculations of mystical philosophy (not least in Iran), the eclecticisms of art and poetry have all conspired to break the grey monolith of the *ulema* into a brilliant cultural and intellectual mosaic. But always, and never more so than today, the advocates of uniformity and strict obedience to a seventh-century ideal have lain in wait for heretics and backsliders and insisted that the world be divided neatly in two between the realm of Islam and the realm of war.

Orthodox Muslims (like all other strict ideologues) find it difficult to understand that such totalitarian systems can and should be subjected to criticism or even ridicule. That is the price you must pay for seeking to control the lives of other men: the possibility that others will answer back. There is no shortage of Muslim criticism of the West, or of other religions from Zoroastrianism and Baha'ism in Iran to animism in Africa or Hinduism in India. Some of that criticism is very offensive indeed, but no doubt those who write it believe they have a right to voice it.

Had Salman Rushdie mocked the private beliefs and inner feelings of a reclusive sect, he might have deserved less sympathy. But his target is a militant, often strident, hugely successful ideology that seeks nothing less than world domination. Islam is big enough and powerful enough to defend itself against such pinpricks without resorting to threats of violence or even calls for the book's withdrawal.

Why, then, the fuss? There is, I think, a symbiosis between *The Satanic Verses* and the fundamentalism that condemns it. Had modern Islam not become so aggressive, had it not given birth to a new and militant orthodoxy, I doubt very much if Rushdie or anyone else would have tackled it in this way. And it is, of course, precisely because the book touches on the sensitivities of a freshly-awakened zealotry that condemnation of it has been so fierce. Neither book nor opponents could exist without the other. 'Where there is no belief, there is no blasphemy,' as Rushdie himself puts it.

It is a mistake to think that Western defence of Rushdie springs out of hatred for Islam, as Kalim Siddiqui and others have argued. Most of his defenders know next to nothing about the subject. They would do the same for any writer similarly threatened by a religious or political system. If the Russian or Polish or South African governments were to issue threats because a British publisher had issued a book by one of their dissidents, we would regard that as unacceptable interference in our freedom, as an attempt to impose external standards of censorship and thought policing in a freer society.

Some British Muslims have said that, since this is not an Islamic country, the death threat is illegitimate, but that, were Rushdie living in a state where Islamic law held sway, his execution would be both lawful and desirable. Technically, they are right. But, if anything, this only makes matters worse. Even if Rushdie were an Iranian citizen living in Iran and facing death there, Westerners would feel compelled to speak out, as we do when writers are arrested in South Africa or killed in Latin America. It is, we believe, not justifiable to put a man to death merely because he has caused offence, however deep, however regrettable. Nor is it acceptable to ban or burn a book simply because it shocks or hurts.

It is not a question of whether Muslims have the right to execute such sentences in their own cultures – of course they do – but of whether a law that condemns a man to death for blasphemy or for abandoning his ancestral faith is a good or civilized law by what we loosely call modern standards. I know this begs many questions: is the West more civilized than the East, are 'modern standards' guarantees of humane behaviour, is this not simple, post-imperial arrogance? Those are serious questions, but I do not wish to consider them here. A more pressing matter calls for our attention.

We are, I think, very near what may prove to be the heart of this controversy. Throughout this century, Muslims have struggled – with little help and sometimes outright hostility from the West – to rediscover and redefine their religion and, with it, their culture and identity. This struggle has been one of the most important undertakings in fourteen centuries of Islamic civilization, with consequences that will affect the whole of mankind for good or ill. It is, in its most intimate moments, a struggle by Muslims for themselves. How could it be otherwise, spurred on as it has been by a vast upsurge of feeling against almost two centuries of direct and indirect oppression by the Western colonial powers?

And yet, to the extent that we now live in a global village and the decrees of an aged *mujtahid* in Qom can reach in moments the streets of Bradford or the pages of my local newspaper, the Islamic renascence cannot remain an enterprise of Muslims alone. To the outsider, it must appear a tragedy that so much energy for renewal has been piped into channels of frenzy, neurosis and outright hatred. A faith that guns down a president in Egypt, that executes its opponents in Iran, and that threatens death to writers and publishers anywhere is in serious danger of tearing itself apart.

One reason why Islam still seems so ill-adapted to the world as it has become in this century is the almost total absence in the writings of its leading modern exponents of serious and informed consideration of contemporary issues. All the well-known Islamic ideologues of this century have espoused an essentially reactionary doctrine. From Muhammad Abduh to Hasan al-Banna, Sayyed Qutb and Shariati, the call is for a return to a 'true Islam', an ideal forged fourteen centuries ago. Our modern dilemma, according to these writers, is that man has strayed from the path laid down for him by God. If only, they say, society could return to God's path, if only men could be governed as they were in the days of the Prophet and his companions, then disorder would give way to order and injustice to justice. If only.

This unredeemed conservatism has been resisted by secularists, but it has seldom been challenged from within the ranks of the faith itself. Even the moderates pursue a basically conservative course. What little attempt there was at genuine reform in earlier years has been all but crushed to death by the juggernaut of fundamentalist revivalism. Basic assumptions remain unchallenged – the inerrancy of the Quranic text, the authenticity of the sacred Traditions, the perfection of early Islamic society, the purity of the classical legal system.

Something desperate, something more than a mere academic discussion of history or exegesis, is needed to stimulate a deep and far-reaching change within the very heart of the faith. Could it be – and I ask this in all sincerity – that the furore over this one book, the imaginative tidal wave unleashed by it, could prove the catalyst for just such a development?

It may seem blasphemous to suggest such a thing, but the book itself cries out for it. It is blasphemous, offensive and at times scurrilous; but it is also serious, profound, moving, sad, clever, preposterous and, above all, irreverent – not only towards Islam, but towards all forms of ideological rigidity. It is most important for moderate Muslims at least to recognize the book's essential seriousness. Just as charges of obscenity may be well met by evidence of the writer's earnestness or the artistic merit of the work itself, so this charge of blasphemy must be reconsidered in the context of the serious purpose so evident in the book's content and style. If *The Satanic Verses* were nothing but crude, inflammatory anti-Islamic drivel, I for one would not be wasting my time defending it.

Next to Rushdie's or anyone else's death, the worst thing that could happen as a result of the threats would be a ban on *The Satanic Verses*. To withdraw it would be to set a precedent whereby anyone, of any creed or political persuasion, who found himself offended by a particular book or play or film, would be tempted to threaten or use violence to force its withdrawal.

Equally serious would be the passing of legislation to extend the law of blasphemy to cover all religions. Superficially attractive as a measure to improve race relations, such a law would in practice prove a massive backwards step for freedom of speech and conscience, and lead to as many abuses as it might seek to remedy. No British court would be competent to decide on what constituted blasphemy for Islam or any other faith, leaving the final word with external bodies tuned to different sensitivities. Before long, no one, whether novelist, academic or journalist, would dare write about any religion other than in the most encomiastic terms. Serious criticism would be outlawed, while religious writers would, no doubt, be allowed absolute freedom of expression.

Before long, there would be chaos. Fundamentalist Christians would take Muslims to court on the grounds that the Qur'an denies the divinity of Christ and rejects the historicity of the crucifixion. Muslims would take Baha'is to court because they deny the finality of Muhammad's prophethood. Baha'is would take Muslims to court because they insist that Baha'ism is the work of the devil. Sikhs would bring cases against Hindus, Hindus against Sikhs. Everyone would have a grievance. Where there is deep commitment to a cause, offence will follow without fail.

I wish to continue living in a society where my legitimate doubts and honest criticisms will not be treated as crimes punishable by imprisonment or death. Freedom of speech, freedom of conscience are the pivots around which our civilization revolves. We destroy them at great peril. *The Satanic Verses* was written in the knowledge that hatred, frustration, anger and irrationality threaten the very heart of things: 'Things are ending . . . This civilization; things are closing in on it. It has been quite a culture, brilliant and foul, cannibal and Christian, the glory of the world. We should celebrate it while we can; until night falls.' Let us pray that Salman Rushdie is not the first victim of his own prophecy.

Review: *A Satanic Affair*

Malise Ruthven, *A Satanic Affair: Salman Rushdie and the Rage of Islam*, Chatto & Windus, London, 1990

If, five years or so ago, I had asked almost anyone, 'What are the "Satanic Verses"?', I might have expected – and deserved – blank looks all round. Today, everyone knows – or thinks they know – exactly what the phrase refers to: 'a novel by Salman Rushdie'. Except that they would be wrong. Five years ago, the Satanic Verses were simply lines of Arabic that had at some point – it is alleged – been included in the text of the Qur'an, only to be expunged and replaced when it was revealed to Muhammad that they were, after all, the inspiration of Satan.

What started life as a debate in the margins of Islamic studies has come to symbolize a virtually unbridgeable divide between two major world cultures. Mr Rushdie and his book are, of course, no more responsible for the present animosity between Islam and the West than they were for the Ottoman conquests, the Crusades or the original Arab invasions of the seventh and eighth centuries. If Salman Rushdie had not existed, he would have to have been invented.

The 'Satanic Affair' about which Malise Ruthven writes is, indeed, much wider than a debate about a book. It draws in its wake centuries of antagonism between Islam and Christendom, the manifold problems of Muslims in the modern world, the resurgence of Islamic (and, for that matter, non-Islamic) fundamentalism, the difficulties faced by Muslims in the West, particularly Britain, the specific dilemmas of Islamic identity in the sub-continent, internal debates about sacred and semi-sacred texts, rural Pakistani traditions of *izzat* or honour, the crisis of faith in a predominantly secular society, the problematic role of Islamic law in contemporary life, and the discomforts occasioned by traditional views of sexuality in a non-traditional context.

Ruthven is well placed to take these and other factors into account. He combines an easy, journalistic style with a genuinely profound understanding of Islam, and his book is as balanced an overview as one might reasonably hope for at this stage. For me, the most instructive feature of this study is the author's willingness to seek out fundamentalist British Muslim opinion and to relate it to Indian and Pakistani Islam as it is actually practised, finding as much significance in a popular (and not particularly Islamic) ideal like *izzat* as in the legal theories of Muslim leaders.

We are returned again and again to the roles of honour and insult in the village communities where so many first-generation British Muslims originated. Particularly intriguing is the link Ruthven postulates between sexual insult (including rape) and religious offence. A number of Muslim spokesmen, referring to the insult offered by *The Satanic Verses*, employ sexual analogy ('What he has written is far worse to Muslims than if he had raped one's own daughter'; 'It's like a knife being dug into you – or being raped yourself').

Both faith and sexuality exist, Ruthven argues, in a guarded, cloistered realm of the hidden (in Arabic, *al-ghaib*). By challenging not only the chief objects of faith itself but the honour of the Prophet's wives (in the famous brothel scenes), Rushdie managed to penetrate to a core of sensitivity whose hurts may not easily be soothed. 'Rushdie enters the sacred space Muhammad occupies in Muslim feeling and affection. That entry is perceived as a violation, as a kind of "rape".'

This sensitivity is all the greater for Muslims living in alien and seemingly hostile societies: 'In Britain, where Muslims are encouraged to see themselves as a small, embattled minority seeking to preserve their identities against the assimilationist pressures of the wider society, the Qur'an and the figure of the Prophet are deeply implicated in the communal *izzat*.' (p. 8). Ruthven sees *The Satanic Verses* as a sort of 'anti-Qur'an', challenging absolutist certainties with its own theology of doubt – Rushdie's own crisis of faith standing, I would suggest, for that of his entire culture. This theme, which Ruthven links to Muslim experience of migration, with its concomitant loss of certainty, is, he says, central to the whole controversy. I would not argue with that conclusion.

With that natural sensitivity one might be sympathetic, seeking, perhaps, ways in which to accommodate it within the broader perspective of an open society, such as ours attempts to be – or, at least, to become. Wounded feelings make some sort of sense, and it is likely that a Muslim campaign based solely on such feelings might have made some headway. Ruthven shows quite convincingly, however, that two factors combined to destroy the original Muslim campaign, and even conspired to make it backfire.

The first was Khomeini's ill-judged *fatwa* for Rushdie's death, originating, as it did, in Iranian internal politics following the country's defeat in the Gulf War. The alienation of international opinion was paralleled by the failure of the Sunni Arab states, in particular Saudi Arabia, to add their voices to that of the Ayatollah, immediately weakening the general Muslim position by introducing a note of disunity.

Secondly, right-wing groups like the Maududist Jamaat-i Islami (operating out of the UK Islamic Mission) used the controversy to enhance their own position within the British Muslim community. The sincerity of the original protesters, who would not even quote offending passages from the novel, was soon displaced by the self-serving rush after controversy typified by statements from the Central London Mosque and Dr Kalim Siddiqui. 'The Maududists and their allies . . . seemed less concerned to protect Muslim sensibilities than to increase the scale of the agitation in order to bring it under fundamentalist control' (p. 107).

Ruthven quotes R.W. Johnson on the effect of what has become a sadly misjudged campaign: 'In most of Europe now, if the right attacks the huddled forces of immigrant Islam, the left will mount, at best, a half-hearted, ambivalent defence' (p. 157). I greatly fear the truth of that statement. For the secular liberal, the Rushdie affair poses almost intractable problems. No one doubts that Muslims suffer gravely from racial discrimination in the West, but the vehemence of their rejection of Western values, not least those on which the whole principle of non-discrimination is itself based, makes it hard to defend them. To defend Muslims on their own terms would be, in the long run, to undermine the very liberties that protect them against greater outrages; but to do so on terms they do not accept (e.g., the priority of free speech over religious sensibility) would be counterproductive.

In the end, Ruthven has no solutions. He is not alone. His critique of the Muslim position will have little or no impact on those whose views it discusses, his analysis of the problems will only confirm non-Muslims in their fear that they are dealing with irrational forces outside their control. Both sides in the debate, ironically, feel powerless: Muslims because they have so long been underdogs, non-Muslims because a liberal culture cannot confront the issues head-on without contradicting itself.

Contradiction, indeed, seems to lie at the heart of the affair. Muslims, deprived of political and social power, feel its loss the more acutely precisely because their faith has traditionally been triumphalist in tenor. As Ruthven so acutely observes: 'The assumption of dominance proceeds from a theology of power which rests uneasily in psyches facing the reality of powerlessness' (pp. 154–5). Non-Muslims are too readily lumped together, fascists with liberals, fundamentalists with secularists, having in common nothing more than a broad opposition to extremist Muslim demands and the death sentence declared on an innocent writer.

Calls for the extension of the blasphemy law are well-meaning (where they are not the work of politicians hungry for the Muslim vote), but gravely mistaken. Even Archbishop Runcie recognized that fact before retirement. Ruthven puts the case for abolition succinctly: 'As it is, the affair reveals a real grievance: as it stands, the law of blasphemy discriminates against non-Christians, as it discriminates against atheists. The law must be abolished' (p. 156). Anything else will lead us into a quagmire from which only the most painful of confrontations with the fundamentalist mind will ever succeed in extricating us. If Malise Ruthven's excellent study does nothing else, perhaps it will alert our legislators to the impossibility of any compromise with fundamentalism, be it Muslim or otherwise.

(First published in the *New Humanist*, 105:2 (1990), pp. 20–1)

Distorted Reasoning

A new species of apologetic writing has grown up recently in the wake of the Rushdie affair. Several authors, disturbed by what they perceive as flaws in the secular establishment's defence of Rushdie, and exasperated by what they see as a continuing Western campaign to present distorted images of Islam, have set out to present the Muslim case. This is a case against not only *The Satanic Verses* but the assumptions of Western cultural superiority as a whole. It involves not just religious arguments against blasphemy, but liberal demands for racial tolerance, social justice and the provision of a louder public voice for minorities in a multi-cultural society.

The most prominent of these works are Rana Kabbani's *Letter to Christendom*, Shabbir Akhtar's *Be Careful with Muhammad*, Richard Webster's *A Brief History of Blasphemy*, and, most recently, Ziauddin Sardar and Merryl Wyn Davies's *Distorted Imagination: Lessons from the Rushdie Affair*. In some cases drawing heavily on the work of Edward Said, the authors put forward very intelligent arguments about the orientalist tradition of the West, the ways in which European writers, artists, churchmen and politicians have created a fictitious Orient, an exotic and unstable world suitable only to be ruled or in other ways controlled by a rational West. The Islam of our literature and our schools, they argue, is not the real Islam but a distortion unrecognizable to Muslims. And *The Satanic Verses*, far from being an aberration, is merely the latest phase in a long-running campaign to pillory the Prophet and denigrate his faith.

But, like the moral majority in the United States, some of these writers are, I fear, making unfair use of liberal ideas in order to promote a case that is actually far from liberal. They do present their case against orientalism well, but go on to use it as a weapon to preach illiberal values. We Westerners may have distorted and still distort Islam; but it is time it was recognized that Muslims have themselves distorted and continue to distort the West – a myopia that may be called 'occidentalism'. Clearing up one set of distortions and leaving another set intact gets no one anywhere. Instead of contributing towards the healthy balance they say they want, these books actually get things more out of perspective and make it increasingly difficult to talk or act with common sense.

Take, for example, the following sentence from the introduction to Sardar and Wyn Davies's book: 'Freedom surely cannot be said to exist nor be defensible where opportunity to exercise this right is unequally held and practised.' This is said in the context of a criticism of Western secularism as a dominant ideology which permits freedom only to its own exponents and denies it to others.

Frankly, I am more than a little fed up with this sort of thinking. A couple of days ago, I was passing Regent's Park, where, as everyone knows, the golden dome of a large mosque rises above the trees. In many British cities, such sights are becoming increasingly common. There are now two million Muslims and over one thousand mosques in France. Germany is roughly the same. Muslims in the West have complete freedom of worship and practice. Islamic missions are active throughout Europe and America, winning large numbers of converts every year.

Now turn to Saudi Arabia, the country which financed much of the building of that mosque in Regent's Park and which pours large sums of money into Islamic missionary enterprises. American soldiers wishing to attend mass there have to do so on board ship. Military padres have been ordered not to wear dog collars or crosses. Jews are not allowed anywhere on Saudi soil, and there are demands for this total ban to be extended to Christians.

When I lived in Morocco, I was forbidden entry to mosques. Once, a Muslim friend was barred from one merely because he had been seen with myself and an American friend. Christian friends were forbidden to preach their religion, let alone win Muslim converts. The punishment for any Muslim who wishes to convert to Christianity or any other faith is still death. A close friend of mine is a former convert to Islam who has since abandoned his faith: he will not reveal that fact to any Muslim for fear of reprisal.

A large part of my library consists of books published by followers of the Baha'i and Babi religious minorities in Iran. They were all illegal publications even when issued under Pahlavi rule: I had to smuggle them out of the country. Even to be in possession of them in Iran today could lead to a death sentence. To import Baha'i books into a Muslim country is still a punishable offence. In 1962, a Moroccan court sentenced three Baha'i men to death and five to life imprisonment for the mere crime of belonging to a 'false' religion. Similar sentences were passed on Baha'is during the early years of the Islamic Revolution in Iran. Other cases can be cited from around the Muslim world.

Yesterday, I picked up a catalogue from a respectable Arabic bookshop in Knightsbridge. Leafing through it, I have already found: a 'Refutation of Judaism and Christianity', an 'Exposure of the Torah' and a 'Refutation of the Torah', a book entitled 'Today's Jews are not Jews' and another entitled 'The Threat of World Jewry to Christianity and Islam'. There are also, of course, plenty of anti-Zionist publications. A bookseller in Cairo, Baghdad, Riyadh, Tehran or Karachi who listed 'An Exposure of the Qur'an', a 'Refutation of Islam', or a pro-Zionist book would be arrested and severely punished.

So I have to ask: where should one look for opportunities to exercise the right to freedom of expression: in an Islamic state or a secular Western state? If I were a Jew or a Baha'i, where would I choose to live: in Saudi Arabia or in Britain? If I were a Sufi Muslim or an Ahmadi, which country would protect my rights and my life: Iran or France? The answer is painfully obvious and has a lot to do with the feelings I and others have expressed in defence of Salman Rushdie.

Sardar and Wyn Davies go on: 'When one's ideology, in this case secular fundamentalism, becomes the yardstick by which reality is measured, one exists in a totally insulated space that permit's [*sic*] no counter reality.' Yes, indeed. If that is true of secular fundamentalism, how much truer is it of religions like Islam which preach absolute truths.

The difference between secularism and religious fundamentalism is that, however strongly people may hold to the principles of the former, they do so freely and in contradictory ways. Secularists have no unchallengeable texts to tell them how they must think, no religious laws to dictate what they should eat and drink, no priests to watch over their behaviour, no unalterable dogmas. Muslims and the followers of other absolutist faiths do.

Paradoxically, what this means in practice is that a secular society is a religiously free society, whereas a religious society (like Iran or Saudi Arabia) is not. To the extent that Israel is coming under increasing orthodox religious influence, it is becoming less tolerant towards both Muslims and unobservant Jews. Secular states, by way of contrast, refuse to recognize any one belief as dominant; as a result, their citizens have complete freedom to believe and act as they wish, provided their actions cause no harm to other citizens.

It is precisely because many Muslims have made their faith 'the yardstick by which reality is measured' that it is so difficult to engage in rational argument with them. The same is true of born-again Christians, orthodox Jews, fundamentalist Mormons, Jehovah's Witnesses and a whole host of true believers. Left to themselves, these groups will anathematize or physically attack one another.

I remember once watching in horror a television interview with a Christian fundamentalist, in which he was asked, again and again, if anyone but a born-again believer would go to heaven. 'Would Anglicans enter the pearly gates?' 'They have not recognized Jesus Christ as their personal saviour, so they will enter the fires of hell and burn therein eternally.' Baptists? Same answer. Catholics? Same answer. Buddhists? Same answer. Muslims, Sikhs, Hindus, Zoroastrians? Same answer. By the end, he had peopled the hell of his imagination with almost every human being who had ever lived or was now living, whether they had ever heard of Jesus Christ or not.

In recent months, we have seen Hindu mobs attacking a Muslim shrine in India, riots because enraged defenders of the Hindu caste system feared that untouchables might be granted some measure of human dignity, Christians forced to flee from parts of Beirut, a right-wing Jewish demagogue assassinated, and a writer forced, at the threat of his life, to embrace Islam.

When did secular liberals last engage in this sort of behaviour? We have our faults, and I think we try to correct them, but outright assault on other people is not one of them. We do not execute people because they are not secularists, we do not imprison them or burn their books, we do not condemn them to hell, we do not deny them the freedom to convert from among us. Instead, we help them. We allow them to publish their books and distribute their tracts and preach their gospels and build their mosques and shave their heads and ring their bells and chant their *adhans*.

Above all, secular liberal societies provide forums for debate that other societies would not tolerate. Sometimes people find it difficult to engage in debate because their voices are too weak, their status too negligible. Akhtar, Webster and the rest are right to say that Muslims, as members of ethnic and religious minorities, are often denied access to the media. They are, as Sardar and Wyn Davies put it, 'a group of people acutely aware of their powerlessness and exclusion from the mainstream of society'.

But they are not alone in that, and I do not subscribe to the view that there is a deliberate secularist plot to misunderstand and misrepresent Muslims: what Kalim Siddiqui has termed 'a crusade of fundamentalist liberal Inquisition against Islam and Muslims' or Sardar and Wyn Davies call 'a deliberate and calculated exercise that impedes mutual understanding between Islam and the West'.

It is axiomatic that minorities will be misunderstood and will find it hard to state their case. In our society, all sorts of people have their views misrepresented. Mormons, Moonies, Seventh Day Adventists, every minority group under the sun, claims that it is misunderstood and denied access to the media. But the fact is that it would be absurd to give Moonies the same access to television as, say, Anglicans or Methodists. That, as the cliché goes, is life.

I myself have been involved for years in the promotion of alternative medicine and the development of a radical critique of orthodox medical practice. Like others in the field, I find it extremely difficult to obtain television, radio or newspaper coverage. And what coverage we get is regularly distorted. That does not lead me to conclude that there is some sort of conspiracy against alternative medicine, merely that minority opinions have a hard time. I feel angry and frustrated at times, but at least I know I am free to speak out as and when I can.

As a result of open debate, minority views may gradually win acceptance. Perhaps as a result of books like those I have mentioned, public opinion will take Muslim offence more seriously and it will be seen as unacceptable to write in unfavourable terms about Muhammad and Islam. That will be a victory as much for secular liberalism as for Islam. The alternative – an outright ban on *The Satanic Verses*, legislation to extend the law of blasphemy, perhaps the creation of public watchdog bodies staffed by Muslims to censor publications and films – would be as damaging to Muslims as to the rest of us.

The Unbeliever in a House of Belief

While on holiday in Italy this summer, my wife and I visited the beautiful ninth-century *duomo* in Amalfi. Inside, we behaved ourselves with the utmost decorum, as all good tourists must. We spoke in hushed voices, we kept our camera out of sight, we deferred to those who had come there for more legitimate purposes: to pray or to visit the relics of St Andrew below us in the crypt. Strolling among candles and the memory of incense, we were acutely conscious of our status as outsiders, unbelievers in a house of belief, unshriven tourists in a place of prayer.

How does such decorous behaviour square with my often-expressed support for writers like Salman Rushdie, the calls I have made for the abolition of the law of blasphemy, my opposition to proposals for the extension of the current law to cover all religions or the creation of an offence of religious insult, or my own iconoclastic writing about Islam, Baha'ism and other faiths? I have, after all, argued at length that the right to offend religious feelings is more or less inalienable, that deeply-held convictions not only may be but should be challenged, that religions have no inherent, God-given right to cordon themselves off from other areas of human activity or to exist in a realm immune from criticism or ridicule. So how can it be that I find myself, Panama hat clutched deferentially in hand, creeping round an Italian church careful not to disturb or offend the faithful as they go about their devotions?

Well, I do so because I recognize that the space of a church or a cathedral (or, for that matter, a mosque or temple) is indeed a realm set apart. I do not enter mosques or churches wearing brightly-coloured Bermuda shorts or sporting a lapel badge reading 'God is dead' simply because they would not be the proper places for such activities. But in doing so, I have not made religion a uniquely privileged arena. I do not go into churches playing a ghetto-blaster at full volume; but no more would I dream of taking one into the theatre or the countryside or the Houses of Parliament. People go to the theatre to watch plays and listen to operas, they visit the country for silence and fresh air, they attend the Houses of Parliament to take part in or listen to debates. And (if they are believers) they go to churches to pray. Even if I think a certain play is rubbish or a political speech a load of hooey, I respect the right of others to watch and to listen as they wish.

But does this mean that I should be denied the right to pen a scathing review of the play or a vicious lampoon of the politician who gave the speech in tomorrow's paper? Of course not. The same applies to the church or the mosque. My respect for other people's right to pray or meditate without disturbance from outsiders does not mean that I think they have some sort of absolute right to immunity from criticism or challenge once they return to the world of normal discourse. The world outside the church is a world we share, believer and unbeliever alike. And just as I feel obliged to respect the norms and conventions that are deemed appropriate within the precincts of a sacred space, so I expect believers to pay at least lip service to the rules of behaviour that apply to the wider world of society at large.

This is where I think certain writers, who have argued in favour of some sort of legislation to protect religious believers from insult, are in error. They have, I believe, confounded one form of right with another. They have tried, in a sense, to translate the internal, special realm of the church and the mosque to the general domain of ordinary public discourse. The absurdity of such a proceeding is, I think, apparent if we put things the other way round: since I have every right to wear Bermuda shorts in the street (not that you'd ever catch me doing so!), why shouldn't I be free to flaunt them in the nearest cloister?

In his generally perceptive study, *The Cost of Free Speech*, Professor Simon Lee discusses this very question of the differences between various modes of discourse. Pointing out that neither Buddhists nor Quakers might have taken much offence had Salman Rushdie written satirically about their beliefs, he goes on to say:

But where I live, in Belfast, Rushdie might find himself exercising a little more self-restraint if he is ever in the happy position of being able to chat on the Shankhill Road about Protestant fundamentalism or to discuss Catholic dogma on the Falls Road. No doubt he could produce some ingenious dream sequence which made fun of these religions but I doubt whether he would think it appropriate to try out his ideas by delivering his barbs in person. Yet he would, up till now, have presumably had no hesitation in writing the same material and publishing it as a novel.

Why is this, and are the conventions changing, or being changed, by Rushdie's experience? It seems that the customs and assumptions of literature are different from face-to-face discourse. Western writers have become increasingly accustomed to writing things they would not dare say in person. Literary kudos is more likely to be won by outraging than respecting.

Professor Lee's argument does, in fact, seem to be supported by several statements made by Rushdie himself in his Herbert Read Memorial Lecture, 'Is Nothing Sacred?', delivered on his behalf at the ICA on 6 February 1990. Openly acknowledging that he has made 'a large number of sweeping claims for literature' in the course of the lecture, Rushdie goes on to say that 'the only privilege literature deserves – and this privilege it requires in order to exist – is the privilege of being the arena of discourse, the place where the struggle of languages an be acted out'. 'Literature,' he concludes 'is the one place in any society where, within the secrecy of our own heads, we can hear *voices talking about everything in every possible way*', and he urges the preservation of literature as a 'privileged arena'.

Both Lee and Rushdie have, I think, got it wrong: the former because he seems to think that the same rules should apply to different modes of discourse, the latter because he is willing to see one arena (religion) as deprivileged and another (literature) as sacrosanct, which is merely to replicate the problems of intolerance and special pleading with which he claims to be concerned.

Professor Lee, like some other writers whose primary (and quite legitimate) concern has been with the insult suffered by Muslims through the publication of *The Satanic Verses*, seems to be trying to extend the rules of face-to-face dialogue to the realm of print. If by that he means that writers should not be able to hide behind their books, any more than religious believers should be able to take cover behind the shield of sanctity, he is perfectly correct. I see no reason why they should. But if he means that writers should be willing to suffer the same consequences for what they write as for what another man might say in the street, he is, I believe, mistaken.

I too have lived in Belfast. Indeed, I was brought up to know that you do not walk down the Falls Road carrying a Union Jack and singing 'The Sash My Father Wore', any more than you take a short cut through Sandy Row draped in a tricolour and wearing a picture of the Sacred Heart pinned to your chest. There are conventions that any sensible person recognizes and abides by, knowing the consequences of non-compliance. But this does not mean that it should be illegal to carry a Union Jack, sing Orange songs, reverence the Irish flag, or hang Catholic icons on your living-room wall. Whether we love them or despise them, those are all legitimate activities that have their place within their own sphere.

Professor Lee criticizes Rushdie (and, by implication, a good many other writers) for being reluctant to deliver in person barbs that he would happily commit to paper and publish in the form of a novel. There is an innuendo here that many writers are cowards taking shelter behind the privilege of print. But let us imagine for a moment a thinker in the late 1930s with unflattering things to say about Adolf Hitler and National Socialism: would he really have been well advised to take the first plane to Berlin and set off down the Unter den Linden carrying large placards setting forth his views? I dislike Saddam Hussein and the Ba'thist regime running Iraq, but I have no plans to go to Baghdad to say so. Does this mean that it would be improper to write about fascism or Ba'thism or to take refuge from retaliation behind British law and the British security services?

Lee's example of what may or may not be said face-to-face with a Northern Irish Protestant or Catholic is, in fact, particularly apposite. No doubt Protestant and Catholic extremists would take unkindly to being told home truths by uncommitted outsiders (including, need it be said, other Irish Christians), but I cannot see how this makes it improper for authors to write critically or mockingly about the manifest absurdities and evils of Paisleyism or Catholic dogmatism. This is important. As Lee himself points out, 'peace-loving Quakers are unlikely to punch Rushdie on the nose for any insults he might launch at their faith'. I rather think I could engage in very straightforward dialogue with Quakers; but – significantly – I doubt very much if I would find much to be critical about. Those groups most likely to make face-to-face dialogue difficult or impossible are precisely those whom society is most likely to need to criticize. By default, such criticism will take place on the printed page or the television screen, at one or two removes from open confrontation.

Of course, this still leaves the problem of insult. There are plenty of moderate Protestants, Catholics and Muslims whose feelings may be hurt by what I or others may write about sacred matters. And this is where Simon Lee's argument appears most pertinent. Why should I, who tread quietly in cathedrals, think it fair to be raucous in print? Why do I not extend the same courtesy that I would show in person to this other, literary realm within which I exist in an even more public fashion? This seems reasonable; but it is not.

If I make a nuisance of myself in a church or engage in a shouting match in a mosque, innocent worshippers have no way of avoiding the offence my words and actions may give. That is why stand-up arguments are so hard to avoid. If I tell you to your face that you are a fool, you may find it difficult to refrain from settling my hash on the spot. And that, of course, is why other forums have been created for debate. Politicians who might lose their tempers with one another in private meet on the floor of the House to engage in sharp and often barbed argument within the framework of rules laid down for the conduct of business in the chamber. Fisticuffs – which might be tolerated outside – are prohibited. Certain types of insult are unacceptable. It is an arena of partially privileged discourse.

Similarly, we have recourse to the printed media as a means of extending and facilitating forms of debate that might be risky or unpleasant in person. The printed word has a particular aptitude for this purpose in that the innocent worshipper is not forced to hear or witness words and scenes likely to cause him or her affront. It is this 'removed' quality that renders offensive writing acceptable. By 'acceptable', I do not mean likeable or immune from criticism, merely tolerable. Religious communities have long acknowledged the value of such removal, usually in a negative sense. Hermits and secluded religious orders are engaged in an act of self-removal from senses, words, thoughts and values they deem harmful to their inner development. Most religions impose bans on activities that may be disturbing to the spiritual life of their followers: there are books that should not be read, acts that should not be indulged in (drinking, dancing, listening to music), places that must be avoided (cinemas, public houses, the temples of other faiths), people whose company should be shunned (unbelievers in Islam, *goyim* in fundamentalist Judaism, 'Covenant-Breakers' in Baha'ism), worldly thoughts that should not be harboured.

Religions, in other words, are particularly clever at keeping themselves remote from threatening currents of thought or activity within the world at large. At one level, it might be said that this is precisely what they are about. The conservatism of religious traditions is one of the most noticeable things about them, from Amish hats to Islamic reliance on seventh-century laws. But, as I have said elsewhere, the idea that religion should remain an untouchable realm immune from outside influence is as unacceptable as that literature should be granted the status of an activity above the law, rather like a foreigner exempted from Ottoman legislation under the old capitulation system.

Now, I do not mean by that that we should feel free to walk into Amish communities knocking off hats or to make our atheistic way into mosques reciting passages from *The Satanic Verses*. That is as bad or worse than playing the ghetto-blaster in Amalfi cathedral. If people want to seclude themselves from the world, they have every right to do so without interference from outsiders.

The problem is that few religions are reclusive in the absolute sense. Islam is the best example of a faith deeply involved in the world. Actual seclusion (*khalwa*) is an activity reserved to certain Sufi orders or, in the restricted sense of the practice of *i'tikaf*, to certain times and persons. But even religions with a much greater stress on other-worldliness may act openly in the public forum, as witness the political role of militant Buddhism in Burma from the early 1900s, or the part played by monks in the Ceylonese revolution of 1956–9. Archbishop Carey's recent observations on the causes of inner-city riots are simply a more Anglican expression of the same tendency.

Religion and society at large impinge on one another at every possible juncture. Many years ago, Emile Durkheim made the observation that religion is an essentially communal activity. Even hermits and nuns in enclosed orders depend on the existence of farmers and others outside their walls to grow and supply the food on which they depend to live. Seen from this perspective, it is too much for believers to expect to get away scot-free, or for their activities and beliefs to remain immune from comment, mockery or even legislative interference. We may make special concessions as, for example, when we exempt Sikhs from the rule that every motorcyclist must wear a crash helmet or that Jehovah's Witnesses may refuse blood transfusions. But we draw the line at introducing prohibition just because alcohol upsets Muslims or at banning contraception in order to appease the Catholic lobby.

It has been said many times that no believer is obliged to read *The Satanic Verses*. Trite as it seems, that is still a valid argument. When believers retire from the world or turn their faces from it, they do so on the understanding that it is still there, that insults to their faith abound in it, and that salvation lies, not in changing the world, but in overcoming it in the heart. But when Muslims protest that the very presence of *The Satanic Verses* is intolerable and that the book must be withdrawn from circulation, they are, in fact, acknowledging their wish to put their finger in the pie of worldly affairs. Clearly, they cannot have it both ways. The rough and tumble of democratic debate means that secularists like myself have to accept the possibility of legislation introduced to pander to religious feeling or to reflect widespread public acceptance of religious opinion (as is increasingly common in the United States). It also means that religious people have to face the same possibilities of censure, mockery or satirical comment that the rest of us take for granted if we enter the public arena.

Nevertheless, it would be crass to pretend that an issue like the *Satanic Verses* debate is entirely like other social and political issues. Muslims object to Rushdie's book precisely because it insults (or seems to insult) figures they hold particularly sacred. It crosses, they say, a threshold of decency, and the same sensitivity to the feelings of others that prevents non-believers from walking naked in cathedrals should alert us to the enormity of the offence that has been caused.

This is still to miss the point. The problem is not the enormity of the insult, but the context within which it occurs. Salman Rushdie did not pin obscene caricatures of the Prophet to the doors of mosques, nor did he burn the Qur'an on television. He wrote a book; that is to say, he entered a space at least as privileged in our society as the precincts of a church, and in that enclosure he engaged in the very proper activity of challenging certain religious assumptions. It may even be argued – as Rushdie himself has argued, and with cause – that he did so with pious intentions and in a manner reverential after its own fashion.

Be that as it may, his opponents refused to recognize the validity of the space he had entered, and, with conspicuous disrespect, dragged him against his will into a different arena. Please do not mistake me: I said above that Rushdie was wrong if he thought of literature as a wholly privileged space. But he was not wrong to ascribe to books at least a degree of privilege, in the same way that religion (or sex or psychiatry or marriage) is afforded its special measure of immunity. The privilege of the writer is considerable, even if it does not extend so far as to protect him from all criticism or, indeed, in exceptional cases, even from prosecution.

This confusion of spaces derives in great part from a more basic confusion about the nature of religious insult and a tendency to conflate it with other forms of abuse. Superficially, religious insult is an easy concept to define and a simple one to judge. In fact, it is a mass of contradictions and anomalies. For one thing, most religious insult has its origins, not in secular polemic, but in religious speech and writing. One need look no further than Christian anti-Jewish diatribes, or Islamic polemics on sectarian movements, to find a level of invective that makes anything in *The Satanic Verses* appear quite tame. Believers are, as often as not, merely tasting their own bitter medicine when they find their beliefs assaulted.

One of the greatest problems is how to determine which individuals, books or beliefs should merit immunity from insult. If we say that only major religious figures like Christ, Moses or Muhammad are of sufficient importance to deserve legal protection, does this mean that lesser figures will be fair game? That is unlikely to appeal to those Muslims who objected to Rushdie's description of the Companions of the Prophet as 'scum and bums'. And it clearly discriminates against the prophets and leaders of small or unpopular religious groups. If, on the other hand, we extend protection to any religious figure, regardless of stature or reputation, we lose our freedom to put the spotlight of censure or satire on apparent charlatans. And we run the risk of moving from a situation where only certain things are sacred to one in which everything is sacred and, consequently, nothing more sacred than anything else.

It is difficult to see how we may legitimately define insult to religion *qua* religion. The law, after all, cannot pronounce on religious truth, cannot really say that Buddha was more inspired than Sun Myung Moon or the Qur'an more divine than the Book of Mormon. A law would make sense and be uncontentious only if it ruled on insult *qua* insult. That, however, would leave the way open to other absurdities.

There are, for example, quite large numbers of people for whom adoration of the late Elvis Presley has come to be something very like a religion. Certainly, serious Elvis devotees (the sort who make a pilgrimage to Graceland once a year and undergo plastic surgery in order to look more like their idol) may feel genuinely hurt and dismayed by some journalistic portrayals of the late great entertainer. Thousands of ordinary people may find 'Spitting Image' representations of members of the Royal Family deeply upsetting.

If we say that such people may not have their icons protected by law because neither Elvis Presley nor the Queen is a religious figure, this would be to argue that feelings of hurt and outrage are valid or meaningful only in a religious context.

If, on the other hand, we go to the other extreme and accept that any form of outrage may be translated into grounds for the prosecution of writers and broadcasters – on the say-so of those who consider themselves insulted – we will introduce into the legal system a totally unworkable principle. Direct comment about personalities and ideas will become all but impossible for everyone except religious people.

Why religious people? Because it would infringe their rights to prevent them speaking openly and on the basis of what they consider to be divine revelation about individuals and ideas they believe to be in error. It is a religious duty for Muslims to 'command what is good and forbid what is evil'. Forbidding what is evil includes speaking out about heretics or unbelievers who threaten the faith with corruption or ruin. Speaking out typically involves the use of invective. Other religious groups have similar obligations, even if there are few today who are willing – as Islamic law still permits – to put their opponents to death.

If the novel or the academic treatise do not invade the sacred space of the mosque or the cathedral, and if zealous believers can be prevented by force of law from laying their hands too roughly on books and their authors, does this mean that modern society is merely an agglomeration of discrete spheres of thought and action, each with its 'Hands Off' sign at the entrance and its security personnel patrolling the perimeter? Manifestly not, or we would not have parades in Bradford or nuns picketing the doors of the Ministry of Defence.

The problem is how to keep things this way, with spheres of interest that interact yet retain their separate identities, rights and ranges of influence. The current model of the Western secular democracy is inherently precarious. The very fact that all groups are granted broadly equal rights leaves open the possibility that one group or another will seek to tilt the balance in its own favour. And that, ultimately, is something even a democracy may not be able to tolerate.

Where Will It All End?

The killing of Hitoshi Igarashi, the Japanese translator of *The Satanic Verses*, and the savage attack on Ettore Capriolo, the book's Italian translator, have woken the world with a jolt from its lazy post-conversionist dreams of a Muslim amnesty and a gentleman's agreement to drop the subject of *The Satanic Verses* and the unprecedented furore it provoked. Once again, nobody connected with the publication, sale or defence of Rushdie's book can feel relaxed or safe. There are translators and publishers in countries all round the world. All must now regard themselves, their friends and their families as once more under threat.

And where exactly does the threat end? Who else is a likely target? Any publisher's rep who handled the book? Any bookseller who has put it on sale? Any librarian who has stocked it? Any university lecturer who has, for whatever reason, put it on his reading list? Anyone who has defended its publication, or just read it, or lent it to a friend? The whole business has been absurd from the beginning, but with this fresh development it threatens to take on dimensions of grotesquerie that can scarcely be contained in rational prose.

And what now of Rushdie himself? With his conversion, however forced, to Islam, it may have been supposed that his life, at least, was no longer forfeit. If he was originally sentenced to death not so much for the crime of blasphemy as for that of apostasy, the same religious law that condemned him equally prescribes forgiveness in the event of repentance and a return to the fold. That, unfortunately, is an ideal that has not always been matched in Islamic practice.

In the seventh and eighth centuries, the Islamic world itself was bedevilled by the sanguinary activities of an extremist group known as the Kharijites, whose policy it was to put to death any Muslim guilty of a mortal sin. The Kharijites accepted no compromise. If a Muslim sinned, he was, by that fact alone, regarded as an apostate. He could never re-enter the faith, and he, along with his wives and children, had to be executed. Short-lived as their movement was, the Kharijites left an indelible mark on all later generations, positing an idealized standard of faith and practice from which all deviation was tantamount to damnation.

More recently, the Ikhwan, the military and religious spearhead of Ibn Sa'ud's conquest of central Arabia from about 1916, took a similar approach to all non-Wahhabi and non-observant Muslims with whom they came in contact. The Wahhabiyya is the strict school of Islam to which the Saudi leadership had adhered from the eighteenth century, and the Ikhwan had no compunction in imposing its puritan ethic at the point of the sword. In the end, Ibn Sa'ud himself had to have the Ikhwan tamed by his other troops, but the mood of intransigence and uncompromising zeal that they promulgated lives on in the religious authorities of the modern Saudi state.

It is in these and similar hardline interpretations of the law – which is otherwise fairly lenient in its treatment of matters of belief – that the threat to Rushdie and others must be sought. Following Igarashi's murder, a spokesman for the Pakistan Association of Japan said: 'Because it is a non-Muslim country, [the murder] is against the law in Japan, but according to the law of Islam it's quite all right. Today we have been congratulating each other. Everyone was really happy.'

Such words are almost too grotesque to be believed, but they seem to be rooted in a Kharijite approach to the law. The killing of non-Muslims may be justified on the basis of legal rulings that prescribe the death penalty for Jews or Christians who dare to insult the person of the Prophet.

Only Jews, Christians and Zoroastrians are, in any case, 'Peoples of the Book', guaranteed the protection of their lives and property within a Muslim state. Hindus, Buddhists, Shintoists and other pagans are denied even these rights. The fundamentalist writer 'Abd al-Mun'am Ahmad al-Nimr makes clear the implications of this position when he writes: 'We reject the notion that there should be Hindu or Buddhist or Baha'i Egyptians, who will steal their rights from Muslim, Christian and Jewish Egyptians by appealing to the resolutions of the United Nations.

The resolutions of Islam which we possess stand above any resolutions taken by any international organization.'

By definition, then, a Japanese writer may be regarded as beyond any pale recognized by Islam. In the words of the Pakistani spokesman just quoted, the Japanese are 'just like animals. They don't respect the religion of other people. They have to learn a lesson.' So a learned interpreter of Islam may be treated as an animal and put to death brutally for no other crime than to have translated another man's book.

This is obscene and criminal thinking. It is now time that the international community stopped shilly-shallying and made clear its position on this whole affair. We have indulged Muslim extremists to the point of absurdity. The Islamic laws of holy war and the execution of apostates (including individuals who convert to other faiths) have no place in any modern state and are notorious obstacles to good relations between Muslims or Muslim institutions and the rest of the world. The widespread Islamic view that human rights are by definition meaningless (since only God has rights), and the persistent defence of human-rights abuses in Muslim countries on the grounds that Islamic law must always override 'Western' notions of natural justice, must now be exposed as the shams they are.

We have just come from a war which, though it was never fought for human rights, inevitably became closely connected to the issue of their abuse in Iraq and, subsequently, Kuwait. The Western victory over Saddam Hussein (if it is not premature to speak of it) brought much-needed succour to his erstwhile enemy, Iran. Our government and that of the United States possess increased moral and political influence in Iran as a result. It is time that we used that influence to spell out to the leaders of the Islamic Republic just how deep is the revulsion of all civilized people – and I include in that number many millions of ordinary Muslims – at the slaughter of innocent people in the name of a faith founded in the name of a merciful and compassionate God and now hijacked by a gang of criminals and cold-blooded assassins.

(First published in the *Bookseller*, 26 July 1991)

III

MARTYRS, MOONIES
AND MONKS

Fi Sabil Allah: Martyrdom in the Path of God

On the face of it, religions win hands down over secular causes when it comes to supplying meaningful deaths. Unlike states or political ideologies, religions claim to explain life and to place it in some sort of meaningful relationship with a hereafter or, in certain cases, with a cycle of birth and rebirth. It seems in a sense altogether reasonable for a man or a woman to embrace death willingly in a religious context, if by so doing life itself may be given a sense of meaning otherwise unattainable.

Indeed, in many religions the whole point of life becomes its negation, if not to the extent of choosing immediate death, at least to that of living a life of abnegation. In the Orthodox Christian tradition, monks are referred to as 'the living dead', seeking in out-of-the-way places to deny the world and their own part in it. In Tibetan Buddhism, *gomchens* will often incarcerate themselves in lightless, airless cells for entire lifetimes, leaving them only when their disciples break down the bricks to remove their bodies.

Such behaviour may be extreme, but it does, as I have suggested, possess a certain rationality. If self-denial even to the point of death is deemed to result in the immediate enjoyment of bliss in another world or in the cessation of suffering by means of escape from the reincarnational cycle, it may arguably be the best long-term policy. After all, we are all willing to undergo lengthy and sometimes painful regimens of medical or surgical treatment in the anticipation of eventual health, or to deny ourselves smoked salmon today for the sake of a new Jaguar XJ6 tomorrow.

The problem is that much religious behaviour of this kind does not seem particularly rational and that many of those engaged in it would be offended to be thought calculating or entirely reasonable. Where reason may itself stand condemned as an obstacle to intuitive awareness, it is unlikely to be cited as a spring for action. Love, devotion, identification, transcendence of self – these are the gears that move the engines of self-denial and death embraced as martyrdom. Certainly, it is hard to discern any overt rationality in the behaviour of Shi'ite suicide bombers or the followers of Jim Jones who drank paraquat in the jungles of Guyana or the devotees of Vishnu throwing themselves beneath the crushing wheels of the juggernaut. But in reality things are never quite that simple.

As Frits Staal has argued, there may be a deeper and certainly a different rationality behind mystical doctrines that presuppose a distinction between appearance and reality. If another level of existence has indeed become more real to the believer than the realm we like to call the real world, even the craziest behaviour may be entirely reasonable.

Among the Sufi mystics of Islam there existed a group known as Malamatiyya, who consciously flouted the laws and conventions of the society around them in order to bring down the condemnation of their fellows on their own heads. Sufi literature abounds with images of drunkenness, madness and unconventionality: the mystic who is in touch with the reality at the heart of things is the true judge of what is rational behaviour, not the *faqih* or *mufti* with his books of law and his predisposition to the demands of externality. In the famous Arabic phrase: 'The good deeds of the pious are the sins of those who have been brought near.' The ultimate goal for the Sufi as for the mystic in most traditions is *fana' fi 'llah*, extinction in God, the final passing away from unreality for the sake of subsistence in the Godhead. That, of course, is the ultimate identification: the human self becomes the divine self, the unreal garment of humanity is divested and an enduring garb of divinity put on.

But what, by way of contrast, does the secular ideal offer its martyrs? Is a mass grave in a Flanders field much compensation for a life cut short? Or a memorial tablet in a village church a permanent possession for the unbelieving soldier? And do the spirits of Rosa Luxemburg and Che Guevara engage in eternal communion with the Dialectic of History? And yet there have been at least as many secular as religious martyrs throughout history, and not a few of those who have died for an ostensibly religious cause have, in reality, gone to the sword and the stake for purely secular ends. Does a meaningful death require a vision of reality and unreality? Or is something else involved?

The sense of contrast between illusion and reality is most sharply felt in Far Eastern religious traditions like Hinduism and Buddhism. The Judaeo-Christian and Islamic traditions have never been so uncomfortable with the world, except in their ascetic and mystical forms. Islam, in particular, has always viewed the physical realm as the ideal arena in which to carry on the duties of faith. For Muhammad and for orthodox Islam after him, God is a distant being; not a *Deus absconditus* perhaps, but definitely remote and unmediated. If this God is to be apprehended at all, it is in the physical signs of His presence with which He has abundantly invested the external world. 'We shall show them Our signs in the horizons and in themselves, till it is clear to them that it is the truth' (Qur'an 41:53). The world is God's creation and, by definition, good. Man's duty is to live here in accordance with God's laws. Every detail of his existence has been worked out in advance and prescribed for him in the revealed Law: not only how to pray and fast, but how to dress and bathe, to buy and sell, to make love to his wife, to eat and drink and defecate. It is the same precisely in orthodox Judaism, from which traditional Islam derived so much of its *weltanschauung*.

Above all, Islam sees the world as a stage for social action. Individual behaviour, individual submission to the divine will, can best be regulated in a social order itself ruled by the laws of God. For Islam, there is no dichotomy between social and divine order, between church and state, between religion and politics. Such a dichotomy, for Muslims down the ages, and more than ever for modern fundamentalists, is a delusion of the Christian West that goes against all sense of reason and justice. It is, therefore, not surprising if today, faced by the phenomenon of suicide bombers or *Basij* volunteers throwing themselves on to landmines in the Iran–Iraq war, Western observers are often at a loss to know just what sort of cause they are dying for. Do Iranian soldiers die *pro patria* or, as they themselves would see it, *fi sabil Allah*, 'in the path of God'? Is there a difference?

In spite of what has just been said, from its inception Islam interpreted the world in terms of dichotomy, all things viewed *sub specie aeternitatis*, heaven and hell, God and Satan, belief and unbelief, faith and rebellion. It is Durkheim's 'absolute dichotomy' between sacred and profane written large and made active in all spheres of life. But within the fold of faith, the effect is to divest the profane of any meaning at all.

In the political realm, this resulted in the division of mankind into two groups and the world into two distinct sectors: *Dar al-Islam*, the realm of Islam, in which God's law held sway, and *Dar al-Kufr*, the realm of unbelief, where man lived in a state of rebellion. In traditional Islamic jurisprudence, this latter realm is also known as *Dar al-Harb*, the realm of war.

Warring in the path of God – *al jihad fi sabil Allah* – was an extension of ancient Arab ideals. The term *islam* itself originally denoted a secular concept, namely defiance of death or heroism in fighting for the honour of one's tribe. Muhammad transmogrified the idea, so that it now meant defiance of death for the sake of God and His Prophet. And in time it came to mean something like submission to the will of God, which is how many Muslims would translate it today. *Jihad* – literally 'effort' – was the active expression of this defiance of death.

What began as raids on Meccan caravans following Muhammad's move to the nearby city of Medina became an ongoing war against unbelief. It has not yet ended. As Muslim armies moved out of the Arabian peninsula, sweeping the Byzantine and Persian armies before them and creating the first imperium of Islam, a mood of triumphalism took hold of the community of faith. Except briefly in its earliest days in Mecca, Islam never faced the sort of persecution that befell Christianity in its infancy. Martyrs and conquerors alike were offered their reward: 'So let them fight in the way of God who sell the present life for the world to come; and whosoever fights in the way of God and is slain, or conquers, We shall bring him a mighty wage' (Qur'an 4:74).

Jihad, then, is a sort of contract between the *mujahid*, the holy warrior, and his God. It is a full-blooded business in which the conqueror wins lands and booty and the martyr a place in paradise. Is there any room at all in this for the pale martyr of Christian tradition and iconography, passively undergoing a painful death to witness to his faith? Certainly, the Arabic word for martyr, *shahid*, means 'witness', just like the Greek. But the Muslim martyr is a witness more to God's conquering power than to His meekness. Islam has no room for the notion of a God willing to become man, much less for one that allows Himself to be slain on a cross by His enemies. Thus the crucifixion of Jesus is declared a fable by the Qur'an. And yet revulsion at the excesses of empire and admiration for the self-abnegation of Christian monks (those 'living dead' of the Eastern tradition) in the conquered territories combined to produce a breed of Muslim ascetic and, by the due process of time, the Sufi mystic. In the image of Hallaj, the tenth-century mystic crucified for his beliefs in the Abbasid capital of Baghdad, Islamic and Christian iconography come closest together. But even the earliest Sufis were also holy warriors. Many of the first mystical retreats were actually located in border garrisons, where ascetics could gather to pray and meditate before riding out against the armies of unbelief. In the nineteenth century, militant Sufism showed what it could do when armies of the Tijani and Sanusi brotherhoods conquered large areas of North and West Africa. And in Central Asia, the Naqshbandi order became synonymous with resistance to Russian encroachment on Muslim territory or, more recently, the communist onslaught on Islam. If we want to find a truly Christian-style martyr complex in Islam, we have to look for it in Shi'ism. Originating as a movement of extreme political protest and opposition in the late seventh century, Shi'ism evolved into a faith of suffering both on behalf of the world and against it. It was the martyrdom of the third Shi'ite Imam, Husayn, in 680 that turned the Shi'a into a people of lamentation. Husayn had ridden out to lead an armed rebellion against the Umayyad dynasty in Damascus. On the plain of Karbala', deserted by a contingent promised by his followers in the city of Kufa, he and his small band of some seventy men and women were brutally massacred by a government army. Today, that bloody event is commemorated by the Shi'a with the most intense seriousness. It is the pivotal event of history, for through the passion and blood of the martyred Husayn, the faithful are brought to salvation. It is the Christ myth in more militant garb.

Every year in the month of Muharram, Shi'ites put on black dress and hold gatherings in which they mourn Husayn's death. Passion plays are acted out to the sound of weeping and shouts of grief. Young men take to the streets in long processions, in the course of which they beat their breasts and foreheads, cutting themselves with knives, and whipping themselves with chains.

Identification with Husayn reaches its apogee in the desire

to die as a martyr in the struggle against injustice. In recent years, that desire has seen a bloody fulfilment for hundreds of thousands on the marshes of southern Iraq, not very far from the plain of Karbala' itself. Others have offered themselves up as living bombs in Lebanon. The rhetoric of self-sacrifice has seldom been so vividly or so effectively articulated.

What has Shi'ism got that other faiths do not? Certainly, not a concern with martyrdom – Christianity renders the concept even more central; or suffering – Judaism, particularly in this century, has more to offer; or denial of the world – Buddhism teaches the best lessons in world-renunciation. I rather think it is the link between all these things and an active political sense. Triumphalist Sunni Islam was never anything but political; but it had little understanding of suffering. Shi'ism found its *raison d'être*, not only in suffering voluntarily embraced as a mode of witness to the truth, but in a determined search after social justice. This can be a little hard for us to take on board, because our media have conditioned us to think of Shi'ism in stereotyped terms: fanatical, barbaric, irrational, violent. In common lore, it has become a psychopathic, even sociopathic, religion. Certainly, Shi'ite notions of what constitutes justice or Shi'ite ideals of what would make a perfect society are unlikely to appeal even to the most liberal-minded of us. Least of all, perhaps, to the most liberal-minded. I personally find it difficult, for example, to accept the thesis that there are no such things as human rights, only the rights of God. But for all that, it is time we understood that the vision of a just society, and not some bloody-mindedness congenital to people of a certain colouring or religious persuasion, is what animates the Shi'ite consciousness and fills to overflowing the graves of Behesht-i Zahra cemetery.

There, I fancy, lies the key to the whole thing. Not just Shi'ite martyrdom, but the search for a meaningful death in whatever context or era. Martyrs do not offer up their lives for their own sakes, any more than soldiers on the battlefield or revolutionaries before the firing squad. There are more congenial religious outlets for those who wish to forsake this world for the chance of bliss in the next. Martyrdom, like other meaningful deaths, is a collective business. The martyr witnesses to both outsiders and insiders. He stands for the whole. His death involves his entire community. This takes us back directly to Durkheim's secondary definition of religion, that it is collective in nature. Distinguishing between religion and magic, he says:

> The really religious beliefs are always common to a determined group, which makes profession of adhering to them and of practising the rites connected with them. They are not merely received individually by all members of the group; they are something belonging to the group, and they make its unity. The individuals which compose it feel themselves united to each other by the simple fact that they have a common faith.[1]

The singular power of modern Shi'ism to generate so many instances of total self-abnegation originates, I believe, not in any esoteric teaching unique to that faith, but in the link that exists, in Islam in general and in Shi'ism in particular, between personal devotion and social order, private faith and public responsibility. All of this is, I believe, closely linked to the American sociologist Peter Berger's theories concerning religion as a primary instrument of 'world construction' and 'world maintenance'. To the extent that it is an artificial construct, society has to be legitimized. In Berger's words, 'religion has been the historically most widespread and effective instrumentality of legitimation'.[2] But all legitimations of social reality can be and are challenged, above all by the fact of death. To quote Berger once more:

> The confrontation with death (be it through actually witnessing the death of others or anticipating one's own death in the imagination) constitutes what is probably the most important marginal situation. Death radically challenges all socially objectivated definitions of reality of the world, of others, and of self. Death radically puts in question the taken for granted, 'business as usual' attitude in which one exists in everyday life. Here, everything in the daytime world of existence in society is massively threatened with 'irreality', that is, everything in that world becomes dubious, eventually unreal, other than one had used to think. Insofar as the knowledge of death cannot be avoided in any society, legitimations of the reality of the social world in the face of death are decisive

---

[1] *The Elementary Forms of the Religious Life*, 2nd edn, Allen & Unwin, London, 1976, p. 43.
[2] *The Sacred Canopy*, Anchor Books, Garden City, New York, 1969, p. 32.

requirements in any society. The importance of religion in such legitimations is 'obvious'.[3]

The primary function of world construction is to ward off a sense of anomy that threatens to destroy us.

> Men are congenitally compelled to impose a meaningful order upon reality. This order, however, presupposes the social enterprise of ordering world construction. To be separated from society exposes the individual to a multiplicity of dangers with which he is unable to cope by himself, in the extreme case to the danger of imminent extinction. Separation from society also inflicts unbearable psychological tensions upon the individual, tensions that are grounded in the root anthropological fact of sociality. The ultimate danger of such separation, however, is the danger of meaninglessness.[4]

From this perspective, the very notion of a meaningful death appears a contradiction in terms. If death is 'the marginal situation par excellence' because 'it threatens the basic assumptions of order on which society rests',[5] it seems a fundamental mistake to seek for meaning in its voluntary embrace, whether as religious martyrdom or as extinction on the battlefield. But paradoxically, it is precisely by seeking such a death that the individual is able wholly and unreservedly to transcend his own separateness, to identify completely with the social whole of which he so desperately needs to become part in order to stave off the threat of annihilation. By thus accepting death, the individual is, in a sense, denying his own separateness. He has already identified himself with the martyred Husayn or the crucified Christ, and in actually dying, he identifies himself with all those others who have flagellated themselves or wept or been persecuted for his sake. It is Koestler's notion of identification with the whole, the self-transcending capacity that produces man's greatest achievements and his basest crimes.

If religion provides the best route to a meaningful death, what has become of dying in our secular age? It has, I think, become something denatured, neither meaningful nor natural,

---

[3] Ibid., pp. 43–4.
[4] Ibid., p. 22.
[5] Ibid., p. 23.

and certainly not a thing to be willingly embraced. Just as life itself has become increasingly medicalized, so death has been transformed into the last battleground of science. Nowhere, perhaps, has this modification been better analysed than by Ivan Illich, in the chapter on death in his study of modern medicine:

> We cannot fully understand the deeply rooted structure of our social organization unless we see in it a multifaceted exorcism of all forms of evil death. Our major institutions constitute a gigantic defence programme waging war on behalf of 'humanity' against death dealing agencies and classes. This is a total war. Not only medicine but also welfare, international relief, and development programmes are enlisted in this struggle. Ideological bureaucracies of all colours join the crusade. Revolution, repression, and even civil and international wars are justified in order to defeat the dictators or capitalists who can be blamed for the wanton creation and tolerance of sickness and death.[6]

Ultimately, death is transformed into a controlled event, just as birth has been downgraded to the status of a medical operation:

> The medicalization of society has brought the epoch of natural death to an end. Western man has lost the right to preside at his act of dying. Health, or the autonomous power to cope, has been expropriated down to the last breath. Technical death has won its victory over dying. Mechanical death has conquered and destroyed all other deaths.[7]

In a sense, this is the result, not of secularization, but rather of the displacement of religious institutions by the all-embracing institution of modern medicine, which has itself become a religion in the process: 'Through the medicalization of death, health care has become a monolithic world religion . . .'[8] The image of medicine as surrogate religion is not an idiosyncrasy of Illich's. Virtually every critic of modern medicine and psychiatry has at some time used it, and I believe it expresses a fundamental truth.

The American sociologist Eliot Freidson argues that 'the hospital is succeeding the church and the parliament as the archetypal

---

[6] *Limits to Medicine: Medical Nemesis*, Penguin Books, Harmondsworth, 1977, p. 205.
[7] Ibid., p. 210.
[8] Ibid., p. 208.

institution of western culture'. But modern technological medicine is constitutionally incapable of giving meaning to either suffering or death, if only because it sees them as essentially evils whose ultimate extinction it seeks to encompass. In an article about AIDS that I read a few years ago, a doctor was quoted as saying that the only thing he was opposed to was death. From that perspective, every death is a failure, and voluntary death for a cause must be seen as the ultimate in pointlessness.

The Palestinian poet Mahmoud Darwish echoes that sentiment:

> If I refuse suicide, you treat me as a coward; and when I accept dying in this way, you treat me as a barbarian. You cannot make up your mind which manner of death suits me best so that I can escape my oppressors. Do you, gentlemen specialists in genocide, wish to deprive me even of the liberty of choosing my death?[9]

In the West, sickness, death and burial are rapidly ceasing to be publicly experienced realities. More and more, we suffer and die alone, and are buried or cremated in a trivalized, deritualized manner: efficiently, hygienically, on a conveyor belt. If death threatens our sense of social order, so our ability to invest it with meaning rescues that order from dissolution.

Malinowski has argued that, just as death threatens the cohesion of the group, so solidarity is saved by making the natural event into a social ritual. We have lost the ability to effect such rituals. Is it, therefore, surprising and ironic that we should find it so difficult to comprehend the forces that lie behind the modern Shi'ite martyr complex? That we should downgrade and stereotype it as fanaticism and irrationality? That we should regard it as barbaric when our own civilization is only a generation away from the death camps and minutes away from nuclear holocaust?

(Originally delivered at an Adult Education
Philosophy Day School, University of
Newcastle, November 1987)

[9] Quoted in Amir Taheri, *Holy Terror*, Century Hutchinson/Sphere Books, London, 1987, p. 90.

Voluntary Suffering and Inflicting Suffering on Others

Most of us are familiar with the humorous paradox of the sadist who obtains satisfaction by refusing to inflict pain on a masochist. No doubt the sadist in question might go one step further and inflict pain on his friend. In reality, of course, there is not much of a paradox here at all because, for the masochist, pleasure and pain have become reversed. But the witticism does help illustrate the obvious fact that we all seek what gives us pleasure and try, as far as possible, to avoid what causes us pain or unhappiness. Suffering results when we are unable to avoid whatever brings us physical or mental distress. And the more severe the distress we feel, the greater will be our efforts to avoid it by whatever means are in our power.

This is, at any rate, the normal response, but it is far from the inflexible rule we sometimes take it to be. Leaving aside the pathological extreme of masochism, it is a most remarkable fact that many human beings will, in fact, voluntarily submit to terrible suffering, even to the degree of sacrificing life itself. At a basic level, this is a standard biological response. The mother who suffers or dies to protect her child is acting in accordance with a fundamental instinct for the survival of the species. But human beings are capable of self-sacrifice for much less basic motives. This is most clearly seen in the voluntary suffering of ascetics within most of the major religious traditions.

All religions teach fortitude and endurance in the face of suffering, but there have always been individuals – sometimes very large numbers of them – prepared to go beyond this and actually seek various forms of suffering as a means of achieving spiritual mastery over the flesh. In the main traditions of the East, Hinduism and Buddhism, the aim of the mystic has been to subdue and discipline the body in order to break free of the world of illusion and to experience reality by means of his higher, spiritual senses.

The aim of Christian and Muslim mystics in the West has been similar, with this difference, that the ultimate goal has been less the cessation of desire leading to rebirth and rather the attainment of the Unitive Life, in which the mystic experiences a sense of union with the Godhead. The Purgative Way, whereby the devotee seeks to weary his physical senses and to control his restless mind in order to open his spiritual senses and his higher intuition, is the first stage of the Path in all mystical traditions.

It has generally been recognized, however, that the unsupervised practice of asceticism has profound dangers, physical, psychological and spiritual. This has led to the emergence of teachers or guides to help the novice avoid the pitfalls of the Path – the guru in India, the *shaykh* or *pir* in Islamic Sufism. And, in their turn, many of the great teachers, men like St Anthony or St Basil, like Suhrawardi or Rumi, founded orders or devised a Rule, a system according to which the mystic could regulate his life and avoid the excesses of extreme asceticism. The Christian monastic orders developed in this way out of the scattered cenobitic communities of ascetics in the Egyptian Syrian deserts, as did the Sufi *tariqas* from small groups of ascetics in Mesopotamia and Persia. At one extreme, asceticism was an unhealthy perversion of the spiritual value of detachment, leading its practitioners to isolate themselves from the world and torture their bodies in the hope of achieving a personal, selfish salvation. At the other extreme, notably in the medieval Christian orders, it formed part of a disciplined life that led the mystic back into the world to help alleviate the sufferings of his fellow men.

It is in the religious context above all that we can observe the extraordinary phenomenon of martyrdom, the witnessing through death to the truth of a cause deemed higher than the self. Unlike the ascetic, the martyr does not willingly inflict suffering upon himself. Instead, he voluntarily submits to all that his enemies may inflict on him, refusing to yield to his natural impulses to flee or recant or fight back. Here again, there are extremes – the longing for martyrdom that leads to activity calculated to bring down the wrath of the persecutor and the quiet acceptance of death in preference to compromise with the Lie.

That men and women can accept unnecessary suffering in this

way is a testimony to the remarkable resources of the human spirit. The very existence of such a phenomenon, however, raises questions of a kind fundamental to the problem of suffering as a whole. If we look at the problem of suffering from a variety of angles, three main responses predominate – coming to terms with the fact of suffering in the world and in one's own life; caring for others and helping them bear their own suffering; and seeking ways in which to relieve the suffering of others or to abolish certain kinds of suffering absolutely. For the philosopher or the theologian, it may be tremendously important to know whether a certain example of suffering is the effect of natural causes beyond our control or the working of blind fate or the pre-ordained decree of an omnipotent deity or the result of human wickedness or carelessness. But from the immediate, practical viewpoint of the victim or those caring for him, it is generally a question of secondary importance, if not of total indifference.

From the point of view of those most concerned with the third response of relieving or abolishing suffering, however, the question has considerable relevance. Sir Karl Popper has argued that our proper aim in the construction of a better society ought not to be the achievement of an impossible utopian dream but rather the minimization of suffering for the maximum number of people. If suffering is to be minimized, it is important to be able to determine which forms of it are most likely to prove amenable to our efforts to decrease or abolish them. A world-view which accepts all disease as God-given and beyond our power to ease or counteract and which refuses to sanction medical science as blasphemous tampering with the divine will can clearly delay the minimization of much suffering from preventable illness. Conversely, a world-view which sees all economic suffering in terms of class struggle may, in its efforts to abolish all vestiges of the class system, cause even greater suffering than it seeks to prevent.

Ironically, however, it is precisely those forms of suffering which it should be most in our power to abolish which prove most intractable – namely those which are directly or indirectly attributable to ourselves. However much we may be able to improve our external environment, our ability to diminish suffering depends as much as ever – perhaps more than ever – on our ability to cope with the results of our own greed or cruelty. It matters little whether we talk in terms of sin or environmentally-determined neuroses – the problems are just as intractable. And in an age when massive weapons of destruction give handfuls of men the power to inflict suffering and death on millions, the problem is more acute than ever.

Both humanists and the followers of most religions have attempted in various ways and with varying degrees of success to overcome this ghastly love our species has to kill, maim, torture or otherwise harm itself. The successes are impressive, but they pale into insignificance beside the failures. Centuries of preaching and exhortation have not changed human nature in the aggregate; this century has witnessed some of the greatest cruelties ever inflicted by man upon man and may yet witness the self-destruction of the human race. The sum total of human suffering has been vastly increased by man's own inhumanity to man, and any account of the problem of suffering must seek to embrace that fact. Burning at the stake or in a forest fire may not differ materially for the victim, but there is a considerable psychological difference both for him and for those who witness his fate.

Curiously enough, the problem of the infliction of suffering is often not the same as the problem of evil. Arthur Koestler has drawn an important distinction between what he calls the self-assertive and the integrative tendencies in the individual. The first of these tendencies, which leads the organism to assert its autonomy, gives us the virtues of independence and creativity on the one hand and the vices of self-interest and egotism on the other. The second, which causes the unit to see itself as part of a greater whole, makes for self-sacrifice and co-operation or blind identification with the mob. It is the latter which is responsible for the greatest crimes of inhumanity, for holy wars and inquisitions, for the burning of books and their writers, for witch-hunts and pogroms, for Belsen and Hiroshima. The crimes of self-assertion are generally petty and limited, those of integration, of religious fanaticism and national chauvinism, vast and uncontrollable.

This may all seem like stating the obvious – although it is curious how few sermons deal with this theme – but what is rather less obvious and of considerably greater importance for the topic of suffering is the remarkable link in the integrative tendency between self-sacrifice for a cause greater than oneself and the commission of atrocities in the name of the same cause or a different one. The evidence is not far to seek. Leaving aside again the extremes of sadism, masochism, and sado-masochism, we can cite a wide range of examples of this tendency. The way in which the persecuted Christian Church became the persecutor of pagans and heretics following its recognition by Constantine and its acquisition of temporal power is notorious. The same devotion that led the followers of Ayatollah Khomeini on to the streets of Tehran clothed in shrouds and eager for the points of bayonets or the tracks of tanks now leads them to imprison and dismember and kill in the name of God and for the sake of revolutionary Shi'ism. The IRA hunger strikers who are willing to die in their beds for the cause of a united Ireland would be capable of killing without mercy in order to achieve the same ends. The bestial cruelties perpetrated in the name of the Third Reich were matched only by the determined fanaticism with which German soldiers and civilians sacrificed everything for the sake of Hitler's Greater Germany and out of devotion to the Führer himself: the death camps were mirrored by the obsession with death and Apocalypse which so typified Nazi ritual and philosophy.

This is not just a cheap paradox. There is a very real connection between willingness to sacrifice oneself for a higher cause and willingness to sacrifice others for it. Let us look more closely at the events of the Iranian revolution. Shi'ism has traditionally expressed itself as a cult of martyrdom, centred on the passion of the Imam Husayn and intensified by centuries of persecution as a minority sect. Even when Shi'ism became the national religion of Iran in the sixteenth century, it retained its fascination with suffering and martyrdom. In the nineteenth century, the Babis, a messianic Shi'i sect, astonished European observers like Renan and Tolstoy by the enthusiasm with which they embraced painful and lingering deaths. And we have all witnessed on our television screens the impatience with which young men rushed to water the seedling of the Iranian revolution with their blood. By losing his identity and casting his life away in devotion to the cause of God, the individual becomes part of something higher and more perfect than himself. But by the same token that the divine cause is sanctified above the things of this world, its sanctity must be preserved from the taints of heresy and unbelief. The deadly emissaries of the Shi'i Ismailis of medieval Iran and Syria gave the world the term 'assassin'; the Babis showed no mercy to their opponents in places where they armed and defended themselves, and they dreamt of a holy war that would rid the earth of infidelity; and the new Islamic order of Iran today is symbolized for many by the grim images of the hanging judge Ayatollah Khalkhali or gun-toting *hezbollahis* quartering the streets of Tehran in search of the enemies of God.

Koestler has discussed at length the reasons for this phenomenon, and I would recommend his works on the subject most keenly. He indicates that we are dealing with two sides of the same coin, that, in both cases, the individual loses sight of himself as an independent entity and identifies himself with something greater – whether it be something concrete such as a mob or a regiment or a nation, or an abstract concept such as 'the cause of God' or 'history' or 'the fatherland'. The spirit of self-sacrifice is either noble and heroic, or foolish and misguided, depending on our evaluation of the worth of the cause it serves. The same is true of the spirit of inquisition and persecution. In 1943, at a meeting of SS-Gruppenführer, Heinrich Himmler said of the annihilation of the Jews: 'All in all we can say that we have completed this painful task out of love for our people. In our own selves, in our souls and in our character we have suffered no damage therefrom.' On another occasion, he said: 'Most of you will know what it means to see a hundred corpses – five hundred – a thousand – lying there. But seeing this thing through and nevertheless – apart from certain exceptions due to human infirmity – remaining decent, that is what has made us hard.'

Of relevance to this phenomenon is a series of experiments carried out at Yale University and later repeated in Germany, Italy, Australia and South Africa. In these experiments, the subjects were placed before a row of dials supposedly connected to a chair in which a volunteer was seated. The subjects were told they were to assist in an experiment to determine whether the infliction of pain could speed up the learning process in certain volunteers; their task was to turn the dials in order to 'punish' those in the chair for incorrect answers to questions. In fact, the electrical apparatus was a dummy and the volunteers in the chair actors simulating pain in response to the imaginary electric current. Before starting the experiments, a number of psychiatrists were asked to predict what percentage of subjects would obey the experimenter to the fullest degree by inflicting (as they believed) a 'severe shock' of 450 volts on the 'victim'. It was predicted that most subjects would not go beyond 150 volts, that only four per cent would reach 300 volts, and that only about one in a thousand would administer the highest shock. In fact, over sixty per cent obeyed the professor in charge right up to the 450-volt limit. In Munich, the figure was eighty-five per cent.

A further series of tests, in which the subjects were no longer exhorted or ordered to go on increasing the voltages, but had complete freedom of choice as to the shock level, indicated that the overwhelming majority refused to go any higher than 150 volts, the point at which the supposed victim made a first mild complaint.

Stanley Milgram, who carried out the first tests at Yale, writes:

> Most subjects in the experiment see their behaviours in a larger context that is benevolent and useful to society – the pursuit of scientific truth. The psychological laboratory has a strong claim to legitimacy and evokes trust and confidence in those who perform there. An action such as shocking a victim, which in isolation appears evil, acquires a totally different meaning when placed in this setting. Morality does not disappear, but acquires a radically different focus; the subordinate person feels shame and pride depending on how adequately he has performed the actions called for by authority. Language provides numerous terms to pinpoint this type of morality: loyalty, duty, discipline . . .[1]

Writing of the mass extermination carried out by the SS under the Third Reich, Martin Borszat says:

> It was the work of ambitious, straightlaced philistines, men obsessed with a sense of duty, faithful servants of the powers that be; they had been brought up in a spirit of soulless conformity; they were incapable of criticism and devoid of imagination; so in all good faith and with a clear conscience, they persuaded themselves, and allowed themselves to be persuaded, that the 'liquidation' of men in hundreds of thousands was a service to their people and their country.[2]

[1] Stanley Milgram, *Obedience to Authority*, Tavistock Press, London, 1974.
[2] Quoted in Heinz Höhne, *The Order of the Death's Head*, trans. Richard Barry, Secker & Warburg, London, 1969, pp. 387–8.

Hannah Arendt has commented that the Reich's extermination organization was manned 'neither by fanatics nor by natural murderers nor by sadists. It was manned solely and exclusively by normal human beings of the type of Heinrich Himmler.'[3]

By sacrificing personal conscience and independence of will to the 'higher' dictates of duty to a supreme cause, these 'normal human beings' were able to carry out acts which they would never have contemplated on their own initiative. And I have no doubt whatever that, if this country were to be taken over tomorrow by a totalitarian regime, there would be no shortage of soldiers, policemen and civil servants to carry out its most objectionable orders without the least qualm of conscience. By delegating the ultimate moral decisions to a higher authority, the individual conscience can reconcile itself to the worst of deeds. What Hannah Arendt calls 'the banality of evil' links inextricably the fanatic and the organization man in an obscene embrace of pain and death.

It would be interesting to devise a series of harmless experiments as a corollary to those we have just described, designed to demonstrate how far individuals may be willing to accept pain when asked or ordered to do so by an authority figure.

But experiments like this really only provide scientific corroboration of what we know already – that man, in transcending himself, can conquer both his moral revulsion to crimes against his fellow man and his natural fear of pain and death. It is not self-transcendence that is to blame, or the tendency to become part of a greater whole – after all, the same tendencies are responsible for some of man's noblest qualities, for self-sacrifice, co-operation, and willingness to help others even at the cost of personal suffering. What is to blame is a lack of balance between the integrative and the self-assertive tendencies, between blind emotion and reason, between unquestioning obedience and independence of spirit. To ask what the key to this balance may be is clearly outside the scope of this essay. I have merely pointed to some of the connections in the hope that the theme may be taken up and discussed at greater length. Perhaps there is, in the end, no satisfactory solution to this

---

[3] Quoted in ibid., p. 382. Cf. Arendt, *Eichmann in Jerusalem: A Report on the Banality of Evil*, rev. edn, Penguin Books, Harmondsworth, 1977, p. 105 (and throughout).

human paradox; but the search for one will not, therefore, lose any of its significance or urgency.

(First published in Mary Midgely (ed.),
Perspectives on Suffering, Newcastle University,
1981, pp. 20–5)

Suffering Revisited

At the end of the previous essay on voluntary suffering and inflicting suffering on others, I remarked: 'It would be interesting to devise a series of harmless experiments ... designed to demonstrate how far individuals may be willing to accept pain when asked or ordered to do so by an authority figure.'

There are, in fact, a few common circumstances in which this phenomenon may be observed: military organizations, especially in peacetime, when there is no immediate external threat; monasteries and convents, and the more extreme new religious movements; and, above all, hospitals.

In all of these, there are, of course, elements of self-interest: ambition to succeed, fear of the enemy in battle, a longing for spiritual attainment, a wish to get better. And there may also be, in many cases, slightly or grossly pathological factors: an obsession with spit and polish, sexual repression, a need to devolve all responsibility for one's own fate. But perfectly normal people become soldiers, nuns and patients, and they are just as likely to submit to the suffering entailed by those roles as anyone.

It may, of course, be argued that patients have no choice in the matter, as the term itself implies. They do not seek injury or sickness, and their submission to therapeutic regimes is merely for the sake of a return to health, whether fully or in part. It would be naïve to suggest that this is not broadly true. Nevertheless, it is clear that a very large measure of collusion exists between medical personnel on the one hand and patients and their relatives on the other. Painful and risky treatments will often be endured, not because the benefit is clear, but because a doctor has insisted on their worth. Chemotherapy may produce side-effects more disabling than cancer, yet patients will endure it without grumbling because it is the proper thing to do. That this is a choice rather than a simple response to the pressures of illness is demonstrated by the numbers of people who choose not to undergo such regimens and even declare that they have received benefits from their abstention.

Medicine, like the army, is a rigidly hierarchical profession. Doctors justify their authority and their practice by reference to the salvific power and overriding value-system of science. It is their role to know and to act, that of their patients to acquiesce and be acted on. Those who die in experimental operations or from the administration of some new drug are martyrs, willing sacrifices on the altar of medical progress.

If we accept that medicine produces side-effects, many of them serious, that iatrogenesis (doctor-induced disease) has even, as Illich argues, become endemic in modern times, and that the harm it causes stretches beyond the individual to society and even to culture, it may not seem so far-fetched to suggest that our acquiescence in medical procedures has in it a degree of masochism. To the extent that medicine does not cure our ills and even produces ills where there were none previously, it is evident that our willing submission to the scalpel and the pill is made for the sake of a greater good, even as the soldier submits to the bayonet or the martyr to the fire or the nun to the flail.

Just as white-coated figures proclaiming themselves 'scientists' succeeded in pressing volunteers to inflict apparent injury on others in Milgram's experiments, so doctors and nurses daily instil in the public the need for suffering that all things may be made well in a medical utopia. This is not mere whimsy, I think. As it was true in the nineteenth century, so it is true today that the dominant system of medicine in Western culture is one that relies on cutting, burning and poisoning to achieve its cures. Rival systems – homoeopathy, herbalism, massage, hypnotherapy, acupuncture – that emphasize gentleness, non-invasiveness, empathy and similar qualities, have, as a rule, been rejected – a rejection that does not lack significance. Authority tells us we must suffer, that there is no virtue in therapies that heal without pain, that there can be no beneficial power in a medicine that does not cause some measure of harm (the dogma of the 'risk/benefit ratio'), and so we suffer.

So, necessarily, doctors learn at an early stage in their training

a measure of hardness, a sense of dispassion, a nobility of detachment that allows them to inflict suffering without undergoing
it themselves. But in that very detachment, as Glin Bennett
has so eloquently demonstrated in his study, *The Wound and
the Doctor*,[1] lie the seeds of very great personal anguish for
physicians themselves. By seeking invulnerability, they open
themselves to wounds that cannot easily be healed. Hence the
irony that a profession with high status, more than adequate
financial reward, and considerable potential for job satisfaction
has one of the highest rates of alcoholism, divorce and suicide.
Once again we are faced with a paradox: those most willing to
inflict suffering without feeling will themselves suffer, above all
on the level of feeling.

Here, as in other respects, the physician has become a priest,
called on to perform 'miracle' cures. He has taken on himself the
role of vicarious saviour, through whose long hours of training
and duty, through whose sacrifice of family and love and friends,
through whose mental and spiritual wounds his patients will find
healing and rest. For the patient not to submit to the knife or the
drug trial seems an act of ingratitude, a betrayal of the faith.

In the hospital, then, and the 'health' centre, we are all bound
in a community of suffering whose focus is a denial of human pain.
We exchange our grief for the emotional deadness of tranquilizer
addiction. We pour out our life histories in five-minute interviews
and are sent away clutching prescriptions. We say we are feeling
better when, deep down, we are heart-sick and fearful that there
is nothing the doctor in his white coat can do.

It has been a long and painful experiment, and there are
few signs that it has yet run its course. There will be new
'wonder-drugs' and new disasters, new procedures and new
diseases. We will continue to play our role as guinea pigs.
While the medical profession, out of the best of motives, and
the pharmaceutical industry, for the keenest of profits, smiles at
us and says 'open please'.

[1] Secker & Warburg, London, 1987.

'Get Thee Behind Me, Satan'

A few days ago, I was involved in one of the strangest radio interviews of my career. Hauled in to the studio in my capacity as chairman of the charity Friends of Homoeopathy and the author of several articles on homoeopathic medicine and science, I was asked to participate in a one-to-one debate with a research assistant from Bristol Royal Infirmary. My antagonist had just published a book on the subject of homoeopathy, in which he claimed that, although there is now much evidence that this system of medicine actually works, it is impossible to suggest a mechanism for its operation while remaining within the bounds of normal science.

Now, this was a rather unusual position for a scientist to take, though by no means unprecedented. It is not surprising for a doctor or pharmacist to express uneasiness with the fact that there really is no observable mechanism whereby homoeopathic medicines should work – they are, after all, diluted far beyond the point where any molecule of the original substance remains: a hard pill to swallow for anyone brought up according to the strict tenets of conventional chemistry. The topic has, nevertheless, become a focus for widespread debate in the pages of scientific and medical journals over the past few years and could very well become the central scientific debate of the twenty-first century.

It is customary, however, for scientists to argue – rather illogically, it should be said – that, if a mechanism has not been identified, homoeopathy cannot work at all, and its apparent effectiveness must be attributed to the operation of the placebo effect, or prior orthodox treatment, or spontaneous remission. (It is, indeed, a curiosity of medical science how many people recover 'spontaneously' after taking homoeopathic remedies! Mind-boggling coincidence appears to be no barrier to scientific credulity.)

My friend from Bristol, however, did not take this common

stance. He accepted – as have several recent researchers – that there is an observable therapeutic effect of homoeopathy that cannot be explained away by reference to placebo or other factors. His rather bizarre conclusion was that, if homoeopathy worked but could not be shown to have a plausible scientific mechanism, it must be 'occult' or 'paranormal'.

At this point, I smelled a rat. Rather a large rat, in fact. As he prattled on about the sinister element of 'vitalism' in early homoeopathic theory or the connections of some nineteenth-century American homoeopaths with the 'occultist cult' of Swedenborgianism (a historical fact of only passing interest today), I began to see the drift of his argument. I had heard this sort of thing before.

When it was my turn to speak again, I challenged the man from Bristol directly. Were these not, I suggested, the views, not of a research scientist as such, but of an evangelical Christian masquerading (for present purposes) as a scientist? And, indeed, he admitted that it was so. He agreed that he was a Christian and an evangelical, but insisted that this had not the slightest influence on his dedication to scientific principles.

That, of course, was hogwash. No scientist, faced with the dilemma he had just described, would resort to claims of sinister occult influences being at work. The homoeopathic problem is fairly simply expressed: if it should be admitted that it works, then it is just a matter of carrying out further research and testing hypotheses until we discover the mechanism. Or, if we think no such mechanism possible (because it would fly in the face of current scientific theory), then claims that the medicines work must be shown to be based on false observations.

(Actually, this latter argument is scientifically the weaker of the two, inasmuch as it depends on a belief that current scientific theory is the last word on the way matter is structured, which sounds dangerously close to religious dogmatism. As evidence for the effectiveness of homoeopathy becomes increasingly strong (as a recent paper in the *British Medical Journal*[1], suggested), it is evident that we are approaching the state of affairs described by

[1] Jos Kleijnen, Paul Knipschild, Gerben ter Riet, 'Clinical Trials of Homoeopathy'. *British Medical Journal*, 302 (9 February 1991): 316–23 ('The evidence is to a large extent positive . . .').

Thomas Kuhn as preceding a major shift in a scientific paradigm: contradictions in the evidence can no longer satisfactorily be resolved by reference to existing theory, therefore the theory itself must be abandoned and replaced by new ideas.)

Be all that as it may, what I was dealing with in my radio discussion was not just a single confused Christian doing his best to make sense out of a scientific conundrum by dragging in spiritism and the occult by the scruffs of their insubstantial necks, but the tip of an enormous iceberg of evangelical opposition to the most bizarre collection of ideas and practices you or I could imagine. Convinced that this world is a battleground between God and Satan, Christ and the occult, these people seek out traces of 'spirit activity' in anything that meets with their disapproval. It is not always possible to follow the logic of this disapproval (because it is not in any sense logical), but some patterns may, nevertheless, be discerned.

The following list represents part of a much larger compendium of subjects which a group of Christian parents in Hampshire recently presented to the headmaster of their local primary school, insisting that he ensure that their children never be taught about them or hear them mentioned, because they are all topics that 'can in one way or another open the way to Satan': Space Invaders; Dungeons and Dragons; oriental carpets and rugs; the World Council of Churches; Care Bears; judo; karate; aikido; T'ai Chi; yoga; cancer-help centres; ET; Superman; the Beatles; CND; Electric Shock Treatment; Stonehenge; handwriting analysis; evolution; the New Age movement; ginseng; aromatherapy; chiropractice; osteopathy; hypnosis; acupuncture; reflexology; copper bracelets; meditation; etc etc.

In most cases, the 'occult' or New Age connections are fairly obvious. Connected to this is an evident distrust of anything of oriental origin, a distrust that seems to be related to the objection voiced by some American evangelicals to the teaching of comparative religions in schools: non-Christian ('Eastern') religions are, to these people, by definition the work of the devil, so children must be protected from all mention of them. The very names of Buddha, Krishna, Muhammad – Antichrists all – must never be uttered in the hearing of Christian children lest Satan enter their tiny hearts. Facts and information – about the beliefs of many of their schoolfriends, about the lives and customs of most human beings who have ever lived – must not be allowed to disturb the sanctimonious self-congratulation of the saved of Hampshire or Oregon.

Eastern religions (are there any Western ones?), as is well known, sometimes involve spiritual practices which, in New Age thought, are translated into methods of 'consciousness raising' or 'self-realization'. But since these practices are, for evangelicals, portals through which Satanic forces may enter the unprotected mind, they must be shunned and their benefits, both bodily and mental, denied or derided – hence the ban on yoga and meditation. In the States, vegetarianism got it in the neck for the same reason. And no doubt spiritual practices within the Christian tradition – *hesychasm* in Eastern Orthodoxy, for example, or the silent worship of Quakerism – get similarly short shrift, as does 'Mary worship'.

Alternative medicine seems to be a particularly juicy target for evangelical wrath. The reasons for this are, I think, rather more complex. First of all, it is well known that several 'alternative' medical systems now growing in popularity in the West have Eastern and (in some cases) religious origins: acupuncture, shiatsu, Ayurveda, Chinese and Tibetan medicine, and yoga (used therapeutically). There is also a broad tendency for people who are involved with New Age thinking to embrace alternative approaches to healing and even to dominate them in some areas.

(Quite emphatically, this is not the same as saying that all those who use or practise alternative medicine are New Age types. My wife, who is a homoeopath, has only ever treated one 'New Age' person in her entire career: her patients have included welders, tanker drivers, barristers, accountants, teachers, merchant seamen and many others whose only interest in homoeopathy has been as a means of getting well. And she herself much prefers a gin and tonic to a herbal tea, or a burst of Verdi to a sugary interlude of New Age musak.)

More deeply, it should not be forgotten that evangelical Christianity has itself a strong tradition of healing outside the sphere of conventional medicine, chiefly through the 'laying-on of hands' and the pursuit of a 'healing ministry' within numerous evangelical churches. Fundamentalist Christians who are doctors or scientists (and there are many of them, as I intend to discuss shortly) appear to have no difficulty about the mechanism of the cures brought about during healing services. The Holy Spirit or the spirit of Jesus Christ are adequate explanations for what are regarded quite openly as miracles. Rational explanations of such cures – the release of endorphins in a trance state, psychosomatic release, or electro-magnetic energy – find little favour among believers, even though they might claim to be scientists in their daily lives.

Many systems of alternative medicine also seem to achieve results by mysterious mechanisms. For the evangelical this can only mean that, since the cures have not been brought about by the action of the Holy Spirit, they must be attributed to Satanic forces. Even where measurable mechanisms have been discovered (as in the case of acupuncture used to produce analgesia, an action now known to be due to the release of endorphins in the brain of the patient), they are routinely ignored in favour of a Satanic explanation. Such a combination of scientific orthodoxy with the most primitive superstition is probably unique.

But there is a relatively straightforward explanation for such an unholy alliance. A very close link exists between religious fundamentalism and scientific dogmatism. In many people, the need for absolute values and inner certainty overrides all other issues. Just as religious dogma comes to be crystallized in books of scripture and exegesis, so the received wisdom of science in any age is set down and frozen in textbooks. They become inviolable repositories of the truth, cordoned off from outside questioning, guarantees of the priceless certainties they contain.

Malise Ruthven observed this phenomenon while interviewing a Muslim fundamentalist in Bradford:

> Anwar the natural scientist had a naïve, unscientific view of what was essentially a literary question [concerning the origin of the Qur'an]. Just as most of the Biblical inerrantists I had met in America – other than religious professionals like preachers or theologians – had been physicians, chemists, computer specialists, or engineers, people whose understanding of reality was rooted in the factualistic realm of applied science and technology, so Anwar, the most articulate of the fundamentalists I met in Bradford ... had been a teacher of biology, a man whose understanding of texts – 'textbook' understanding – came largely from manuals devoted to specific branches of science. Social surveys confirm that it is much more rare for fundamentalists

to belong to professions such as law, where the use of language is value-oriented.[2]

Everyday science, science based on 'established facts' can, manifestly, co-exist with faith, even reinforce it. But radical science, science that asks questions, science that, in Kuhn's terms, breaks old paradigms and replaces them with new ones, can never rest easy with a world-view based on the revelation of truth from above, let alone with taboos about what may and what may not be asked or postulated. If I am right in thinking that homoeopathy, acupuncture and several other energy-based systems of medicine are functioning on the far limits of conventional science, right on the edge of what may be the next major paradigm shift, then it is inevitable that their chief opponents will be found among those who have invested most in the certainties of 'normal', textbook science and, above all, those who manage to combine religious and scientific fundamentalism.

It is interesting that evangelical religion seems to have little difficulty in co-existing with orthodox medicine and that, in fact, so many doctors are born-again Christians. Significantly, it was a radical Catholic thinker, Ivan Illich, who identified modern medicine as a 'world religion' which seeks to extend its control over more and more aspects of human life and, above all, to appropriate the processes and meanings of death.[3] Evangelical

[2] *A Satanic Affair*, Chatto & Windus, London, 1990, p. 142. The role of the textbook in the creation of 'normal science' has been meticulously studied by Thomas Kuhn in his indispensable study, *The Structure of Scientific Revolutions*, (2nd edn, University of Chicago Press, 1970).

[3] See Ivan Illich, *Limits to Medicine: Medical Nemesis: the Expropriation of Health*, Penguin Books Harmondsworth, 1977. 'The religious use of medical technique has come to prevail over its technical purpose . . .'; 'Even in those circumstances in which the physician is technically equipped to play the technical role to which he aspires, he inevitably also fulfills religious, magical, ethical, and political functions'; 'Through the medicalization of death, health care has become a monolithic world religion . . .'; 'In the pursuit of applied science the medical profession has largely ceased to strive towards the goals of an association of artisans who use tradition, experience, learning, and intuition, and has come to play a role reserved to ministers of religion, using scientific principles as its theology and technologists as acolytes.'

Christianity places authority in the individual, seeking guidance in the promptings of the spirit rather than the deliberations of counsels or the authority of a priestly hierarchy. From that perspective, orthodox medicine and science are either neutral or positively benign inasmuch as they expound a world-view that is profoundly mechanistic. Conventional science avoids comment on matters of the spirit, while laying down the law about the structure of the physical universe in a manner that leaves room for miracles as events outside the ordinary. Science can, of course, come into conflict with fundamentalist religion – classically in the case of evolutionary theory – where scientific dogma impinges on the religious sphere. But real clashes are much more likely between religion and the soft sciences such as history, psychology or sociology.

Catholicism and other established churches place authority in the Church and are suspicious of inner promptings. The spirit, as Peter Berger puts it, is remote. To the extent that doctors have come to take on the role of priests (as Illich and others have argued) and hospitals to supplant the role of churches,[4] established religions are more likely to see the medical establishment as a direct threat. Paradoxically, relations between alternative medicine and some sections of the Anglican Church have at times been harmonious, as in the cases of complementary medical clinics set up in Marylebone and St James's in Piccadilly. The paradox lies precisely in the fact that a hierarchical and authoritarian church should provide such willing shelter to philosophies of health care which stress so heavily the need to empower the patient; while sectarian groups, whose ethos leans towards the authority of the individual, have tended to oppose the autonomy of patients while defending an authoritarian and hierarchical medical system.

One might ask, indeed, why on earth God should be the staunch supporter of orthodox medicine that so many evangelical Christians take Him for. He has, after all, been around a great deal longer than any medical system now in use. Did He, in the old days, back the phlebotomists against the herbalists? Or the users of mercury against the Mesmerists? Or has His conversion

---

[4] 'The hospital is succeeding the church and the parliament as the archetypal institution of Western culture': Philip Rieff, *Freud: The Mind of the Moralist*. University of Chicago Press, 1979, p. 360.

to 'scientific' medicine been more recent? Since around the time of thalidomide, perhaps, or Valium, or Opren, or any of the other wonder drugs our civilization produces in such quantities.

If God does have a bias in favour of Western orthodox medicine, does that mean He approves of the widespread havoc caused by iatrogenic illness, illness brought about by the action of doctors or the drugs they use? Iatrogenesis accounts for an increasingly high percentage of modern suffering. It is endemic to mechanistic medicine, a necessary product of its values and priorities. I want to know how it is supposed to be in the order of things that a loving Creator takes the side of a medical system so productive of unwanted misery, while other, gentler methods of healing are rejected out of hand as 'occult' and 'Satanic'.

It would be possible to take this argument many stages further. But it is likely to grow academic, even sterile. What really matters to me in the last analysis is the simple sense of outrage I feel at the behaviour of these self-appointed guardians of the public good. They have already turned the serious business of identifying child abuse into a bizarre trawl for Satanists and witches, not on the basis of facts, but because their beliefs demand some sort of fictive reality to sustain their fantasies of a cloven-hoofed Beelzebub luring mankind into his web.

It has to be asked how Christian, how charitable, how moral the behaviour of these sad, obsessed people really is. I have listened to my wife and other homoeopaths describe the cases of patients who have come to them on the verge of suicide, or in deep despair in the face of unendurable suffering, people whom orthodox medicine has consigned to one of its many dustbins of the untreatable or difficult. And I have listened in admiring humility to accounts of the changes homoeopathy has wrought in the lives of these people, giving new leases of life to people who had been abandoned as hopeless cases. Last year I attended a lecture by an Indian homoeopath, whose clinic in central Bombay has become a leading centre for the management of some of the city's many drug addicts, achieving remarkable success in restoring its patients to health. Throughout India, there are hundreds of homoeopathic clinics and hospitals treating prostitutes, drug addicts and the poor in general.

And yet my cosy Evangelical could sit back and condemn homoeopathy as Satanic, evil and harmful. All for no better reason than a poor historical understanding mixed with a superstitious belief in demons and evil spirits. I find myself appalled, sickened and angry that so much of real benefit can be condemned in the name of a faith that, in its better moments, has done so much to relieve human suffering. And I think of all the harmless pursuits, all the enchanting fairy stories, all the proclamations of life that have come under the stern interdict of the smugly saved. And I wonder who will save us from them or save them from themselves.

(First published in the *New Humanist*,
December 1991)

The New Religions: A Growing Force in Politics?

The best revolutions are quiet ones, the kind that sneak up on you before you know they are there. Quiet revolutions do not make the headlines, but perhaps they should – and religious revolutions more than most. When the latter are big and noisy and disruptive, like the Shi'ite revolution in Iran, they attract attention and comment. More often, however, they are peaceful movements of change that burgeon slowly in fertile soil until they are ready to reveal themselves.

Since the consensus is that we live in a secular age, major shifts in religious behaviour can go unnoticed for decades. Sometimes it takes an event like the Iranian revolution to bring long-term developments to general consciousness. And yet the consensus regarding secularity is, in many ways, a false one. Revivalism and relevance are not confined to the Islamic world. Turbans need not be more revolutionary than mitres. Neo-fundamentalism is a force to be reckoned with in modern American life and politics; liberation theology has radicalized whole sections of the population in Latin America; religious forces still shape life for many Hindus and Sikhs; the Catholic Church is a major component of the political scene in Poland and seems set to play an increasingly vital role in Eastern European politics generally; clerics like Desmond Tutu play an important role in South African affairs – the list is a long one and appears to be growing longer.

If all that seems like old faiths seeking to give themselves a patina of relevance through activity in the political arena, there remains the phenomenon of new religious movements – sects and cults whose very presence provides a cogent demonstration of the inadequacy of the consensus view that this is not a religious age. For quite a few people, it has become the Age of Aquarius.

New religious movements – NRMs – have been with us for some time now. They came to the fore in the aftermath of the hippy counter-culture and civil-rights movements of the 1960s, and their followers became familiar figures on the streets of many Western cities for several years during the 1970s, with their saffron robes, pamphlets, candles and wide eyes hungry for converts. Several attained fame or notoriety, from Maharishi Mahesh Yogi, who numbered the Beatles among his adherents, to Sun Myung Moon, whose Unification Church (the Moonies) came to be associated with stories of brainwashing and financial corruption, or the late Bhagwan Shree Rajneesh, whose followers became embroiled in tales of sexual scandal and bizarre manipulations at Rajneeshpuram in Oregon.

Not only have movements like the Unification Church or Rajneesh devotees shown extraordinary vitality since the 1960s, but as they settle down and learn the techniques of organization, some of them are beginning to develop a social and political consciousness the implications of which are still for the most part unrecognized or derided. Many new religions, like millenarian sects in the Middle Ages, want to change the world and are no longer content to sit on the sidelines of international affairs chanting mantras and contemplating their navels.

In the years since the public at large became aware of them, the new religions have undergone a variety of transformations. Most have adopted a much lower profile than before, many have learned to cope with declining numbers, and a few have adapted well to the society around them, partly in order to attract a more respectable and stable clientele. But if they are less conspicuous, they are far from spent forces, and there are signs that the better organized and more diversified among them have only begun to play what may prove to be an increasingly important role within modern society.

By 'society' I mean not just the affluent West, but equally and possibly more so parts of the Third World. One significant aspect of the activities of many of these movements is their growing concern with political influence in underdeveloped regions, and there is mounting evidence that some of them are starting to obtain leverage in some areas disproportionate to their size or perceived status.

* * *

The spread of sects and new religions in the Third World is a phenomenon still seldom noticed outside academic circles, and where it is seen it is frequently underestimated by independent observers. But the activities of these movements do have serious implications for the political and social processes of those countries in which they operate. In an article published in *New Blackfriars*,[1] a Dominican writer, Gilbert Markus, identifies what he calls 'theologies of repression'. By this he means principally a number of fundamentalist evangelical sects active in Latin America, whose doctrines are beginning to be seen by some right-wing politicians as valuable counterbalances to liberation theology.

The 1969 Rockefeller Report on Latin America stated that the Catholic Church there could no longer be trusted to support pro-US regimes. In 1980, the Santa Fé Report on US foreign policy argued that liberation theology and its exponents had to be 'counteracted'; and in 1983 General Schwaeker, the Pentagon's co-ordinator of Latin American forces, suggested a possible source for this counteractivity: 'We can no longer rely on the Catholic Church in Latin America. We have to rely on the Free Churches.'

The attractions of these 'Free Churches' are not far to seek, least of all in an era of 'Moral Majority' revivalism in the United States itself. On the one hand, they uniformly tend to be vociferously anti-communist, while on the other they preach political quietism, at least as far as the status quo is concerned. As Márkus astutely puts it, 'to be "saved" is to be saved from the world of social and political problems, and so to be relieved of the obligation of engaging in any form of political activity'. 'This kind of theology,' he adds, 'is designed to bring about the political demobilization of the people, reducing them to an apathetic and disorganized collection of individuals, concerned only with a very personal and individual morality.'

A few years ago, news came that President Marcos of the Philippines had publicly declared himself a supporter of Maharishi Mahesh Yogi's organization, becoming the first head of state to enter into a formal relationship with it. On 13 September

[1] *New Blackfriars* 67:787, January 1986, pp. 37–45.

1984, Marcos was declared 'President of the World Government of the Age of Enlightenment in the Philippines'. The 'World Government' proper is a European-based organization whose governors form the top echelon of the Maharishi's international movement, best known for its promulgation of the techniques of Transcendental Meditation.

Marketed as a secular and 'scientific' method of relieving stress and improving individual personality, TM has acquired an enormous following and much respectability. But the long-term objectives of the organization go far beyond the provision of a meditational system for men and women suffering the effects of overachievement. Society itself must be changed and a World Government established to manage human affairs in a new Age of Enlightenment.

With Marcos's blessing over one thousand TM adherents entered the Philippines to engage in a country-wide campaign of proselytization for the movement. Meanwhile, the local TM organization began to buy up private schools and universities, using foreign currency brought in from the Maharishi Educational Foundation in Switzerland. It is difficult to know what Marcos hoped to achieve by this espousal of the Maharishi and his claims. Absolute rulers often show a penchant for putting gurus on their payrolls – witness the Sultan of Brunei's patronage of the Indian holy man, Shri Chandra Swamiji Maharaj or Nancy Reagan's well-known reliance on the advice of her personal astrologer.

What cannot be ruled out is the possibility that Marcos, not far away from the upsurge of public protest that ousted him, may have seen in TM a means of keeping himself in power, either because he really believed in the power of group meditation to influence the course of material events, or because he saw in the movement a lever with which to raise a fresh power base. All we do know is that it did not stop him being overthrown.

In 1983, a similar breakthrough was made in Honduras by Moon's Unification Church, one of the most widespread and politically influential of new religions. In January of that year, General Alvarez, head of the Honduran military, announced the establishment of APROH, the right-wing Association for the Progress of Honduras. APROH has been described as 'the political wing of the [Honduran] armed forces'; its avowed aim, like that of Moon's church, is militant opposition to the spread of communism.

At the opening ceremony, Colonel Bo Hi Pak, Korean head of the Latin American division of the church, presented APROH with a cheque for five million dollars to support its anti-communist activities (which may have included the financing of paramilitary squads). One month later, APROH invited Bo Hi Pak to hold a seminar on behalf of the church, marking the first official appearance of the Moonies in the country. The colonel subsequently held a series of favourable meetings with the president, Dr Suazo Cordova, and with General Alvarez, as a result of which the church received wide publicity as 'the religion which fights communism'. Leading members of the government and the education sector became Moon sympathizers and spoke publicly in the movement's favour.

There have been setbacks since then for the Moonies in Honduras, following a campaign of counter-publicity initiated by a Catholic bishop. But in Uruguay, where it controls several businesses and the country's third-largest newspaper, and in other Latin American states, the Unification Church continues to foster close relations with right-wing governments and to engage in large-scale commercial enterprises.

Nor are the church's activities restricted to South America. There are close links with Park Chung Hee's regime in South Korea, where the sect originated, and with several influential Japanese political figures. In 1973, Moon stated that his dream was to create a Christian political party that would incorporate Protestants, Catholics and smaller denominations, as a counter-force to world communism. The world must be ruled by a theocracy: it is no longer possible to separate the political and religious spheres.

Some American sociologists, including Thomas Robbins and Dick Anthony, have described the Unification Church as 'the last civil religion', using as their model Robert Bellah's theory about American civil religion and its belief in a community of righteousness through which God's will is implemented in history. Speaking in New York in 1976, Moon referred to America as 'God's final bulwark on earth'. Elsewhere, he speaks of how 'America is in the centre of the God-fearing free-world nations. America has been chosen as the defender of God . . .' Following the defeat of communism, the Unification Church will usher in a benevolent theocracy in which all mankind will be united in a single faith. In recent years, the church has sought to offset its generally poor public image and declining growth rate in the West by expanding its activities in the Third World, particularly through its own aid organization, the International Relief Friendship Foundation, which is currently active in over fifty countries.

At about the time the Moonies were appearing on the scene in Honduras, an adherent of a fundamentalist Christian sect was in control of neighbouring Guatemala. General Efrain Rios Montt became President of Guatemala following a military coup in March 1982. Four years earlier, he had become a 'born again' Christian on his conversion to the Church of the Complete Word, a branch of the California-based Gospel Outreach Movement. Rios Montt's sect numbered only about eight hundred in Guatemala at the time he seized power, but fundamentalist Christianity threatened to become a major factor in the country's politics before very long.

In May 1982, the general stated that the junta had not asked for US aid because it had already been offered millions of dollars by Christian organizations in the United States. This money was to be used to develop a social, political and economic system to be known as 'communitarianism', under which fundamentalist missionaries would go into the countryside to build model villages – and, no doubt, a model political order. While Rios Montt remained in power, right-wing Christian organizations in the US lobbied on Capitol Hill for military aid to be extended to his regime.

Before long, the general's opponents began criticizing the 'religious sectarianism which is practised at the highest levels of government'. In June 1983, the Guatemalan Episcopal Conference issued a pastoral letter condemning the government's attitude towards Catholics and warning against the possibility of 'a religious war of incalculable consequences'. Even the right-wing MLN (National Liberation Movement), a party which had originally been in broad agreement with the general and his policies, came to call for a 'holy war' against any attempt by him to create an evangelical political party to contest the elections to have been held that year.

In the end, and in spite of support from Ronald Reagan, who visited in December 1982, Rios Montt's opponents proved too powerful and he was ousted by another coup on 8 August 1983, leaving the Church of the Complete Word without a protector. But what if the next Rios Montt is, let us say, a member of the Unification Church, with such vast wealth, manpower and organizational capability at its disposal?[2] The Rios Montt affair was no flash in the fundamentalist pan: Márkus estimates that some twenty per cent of the Guatemalan people are now members of new sectarian groups.

Less well known but highly significant was the conversion about fifteen years ago of Malietoa Tanumafili II, the king of strategically-important Western Samoa, to the Baha'i faith, a religion of Iranian origin that views itself as the world religion of the future. Although described in its literature as a 'non-political' movement, Baha'ism does, in fact, embrace some fairly radical political aims in its overall programme of world salvation. By 'non-political', adherents of the sect really mean that they do not stand for political office or directly engage in party-political activities, in particular those of an oppositional nature. Baha'is are invariably loyal to the governments of the many countries in which they reside and proselytize.

That, of course, does not exhaust the spectrum of what may generally be included under the label 'political'. Islamic in origin, Baha'ism perpetuates the Muslim theory of society as a unity, without the distinction between 'religion' and 'politics', 'sacred' and 'secular' characteristic of Christianity.

Though generally less well known than the Unification Church and other, more controversial movements, Baha'ism is in fact the most widespread, largest and fastest-growing of the new religions active in the Third World. With a claim to five million members worldwide and a geographical diffusion said to be second only to that of Christianity, the faith has, in the words of one British Baha'i sociologist, Peter Smith, 'started to become a predominantly third world religion'. In the past ten years or so, there have been around one million conversions to the sect in India alone, and mass conversion is a common feature of

---

[2] Recent reports state that Rios Montt himself is about to stage a comeback.

Baha'i growth in parts of Africa, south-east Asia, and Latin America.

Between 1974 and 1979, the numbers of Baha'is worldwide increased by forty-three per cent. Some regional rises in membership were even higher: 11% in Australasia, 53% in Africa and 44% in Asia. According to internally-produced statistics, by 1979 Baha'is resided in 49,597 separate localities in Asia, 26,111 in Africa, 22,577 in the Americas, and 2,573 in Australasia. Though they still constitute a very small percentage of the population in any country (the highest claimed is 8.77% in the Gilbert Islands), the Baha'is have clearly laid impressive foundations for future growth.

Born out of a fusion between the radical millenarianism of nineteenth-century Iranian Shi'ism and modern Western rationalism, Baha'ism was one of the first Eastern faiths to make a bid for converts in the United States and Europe, beginning its mission to the West in the 1890s. Under the highly effective leadership of the founder's grandson, the Western-educated Shoghi Effendi (1897–1957), who headed the movement from 1921, Baha'ism pioneered the use within a religious system of modern management techniques in order to create a highly organized non-clerical administrative system. During the thirty-six years of his leadership, Shoghi Effendi transformed a thinly scattered and largely disorganized group of religious eccentrics and cultists into an internally cohesive, mission-conscious band of visionaries dedicated to the task of preaching Baha'ism as the dynamic world religion revealed for a new age of human development.

Baha'is learned to organize their efforts along the lines of a business corporation. Religious assemblies (locally and nationally constituted) were legally incorporated, by-laws and articles of association were drawn up, regular conventions were held, and committees proliferated. This hard-headed approach lost the sympathy of those on the run from organized religion, but it enabled the Baha'is to cope well with the threats to unity and stability that face any movement without a firm constituency and a recognized place in society at large. It also meant that the movement was in the hands of those least alienated from that wider society, people educationally and technically better equipped to steer their faith to a position of greater acceptance.

What the Baha'is started learning in the 1920s, the leaders of many other new religions are just beginning to realize: if you want to sustain growth and cohesion after the first generation of starry-eyed converts, planning, organization and even marketing strategies are indispensable. This is more than usually true in a society that is, in Bryan Wilson's words, 'increasingly pre-occupied with conscious and deliberate planning, with long-term investment, with the attempt to construct the social order – once thought to be in some way "natural" and "given", perhaps "God-given"'.[3]

Well before the rise in popularity and influence of the post-war wave of new religions in the late 1960s, the Baha'is had already embarked on ambitious international projects designed to plant their faith in every conceivable corner of the globe. For reasons that are not altogether clear, Baha'ism escaped the attentions of the anti-cult and deprogramming movements in America and Europe, and never attracted the controversial and unfavourable media coverage accorded other groups like the Moonies or Scientologists (despite extreme unpopularity in its native Iran and other Muslim countries). In parts of the Third World, Baha'i belief in the 'oneness of all religions' and the claim to be a 'new world faith' have helped avoid some of the problems encountered by Christian sects demanding wholesale conversion to a creed linked culturally and often economically to former colonial powers or the United States.

Until recently, the Baha'is assiduously avoided any activities that might seem, however innocently, to involve them in politics. The movement's uncompromising apoliticism was seen – quite correctly – as a major selling point in countries plagued by political controversy or subversion, as it has been for Protestant sects in Latin America. But, in the light of Márkus's concept of 'theologies of repression' linked to political inactivity and my own observations of Baha'i theory and practice over many years, I believe it is time to re-evaluate the position of the movement and to assess the implications of some of its doctrines for its growing Third World membership.

In 1983, the Baha'i leadership for the first time instructed members to embark on activities within the sphere of 'social

---

[3] *Contemporary Transformations of Religion*, Oxford University Press, 1979, p. 5.

and economic development'. An Office of Social and Economic Development was established at the Baha'i world centre in Israel, and plans devised for increasing Baha'i involvement in a wide range of areas, from educational and rural development programmes to agricultural and medical projects. Significantly, all such activities were to be seen as a 'reinforcement' of the Baha'i missionary enterprise.

Baha'i involvement in social and economic development is, however, construed as taking place within the context of the faith's absolute insistence on 'complete obedience to the government of the country [Baha'is] reside in, and no interference whatsoever in political matters or questions'. What this means, in effect, is much the same as what is meant by the attitudes of the Protestant sects referred to by Márkus: a willingness to acquiesce in the rule of even the most dictatorial regime on the grounds that salvation must be sought elsewhere – in this case, a long-deferred earthly utopia rather than pure pie in the sky.

If Baha'ism is, therefore, a movement whose spread is bound to be attractive to rulers only too happy to have large numbers of their rural and tribal populations embrace an ethos of political quietism, the Baha'is themselves are eager to court government favour wherever possible. As one Baha'i publication puts it: 'Far from rejecting "the world" and the institutions that govern it, the Baha'i community has deliberately pursued a close relationship with civil authorities as an integral part of its development.'

Since the days of Shoghi Effendi, the Baha'i leadership has regularly sought to enhance the prestige of the movement by winning the sympathy of national and local dignitaries and government officials. The pages of Baha'i journals bear eloquent testimony to the assiduity with which this policy is pursued: Baha'i leaders are fond of being photographed presenting books to or having audiences with presidents and other men of power, even if they should be dictators like Pinochet or Idi Amin.

This was, indeed, the original Baha'i mistake in Iran, where the movement's all-too-ready support for Reza Shah and his often ruthless reform projects ended in alienating Baha'is (the largest religious minority in the country) from the population at large.

In the Third World in general, however, Baha'ism represents a challenge to liberal forces in a way that is not true of most fundamentalist Christian sects. Unlike the latter, whose reactionary policies are generally closely linked to their overt message of personal salvation and an often narrow cultural chauvinism, the Baha'i movement is, on the surface, manifestly liberal in outlook and internationalist in scope. Its basic principles of world unity, world peace, the oneness of revealed religion, equality between the sexes, the abolition of racial prejudice, or the abolition of the extremes of wealth and poverty align the movement with progressive causes.

To the extent that such principles are pursued or implemented, Baha'ism is an undoubted and powerful force for radical social change. The problems emerge only at a deeper, less public level. Not only is there a perceptible tension within the religion itself between its avowed liberalism and a very strong authoritarianism centred in 'infallible' laws and 'divinely-ordained' institutions that can expel the heretic or remove the voting rights of those who challenge authority or transgress the faith's strict moral code (including, of course, the ruling on political involvement or even publishing something without approval); but in its attitude towards secular authority, Baha'ism betrays an anti-liberalism that is disturbing indeed.

In one passage of Baha'i scripture we read that 'God . . . hath bestowed the government of the earth upon the kings. To none is given the right to act in any manner that would run counter to the considered views of them who are in authority.' The very concept of liberty is derided as inherently faulty:

> We find some men desiring liberty, and priding themselves therein. Such men are in the depths of ignorance. Liberty must, in the end, lead to sedition . . . That which beseemeth man is submission unto such restraints as will protect him from his own ignorance . . . Regard men as a flock of sheep that need a shepherd for their protection . . . Say: True liberty consisteth in man's submission unto My commandments.

Such attitudes are, perhaps, disturbing enough in themselves, but it is important to remember that there is yet another dimension to the Baha'i mission. Whereas the average Protestant sect is content to collaborate with regimes that support its ends and wait for the future return of Christ, the Baha'is are actively working to establish religious states in which the functions of government will be taken over by Baha'i institutions.

Shoghi Effendi writes of the emergence of a 'Baha'i theocracy' or a 'Baha'i World Commonwealth' ruled by the laws and institutions of the true faith, and envisages the creation of individual states as steps toward the creation of this 'new world order'. He looks forward to the time when 'humanity will emerge from that immature civilization in which church and state are separate' and to the day when Baha'ism will be recognized, 'not merely as one of the recognized religious systems of the world, but as the State Religion of an independent and Sovereign Power'.

However familiar and chilling that sounds, it is likely to remain a utopian dream; but the spread of Baha'ism in countries with unstable regimes holds out the possibility of small-scale theocracies by the next century. The collapse of communism as a utopian ideal has left a massive vacuum into which movements like the Unification Church and Baha'ism may easily fit. All it may take is for one dictator to recognize the possibilities inherent in a movement that preaches liberal values to the world but retains, not far beneath its skin, an abiding admiration for and a divinely-sanctioned endorsement of absolute and unchallengeable authority.

The range of politically-involved or politically-motivated new religions is vast. In Japan, Soka Gakkai (Nichiren Shoshu), which claims over fifteen million members (and has flourishing branches in other countries), bases its activities on the principle of the fundamental unity of religion and politics. It controls the right-wing political party, Komei-to, which it founded and which in 1965 became the third largest party in the country. In Spain, Opus Dei, an extremist Catholic group, seeks to return the country to its Christian roots by infiltrating political and economic institutions on a wide scale. And in America the rise of neo-fundamentalism has provided fertile ground for increased political activity on the part of groups like Moses David's Children of God, let alone the much broader involvement of the 'Moral Majority'.

The phenomenon is too widespread and well entrenched to be ignored any longer. The use of modern management and communications techniques in what is effectively a religious marketplace has brought to the fore a new generation of sect leaders eager to abandon the weirdo image of yesterday. Each of the groups discussed above now possesses an elite cadre of highly intelligent and well-trained religious executives who are well able to make their movement appeal even to hard-bitten politicians. As the American sociologist Peter Berger once expressed it: 'There have been very cool minds indeed in the history of religion.'

What are the likely consequences of the entry of such movements into the political arena? That is hard to say, but there is reason to think they could be serious. We are witnessing a broad revival of religion around the world. The decline of communism in Eastern Europe and, as is probable, elsewhere in the next few decades, has left and will leave a gap that may well be filled by religious adventurers. Some will opt for traditional modes of worship and belief, others may seek something more consonant with their need for a faith in tune with modern problems. George Bush's vision of a 'new order' is precisely mirrored by the thinking and terminology of groups like the Baha'is and the Unification Church. That it has other, darker, echoes should not surprise us. So too, the monumental neo-classical architecture of German fascism and Stalinist totalitarianism find echoes in the grandiose buildings that grace the Baha'i world centre in Israel.

As a confirmed Baha'i, Malietoa Tanumafili is expected to render unquestioning obedience in all matters to a supreme Baha'i council known as the Universal House of Justice, based in Haifa, Israel, the world headquarters of the movement. What would happen if George Bush became a convert tomorrow? And what will happen if a small Baha'i state does eventually emerge somewhere, ultimately subject to the overriding authority of an outside body deemed infallible in all its judgments and governed by a canon of laws divine in origin and unalterable? Baha'i dissidents are at present shunned utterly by members; what would be their fate in a Baha'i state?

Perhaps the most significant – and in some ways the most disturbing – fact about many new religions is their commitment to a future order of things on earth. The present systems are of no concern to them: they are mere barriers to the realization of the utopian order of the future. In power, such people, however well-meaning, could become dangerous for, rather than try to cope with social and political problems as they arise, they will feel committed to press on with the implementation of their vision of the new order – and so much the worse for anyone who does not fit into that vision or chooses to dissent from it.

If the new order, whatever its precise orientation, should be regarded as the kingdom of God on earth (or a near approximation), then those who are less than satisfied with what is on offer must surely fall into two categories: rogues and the mentally ill. In which case, they must be either punished or treated.

It has happened before in the history of this century: in Russia in 1917, in Germany in 1933, in China in 1949, in Iran in 1980. Let us hope that the next century will not see it happen again in a new guise.

(Based on an article first published in the
New Humanist 102:2, 1987, pp. 9–11)

Living without Certainty

The loss of faith, like the amputation of a limb, leaves a pale, tugging ghost behind. Severed hands go on clutching, withered legs walk – traumatized faith goes on dreaming even after reason has taken hold of life and shaken it firmly awake.

I do not know which is worse: to have had a childhood faith and lost it, and with it so many associations of infancy and youth; or, like myself, to have been converted, lived a life one would never otherwise have lived, and then watched one's new faith turn, like Dead Sea apples, to ashes in the hand.

I did the impossible: I was born and brought up in Belfast without imbibing any strong sense of religious loyalty. My parents were Protestant but strangely lacking in any sense of communal identity: drumless, sashless creatures marching to the muzak of suburbia. My first friends were a Jew and a Catholic. If you're out there, Maurice Sampson, I never did get circumcised!

In my teens, however, a liberal conscience combined with a taste for the exotic to lead me well astray. I read about Buddhism and fancied donning a yellow robe for a while (my other, wholly inconsistent, dream was to learn Swedish and emigrate to the great socialist utopia of *smörgasbord* and free love). I spent a musty evening or two poring over maps of Atlantis with geriatric members of the Theosophical Society. I tried to learn Chinese.

And then, barely turned seventeen, a year away from the great unknowns of university and adult life, I encountered the Baha'i faith. Three weeks later, I signed my name on a dotted line and joined the ranks of the converted. Baha'ism is, in some ways, the ultimate turn-on in new religions. At seventeen, I was intoxicated by its heady mixture of oriental mystery and down-to-earth liberal modernism.

There is a fullness about Baha'ism that you just do not find at other religious feasts. All religions are true, we were told, but Baha'ism is the latest and best, the fulfilment of thousands of years of prophecy. God had sent his latest prophet for the express purpose of unifying mankind and ushering in an era of universal peace and world brotherhood. We were taught to abandon all prejudices, to regard men and women as equals, to work for the establishment of world government. We preached a liberal faith for modern man, we had converts in every corner of the globe. 'Bliss was it in that dawn to be alive, But to be young was very heaven!' And it was.

It took me almost fifteen years, some very hard knocks, and a lot of difficult reading in Persian, Arabic and English to reach the skull beneath the skin. I don't mean the usual SHOCK HORROR GHASTLY CULT SECRET sort of thing. Baha'ism is blessedly free of that sort of nastiness. No brainwashing, no orgies, no money-hungry guru hustling for my cash. A pity in a way: I would have enjoyed a good orgy.

On the contrary, Baha'is are, by and large, very nice people. Terribly sincere. Idealists. There is, of course, the usual mixture of hypocrisy, historical rewriting, and bureaucratic horse-shit that you find in any fairly developed movement, be it religious or political. I could have coped with that. What finished me was the realization that the very ideals that had so attracted me at first were themselves responsible for the growing chill I felt as I contemplated the future Baha'i world I had been working for so many years to build.

You start with God: a single, all-powerful, all-meddling Deity who has plans for everyone. You move on to his prophet (in Baha'i-speak, his 'Manifestation'): in this case the nineteenth-century Iranian holy man Baha' Allah: absolutely infallible, so holy not even his photograph may be published, so divine his word may not be questioned. You add a complex religious organization with nine men (no women) at the top, getting their instructions straight from God Himself. You finish with a layer of pure Popperian historicism: history is moving in a divinely-ordained direction from which nothing must be permitted to deflect it.

And what do you end up with? A dream of a new world order that no one can be allowed to question: if, after all, the new political system created by the Baha'is is the Kingdom of God on earth, who could ever be allowed to say or think otherwise? A rigid body of laws, many taken from Islam: unchanging, unchangeable and in many cases extremely draconic. An authoritarian hierarchical system demanding 'instant, exact, and complete obedience'. No freedom to say or publish one's own ideas. Total censorship disguised as 'protecting the best interests of the faith'. Religious Stalinism at its worst.

In their desperation to bring us all to a state of brotherly love and universal harmony, the Baha'is offer the complete antithesis of all my seventeen-year-old liberal conscience ever stood for. History is littered with such transformations of the radical ideal turned against itself: I have no reason to feel singled out by Fate, no reason to mourn lost youth or missed orgies. If anything, my Baha'i experience taught me things I might not otherwise have learned. Persian, Arabic, how to make fruit cocktails, a little geography, a desperate passion for the freedom to question, to dissent, to stand alone.

The phantom limb of faith will always be there, twitching. But far better that than not to have known the inebriation of absolute certitude, not to have seen into the cold heart of God made man and man twisted to be like God. Better a phantom limb than a noose around the neck and a straitjacket about the heart.

The Thriller in an Age of *Détente*

It used to be so easy. The writer of thrillers in search of a theme needed look no further than the barbed and tangled wire of the Berlin Wall or the snow-encrusted pavements of Dzerzhinskii Square. Half the world was busy projecting its Jungian shadow on to the other half, and writers could make a living in the shadow of that shadow. The thriller played its own part in the cold war process: it admonished us of past and present danger, it indulged dark fantasies of evil empires and Stalinist plots, it satisfied an atavistic craving to people the world with heroes and villains, cops and robbers, us and them. The *reductio ad absurdum* of James Bond, the cynicism of Deighton and Le Carré, the jingoism of Rambo, or the blatant anti-Russianism of de Mille – all served to mark out the territory within which we, as citizens, visualized a war without battlefields or heavy artillery.

Now the walls are coming down, lights are going up in the once-dark theatre, and the long play is over. Or so it seems. Sinister Russian agents inspire pity where they once instilled fear, deeds of derring-do on the borders of Eastern Europe sound like something from Enid Blyton. So what do we do now, those of us who depend for our living on the thrills and spills of international skulduggery? Where may we find the scenarios and characters on which our continued existence – and the ongoing pleasure of our readers – must depend?

The answer is, I fear, all too simple. Even before the cold war ended and the second Gulf War began, the old East–West skirmish between capitalism and socialism was already giving ground to a renewed state of tension between older enemies – the West (including Russia) and Islam.

The late great division of the world between a capitalist West and a communist East was from its inception no more than an historical aberration. The real divide has always been further to the south: between the Hellenic and Persian civilizations, then the Byzantine and Sassanid empires, and finally Christendom and Islam: the Arab conquests, the Crusades, the Reconquistida, Europe versus the Ottomans, Israel and its allies against the Arab states, Suez, the Tehran hostage crisis, PLO terrorism, bombs against Ghadhafi, 'world opinion' against Saddam Hussein.

It is a division that has never really gone away. During the long periods of truce between Muslims and Christians (or, in the modern period, Western secularists), both sides have got on with the business of prosecuting a cold war through propaganda and the making of myth: on our side the threat of an 'Islamic peril', oriental fantasies from the *Thousand and One Nights*, genies, harems, the lechery of sultans, the romance of the desert, a harsh God, a debauched prophet, bearded fanatics, oil sheikhs, ayatollahs and terrorists. On theirs, a belief in an ongoing Crusade, Americans, communists, and Zionists joined in an unholy cabal, the perfidy of Europe, sexual abandon in the streets of London and Paris, whole nations drenched with wine and corrupted by gambling, knowledge suborned for the sake of power, *The Satanic Verses* as part of a wider campaign against Islam.

Now, the withering of old enmities and the evaporation of Ronald Reagan's vision of an evil empire of the Steppes have coincided with the recrudescence of Islam as an ideological and political force, not only in the religious heartlands of the Middle East, but in Africa, parts of the Soviet Union, the Far East and the North African enclaves of France.

Inevitably, thriller writers will be drawn in ever-growing numbers to the theme of an embattled West hand in hand with a decaying Soviet imperium threatened from without and within by the hordes of militant Islam. Several have already entered the lists: Clavell with *Whirlwind*, Follett with *On the Wings of Eagles*, Uris with *The Haj*, Quinnell with *The Mahdi*, myself with *The Last Assassin* and *The Seventh Sanctuary*.

It seems almost too easy. Like someone whose dog has died, we need only go out and buy another one. New plots for old. For Russians, substitute Arabs; for zealous communist party apparatchiks, cadres of Islamic Jihad; for the KGB, the various Arab *mukhabarat*; for the Berlin Wall, the sun-kissed shores of

North Africa or the gun emplacements of Kuwait City. *Plus ça change* . . .

But we court disaster of a sort in all this. Just as the modern confrontation between Western 'civilization' and Islamic 'barbarism' offers little more than an action replay of centuries of conflict, so the fictions it will engender may replicate the distortions, mystifications and innuendos of earlier Western writing about Islam and Muslims. Not only that, but turning Muslims (or Pakistanis or Arabs or Iranians) into the new enemy of the American (or British or French) way of life threatens to bring in its wake dangers of a new kind. The Soviets were an enemy 'out there', unknown to most of us, lost in a sort of mist of space and ideology. Muslims, however, are not just out there: they are, increasingly, here with us, as immigrants, as refugees, and even as converts from within our own society.

So what is the thriller writer to do? There can be no denying the appeal of Islam and the Middle East as locales within which the suspense novelist may find rich material for decades to come. Lebanon, the Gulf, Iraq, Iran, Libya are all areas of intense political, religious and military activity, where bloodshed is endemic and Western intelligence activities subject to enormous risks. Hostage taking, suicide bombing, the *intifada*, the execution of dissidents and the burning of books all form an ideal backdrop to ripping yarns of suspense and intrigue.

Perhaps we can rise to the challenge. Perhaps we can provide the thrills without the stereotypes, the blood without the blood libels, the criticisms without the insults. Sadly, recent reporting of events in the Gulf gives little room for hope. The demons of the new cold war have been Khomeini, Ghadhafi, Arafat, and now Saddam Hussein. Demons call for demonologists. I fear it is a call that will not go unanswered.

(First published in the *Independent*, 10 November 1990)

The New Anti-Semitism

Last night on television, I watched a party of Russian Jews making *aliya*. People were singing as they arrived. They looked happy, if bewildered. It served as a symbol of sorts for a world on the move. As walls come down all over Europe and the cold war gives way to a shaky new world order, we are all forced to rethink our stereotypes and to find new ways of talking about the world. The journey from Russia to the Middle East involves a great deal more than a ride on an Aeroflot jet.

As an Islamicist and a thriller writer several of whose books have had Middle East settings, I am particularly conscious of the way in which the shift in the international power balance has focused all our thoughts on the Arab and Islamic worlds.

Inevitably, that image of the *aliya* from Russia stays uppermost in the mind. In the popular mind, all Middle East conflict centres on Israel. Armageddon is only a short drive from Jerusalem. Although Israel figures only occasionally in Middle East thrillers (most successfully in two wonderful books from Lionel Davidson, who made his own *aliya* several years ago), the country and its conflicts casts a shadow over the entire region.

My second novel, *The Seventh Sanctuary*, had for its setting Israel and Saudi Arabia. I had visited Israel three times – in 1967, 1970 and 1975 – and developed an affection for the place and the people. I already had particularly strong feelings about the Holocaust as a major – possibly *the* major – event of the twentieth century. The plot of *The Seventh Sanctuary* was a little over the top (*all* my plots are over the top), but I was trying to say some fairly serious things about Israelis and Arabs. If there was a message in the book, it was that both Jews and Arabs face a common danger in fascism, right-wing bigotry and the tendencies of political leaders on all sides to exploit prejudice for their own ends.

The hero is an American Jew, an archaeologist called David Rosen, the heroine a Palestinian academic called Leyla Rashid. In the course of the novel, David comes to understand more of the Palestinian position, Leyla to grasp the enormity of the forces that brought Israel into being.

Not everyone liked this approach. In Australia, two pro-Palestinian academics condemned the book as racist and anti-Arab, and all but accused me of receiving funds from MOSSAD. That saddened me enormously. One of the great dangers in writing about the Arab world or Islam is that of falling into the trap of employing stereotypes, of using the sort of language and imagery that has been condemned by Edward Said and others as 'orientalism'.

There is no question that Said is correct, that the stereotyping of Arabs and Muslims in the modern West is ugly, distorted and widespread. Europeans and Americans are (largely) sensitive to anti-Semitism, but unflattering images of Arabs, Iranians and other Middle Easterners still crowd our newspapers and television screens. None of this matches the excesses of, say, Nazi anti-Jewish propaganda – and God forbid that it ever should – but it is dangerous and pernicious for all that.

It is all the more ironic – and disturbing – then that, having attempted to be sensitive to anti-Arab prejudice in my novel, I should be accused of precisely that. The reason, tragically, seems to be that, for some critics, any form of compromise is anathema. My own approach to the Israeli–Arab dilemma is to avoid taking sides and to seek ways in which Palestinians and Jews may live together peacefully. Israel has its place among the nations, and Israelis have a major role to play in the future structuring of the Middle East. I see no future for anyone in an extreme anti-Israeli position, any more than in a Kahane-type anti-Arabism.

Writing thrillers about the Middle East is fraught with difficulty. There are extremists on all sides waiting to condemn the unwary. For my own part, I will not worry so long as I can avoid the blatant stereotypes and create living characters to populate my fictitious universe. For any writer, the centre lies in mankind and not in particular causes. My admiration for Israel is based, not on particularism, but on the symbolic power of Jerusalem as a home for Jews, Muslims and Christians alike. And beyond that on a belief that the Holocaust represented and still represents a watershed in human affairs. In *The Seventh Sanctuary*, this feeling is expressed by Harry Blandford, an English convert to Judaism, when he explains the reasons for his conversion:

> We're all Jews now, David, every one of us. Not just you and your people, that's only in the blood. There's more to it than that. When they killed so many, they made Jews of everyone. Whether we wanted it or no, we were made children of Abraham by the Holocaust. It's so simple, David. Surely you can understand. Once they did it to you, they could do it to anyone. How many did Stalin massacre in Russia? The Cambodians after Year Zero? How many are in camps today, or in torture chambers? God has taken the foreskin from every man on this planet.

At the end of the book, the imagery is reversed, and I write how Muslims have all become Palestinians at heart. That message is particularly poignant today. Not only is there a recrudescence of anti-Semitism in Eastern Europe – the flip side of liberation – but anti-Arab and anti-Muslim feeling is growing in Britain, France, Spain, Italy and elsewhere. Had the Gulf War continued and had it led to widespread terrorist attacks by Muslim extremists, there might have been widespread internment and worse.

Meanwhile, the situation is much complicated by the growth in Arab countries of a form of anti-Semitism for which I can find parallels only in Nazi Germany or in the activities of the still much-admired Mufti of Jerusalem, Hajj Amin al-Husayni. Political anti-Zionism is being increasingly displaced by the crudest type of anti-Jewish polemic. Books and pamphlets – among them Arabic editions of the *Protocols of the Elders of Zion* – litter the shelves and tables of shops and bookstalls from Morocco to Pakistan.

According to these lurid productions, 'world Jewry', hand in hand with Britain, Russia and the USA, the Freemasons, and (in an increasingly sizeable body of writing) the anathematized Baha'i sect, is engaged in a conspiracy of mammoth proportions to eradicate Islam.

What is worse, intelligent Muslims believe this nonsense. I have just finished reading a book by an eminent Egyptian literary critic, in which historical distortions and racist fantasies are trotted out as naïvely as in the outpourings of Julius Streicher. Traditional Islamic concepts of the Jews as People of the Book, as

Ahl al-dhimma, a people guaranteed protection by the law of Islam, and as co-heirs of the Abrahamic faith, have been abandoned in an increasingly mindless rush for certainty in the grip of paranoid conspiracy theory. It is highly disturbing and highly dangerous. Dangerous not only for Jews, but even more for ordinary Muslims who will, in the end, have to come to terms with a real world for which such fantasies are no preparation.

The Middle East has become critically important for all of us in Europe and America. Its conflicts can no longer be confined to its own territories. Jews and Muslims alike are British and German and French citizens. Synagogues stand side by side with mosques in our high streets. The scandal of *The Satanic Verses* has its counterpart in the scandal of anti-Semitic writing in Cairo and Damascus. We are not just Jews and Palestinians in our hearts, we are actual participants in their struggles. The real challenge is not how we should help one side or the other, but how we can defend both sides – and ourselves – from the greater threats of bigotry and political extremism.

(Based on a piece originally published in *Israel Update* 1, Spring 1991, published by Front Page Creations, Newcastle)

Warrior Monks

Did victory in the Gulf War exorcize the ghosts of Suez and Vietnam? And all those other smaller ghosts, the ghosts of Lockerbie and Terry Waite and the embassy hostages, the phantoms of Desert One, the Beirut suicide bombers, and the *Achille Lauro*. Just what sort of new age is slouching towards Washington (or, for that matter, London, Jerusalem, Paris or Baghdad) to be born?

Wars end the way wars begin: with a peace no one knows how to handle, with problems that cannot be solved by sending in the SAS. The cold war is over, the Gulf War has ended unpredictably, and the future looks as uncertain as ever. Why? Why, when so many speak of the end of history and herald the advent of a new world order, does the world feel as insecure as ever and our place in it as unassured?

The answer is, I think, that when Western pundits speak of 'the end of history' or a 'new world order', they leave out of their calculations the historical perspectives and future aspirations of the non-Western world. Above all they forget that Islam, with which we are moving into closer and closer conflict, is tied to history in a way that no other religion and no other ideology (except perhaps Marxism) has ever been.

Wilfred Cantwell Smith once observed that 'the fundamental *malaise* of modern Islam is a sense that something has gone wrong with Islamic history'.[1] I would go further and say that it is a feeling that history as such has gone awry, that mankind has been deflected from its destiny, a destiny that may be summed up as the Islamization of the planet.

'The fundamental problem of modern Muslims,' Smith went

[1] *Islam in Modern History*, New American Library, 1957, p. 47.

on, 'is how to rehabilitate that history: to set it going again in full vigour, so that Islamic society may once again flourish as a divinely guided society should and must.' Since the beginning of this century, Muslims have been trying to do just that, sometimes by secular and sometimes by religious means. The creation of Pakistan, the experiments of Nasserism and Baathism, the Ghadhafi and Khomeini revolutions were all attempts to generate a renaissance, to throw off Western hegemony, to set history back on its 'true' course.

Such efforts have without exception fallen far short of the ideals at which they originally aimed. None has ushered in the millennium. Not even oil has lived up to its promise as a divine (if Thatcherite) bestowal destined to redeem history through the creation of wealth. Time and again, the tide of Islamic history has fetched up on the reef of the West: the West as culture, as education, as entertainment, as ideology, as economics, as naked military strength. Karl Popper would probably point out that the reason for failure is simple: history does not have a 'true' course, it is not going anywhere, and attempts to force it in one direction or another are doomed.

Saddam Hussein may be a villain and a fool, but we will not need reminding of how he came to represent to thousands of ordinary Muslims the hope of a new dawn in international affairs. It is a perspective that no Western statesman – and certainly no military commander – thought to introduce into the equations for building a new order. Iraq's defeat may have been merited and timely, but it was for all that another blow to the pride of people for whom greatness seems always to be just beyond reach.

The sheer weight of destructive power unleashed on one Third World country in the name of liberty and democracy must be for many a more visible expression of that even more oppressive burden of Western political, economic and social control or what the Egyptian fundamentalist A'isha 'Abd al-Rahman terms 'the intellectual crusade'. The uppity Muslims have been knocked down to size once again, and many must be wondering if they can ever be more than second- or third-class citizens in the West's new order.

There is a grave sense in which our walkover victory in the Gulf may prove to have been precisely the worst outcome to the conflict. To have achieved such a rapid and total conquest at such small cost to ourselves and such a great physical and spiritual price to an Islamic state is certain to aggravate the already deep-seated sense of inferiority and subordination that has turned to resentment and detestation in the minds of many Muslims.

The crucial problem lies, I think, less in the West's physical power than in its assertion of moral superiority. Or, rather, it lies in the linkage of the two. A merely brutal and morally bankrupt West might be combated by an assertion of Islam's spiritual heritage, in a Holocaust theology similar to that of modern Judaism. A morally upright but militarily weak West might be seen off by defensive or offensive *jihad*. But a West that claims the moral high ground while raining high explosives on a beaten and abject enemy presents an almost insuperable dilemma.

It is this link between moral rectitude and military prowess that explains not only the roots of the Gulf War but also the shape of the combat that lies ahead. For me, it was summed up in the early days of the war by a young American pilot who expressed grief at having killed an Iraqi but went on to say that he could cope with it: 'That,' he said, 'was the advantage of being brought up in a God-fearing country and being on the right side.' Right, white, and way up in the sky.

You may have seen a photograph in the *Guardian* of American soldiers attending a briefing somewhere in the Gulf. Their backs are to the camera, and all the viewer can see are their heads and shoulders. The first impression one has is not of soldiers at all, but of monks – in particular, Buddhist monks. The irony is obvious, but the similarity is neither coincidental nor superficial.

Soldiers and monks have much in common. They shave their heads, they observe strict codes of discipline, they wear identical, drab clothing, they take vows – above all vows of obedience to their superiors – they are celibate (in the case of soldiers, only when on duty), they perform communal rites, they undergo various forms of penance. In a ritual disturbingly similar to that in which nuns are wed to Christ, American marines take their rifles as brides and bring them to their beds.

It isn't just that soldiers sometimes look like monks or behave like them. Throughout history there have been religious orders that have devoted themselves to military activities: the Tijanis and Sanusis in Islam, Tibetan and Japanese Buddhist sects, the Knights Templar.

If we think of the US marines as a quasi-religious order, it helps understand what has been happening and what I fear may happen in the months and years to come.

The United States of America is a place of strange contradictions. It is the most materialistic civilization on earth, yet figures for church-going are higher than anywhere in Europe. Church and state are constitutionally separated, yet Christian fundamentalists exercise enormous influence over right-wing politics. Americans worship God but in their schools they pledge allegiance to their flag. The Stars and Stripes is, as Simon Lee recently expressed it, 'the nearest thing to a sacred icon that a secular state can have'.[2] American religion is, in Robert Bellah's phrase, 'civil religion',[3] a curious mixture of Christian pietism and idolatry of the state.

But American adoration of the nation and its symbols goes much further than putting your hand over your heart when they play 'The Star-spangled Banner'. The state's founding fathers called America 'God's New Israel'. Its inhabitants were His new Chosen People marked out to do His will among mankind. Immigration from Europe came to be regarded as a second Exodus, the Revolution as a struggle to establish Zion in the wilderness.

Since the end of the Second World War, Americans have been searching desperately for an international role commensurate with this conviction of a divine destiny. The communist menace, at home and abroad, had overtones of a Satanic conspiracy against God's own people. In the rhetoric of fundamentalist preachers and the Unification Church, the war against communism became a last crusade that would end in the second coming and the establishment of God's Kingdom.

Within the USA, traditional religion was always deeply affected by the state of the cold war. As Robert Wuthnow once put it: 'Periods of moral conflict with the Soviet Union have always been associated with a reassertion of American religious traditions,

---

[2] *The Cost of Free Speech*, Faber and Faber, London, 1990, p. 44.
[3] See his *The Broken Covenant: American Civil Religion in Time of Trial*, Seabury Press, New York, 1975.

while detente and peaceful coexistence have invariably required us to rethink those traditions.'[4]

In a sense, nothing could have been more disastrous for America than the end of the cold war and the apparent collapse of communism as a viable ideological alternative. Dualistic religions do not fare well without a devil to confront, without an Other against whom to pit the forces of righteousness.

And, in a sense, nothing could be better than what has taken communism's place: Islam. American religiosity and American utilitarianism had a tailor-made enemy in dialectical materialism, with its militant atheism and fervour for worldwide revolution. But Islam is one better. It is the traditional enemy, the enemy of Tours, the Chanson de Roland, the Crusades, the Reconquista, the Siege of Vienna and the Cruel Turk.

Islam has pedigree. Not only that, but it looks as if it has pedigree. Turbans and beards, veiled women and medieval shrines, mullas and executions with the sword: the enemy seems to have stepped out of the history books. With the Europeans out of the way (more or less), the United States at one stroke becomes the heir to a conflict as old as the last days of the Roman Empire. At last, God's own country steps on to the world stage as Rome reborn, ready to spread the mantle of Pax Americana over the entire globe.

Islam has the edge over communism in another respect: for all its differences, it shares many features with American Christianity. Like the faith of the Pilgrim Fathers, Islam is puritan; it is monotheistic; it is scripturally fundamentalist; it has no priesthood; it divides the world between the realms of belief and unbelief. It is America's mirror image, and the more potent for that. To be effective, Antichrist must not be too different from Christ.

Is it, then, surprising that, within so short a time since the fall of the Berlin Wall, we should have found ourselves led by the United States into an all-out war against an Islamic state? The sincerity or otherwise of Saddam Hussein's faith is not at issue here. By the very act of waging war against him, we reawakened images

[4] 'Religious Movements and the Transition in World Order', in Jacob Needleman and George Baker (eds.), *Understanding the New Religions*, Seabury Press, New York, 1978, p. 74.

of Crusading armies wresting the Holy Land from the infidel. The immediate enemy was Iraq, but who can fail to see that in conquering we have incurred the lasting hostility of a large part of the Muslim world?

It is there, in that widespread hostility, that the inevitability of this conflict lies. For Islam mirrors the religion of America in one other crucial respect: it too is a sort of civil religion. Just as the United States transcends the boundaries of its constituent states and the mix of ethnic groupings out of which it has forged a nation, so Islam is, in its ideal formulation, a religio-political whole embracing Arabs, Turks, Iranians, Pakistanis and others in a single system. The reality has never been quite that simple, of course; but then neither has that of the American melting pot.

Islam – as Ayatollah Khomeini never tired of pointing out – is not just a 'religion' in the restrictive Western sense, something to do with God and the next world and practised only on Sundays. It is also a pattern for constructing (and reconstructing) all of social and private life. Religion and politics, religion and law, religion and economics mesh and entwine in an unbroken fabric that is to believers God's plan for a new world order very different to that of George Bush.

The Islamic *umma*, the commonwealth that unites all believers in a pattern of religious and political harmony, has never existed, nor is it ever likely to. But the dream of a pan-Islamic federation has inspired more than one reformer in the modern period and remains a powerful focus for thought and action from Morocco to Indonesia.

Meanwhile, believers in another utopia are also dreaming dreams. American civil religion has entered a critical phase. It has assumed global responsibility in a world descending into political chaos. America's choice, Bellah argued, would be either to internationalize its civil religion or to join it to a new world civil religion. But that second option is no longer viable, since it is now clearly blocked by an insuperable obstacle: Islam. If the West's new world order is ever to come on earth, battle must be joined.

The first stage in that battle is the subordination of mere Christian values to those of Americanism. Just before the ground offensive began, in Kennebunkport's First Congregational Church, where President Bush was attending the weekly service, a lawyer called for an end to the war and for repentance. He was told to get out because 'this is not a political forum, this is a church of God'. Members of the congregation stood and sang, not a Christian hymn fitting for a 'church of God', but the anthem of another faith, 'God Bless America'. Repentance and calls for peace, it seems, have no place in God's house if they are likely to bring the true faith, the faith of America triumphant, into disrepute.

Not surprisingly, the other side has wanted a fight as much as America. Muslim writers have for some time now spoken of a new Western crusade against Islam, a post-colonial enterprise to subjugate the Muslim world or keep it under Western control. More recently, the Rushdie affair has seen several Muslim apologists – men like Kalim Siddiqui and Ziauddin Sardar – conjure up a 'fundamentalist liberal Inquisition' against Muslims and their beliefs. There is a widespread belief in a secularist/Zionist/Baha'i conspiracy against Islam, orchestrated since the last century by that ever-popular demon, World Jewry.

Attitudes are hardening, and not only among extremists. Muslims feel beleaguered, denied their historic destiny. If it is God's will that the new world order be the order of Islam, then the West, in its obdurate refusal to leave the heartlands of the faith alone, must be challenged, faced up to and seen off. Why else did a thug like Saddam Hussein become such a hero? Writing in the *Guardian* a few months ago, Martin Woollacott spoke of Islamic fundamentalism as 'the great opposition movement – anti-Western, anti-Israeli, anti-modern, and anti-rational – which is waiting in the wings in the Middle East and whose day may come if the Arabs and the West do not learn the right lessons from the disastrous war which has just ended'.

The debacle of Vietnam led to a loss of confidence in the American civil religion. Young people turned to the East, to meditation and drugs, to an un-American way of life. Then along came Ronald Reagan with his talk of evil empires, and lo! Americanism was granted new life, only for the end of the cold war to take away much of its *raison d'être*. Now, victory over Iraq has given George Bush a mandate to reassert the faith with renewed vigour.

At a debate in London during the Gulf War, I heard the right-wing historian Norman Stone describe it as a struggle for civilization. But for what civilization, whose civilization? The civilization of *Rambo* and *Top Gun*, of Disneyland and 'Dallas', of TV evangelism and the Moral Majority, of napalm and fuel air weapons? Think of it that way, and you can see why many Muslims fear rather than welcome a new order.

But just as there is another civilization behind Saddam Hussein and Hezbollah terrorism, so there is another West behind Stormin' Norman and his marines with their shaven heads, another America behind the jingoism and the flag-waving religiosity. Both Western liberals and Arab moderates are haunted by the spectres of extremism and intolerant fundamentalism. The real war is the one we can fight together for a shared civilization and shared values of freedom, tolerance and an open society. The alternative will be a new cold war that will have no winners.

Still Lives

The writing of biography has become a major feature of modern literary life. Biographies win prestigious awards and sell in large numbers. They range from the scholarly (Ackroyd, Gilbert, Bullock) to the tawdry (Kitty Kelley), from lives of great men and women to flimsy gossip-sheets about the Pet Shop Boys and Madonna. We take them for granted, as though there is something utterly natural about this huge interest our culture has in the lives of the living and the dead. But is it natural? Is biography inevitable?

I have just finished reading Rima Handley's excellent study of Mélanie and Samuel Hahnemann, *A Homoeopathic Love Story*. There have been lives of the founder of homoeopathic medicine before this, of course: semi-hagiographic accounts of a great but sadly neglected figure in medical history. But his second wife Mélanie, whom he married at the advanced age of eighty and with whom he spent the last nine years of an already outstanding life, has until now been something of a cipher. Now, out of what once seemed impenetrable mists, she has emerged to take her rightful place as one of the most remarkable women of the early nineteenth century, someone deserving recognition far beyond the narrow cliques of homoeopathic practitioners and enthusiasts.

Born the Marquise Marie Mélanie d'Hervilly, she visited Hahnemann in 1834 as a patient, travelling dressed as a man to his home in Köthen, near Leipzig. She was then thirty-four and already enjoyed a reputation in her native Paris as a woman of exceptional talent, above all as a poet and painter. Following her marriage to Hahnemann at the beginning of 1835 and the couple's departure for Paris soon afterwards, Mélanie herself undertook the study of homoeopathy. At first assisting her husband, she eventually began to practise medicine in her own right – one of the first women to do so.

Dr Handley – a medievalist by training, now a practising homoeopath and psychotherapist – has performed a gargantuan task in rescuing Mélanie Hahnemann from obscurity. She uses letters, case notes, poems and an autobiographical account by Mélanie herself to paint a vivid and rounded portrait of her subject. The book is literate, readable and informative. But it is, in a sense, run-of-the-mill. It is just what we would expect such a book to be.

Reading it set me thinking of a biography I myself started work on many years ago. My subject was to have been an Iranian woman almost exactly contemporary with Mélanie Hahnemann: Qurrat al-'Ayn, famous in certain circles as a leading figure in the short-lived and ill-fated Babi movement, a revolutionary sectarian group in nineteenth-century Iran. There have been a few plays about her, and Sarah Bernhardt once wanted her own drama, in order to play the role. But no biography.

Like Mélanie, Qurrat al-'Ayn was a highly talented woman forced to struggle against male prejudice. Where the former became (not quite legally) a woman physician, Qurrat al-'Ayn succeeded in breaking down even more formidable barriers against her sex by practising (also not quite legally) as a Shi'ite religious scholar. In Iraq, she gave lectures to male students from behind a screen. After her conversion to Babism, she became a leader in her own right, with an influence on the doctrines and politics of the sect second only to that of the founder himself. And in 1848, she was instrumental in calling on her fellow converts to abolish Islamic law, an event she marked by appearing in public without a veil.

Like Mélanie too, Qurrat al-'Ayn was a poet, and a fine one at that. Many of her poems are still published in anthologies, and it is likely that they would be better known were it not for her reputation as a heretic. Her end was tragic, strangled on the orders of Nasir al-Din Shah in a garden in Tehran, her body thrown down a well.

Qurrat al-'Ayn has been thought by some – with very little reason, it should be said – to have been a pioneer of women's rights in the Orient. That is an assessment based on wishful thinking more than anything. Babism did not teach and Qurrat al-'Ayn did not preach the emancipation of women – there is, indeed, good reason to suppose that she would have found the aims of the suffragette movement socially and morally unacceptable. Yet, by her own behaviour, she achieved something that an out and out feminist could not have achieved in her time and place – she demonstrated that a woman might think and act much as a man, might even lead the hearts and minds of men. She was, in a sense, oblivious of her sex, and, for that reason, female emancipation was extraneous to her modes of thought and action.

Looking over my unfinished biography I find it quite dense and stale, and certainly unpublishable in its present form. The reason is not hard to find. It is less a biography of Qurrat al-'Ayn than an academic treatise on the history of the Babi movement, with occasional glimpses of the role she played in it. And the reason for that is quite simple too: there is virtually no material of a personal kind on which to base a developed biographical study. The movement and not the people in it is what contemporary chroniclers thought important. Even where we possess letters and poems by Qurrat al-'Ayn herself, they deal with doctrine or polemic. She never talks about her husband, who divorced her, her children, who became estranged from her, her uncle, who became her greatest enemy, her feelings as a woman, her childhood, herself.

Why was it possible for Rima Handley to write a satisfactory biography of a fascinating but relatively obscure woman of early-nineteenth-century France while I ground to a halt in my attempt to describe an equally fascinating, equally obscure contemporary who lived in Iran? Was it mere chance, the survival of private manuscripts in one case and their loss or destruction in the other? Only partly, I think. The real reasons have, I believe, more to do with fundamental differences in how the individual is perceived in Western and Islamic society.

In *A Lonely Woman*, a study of the life and poetry of the modern female Iranian poet Forough Farrokhzad (1935–67), American Iranologist Michael Hillmann makes the following observations:

> ... in the growing number of essays on contemporary Iranian literary figures and movements, scholars make little effort to go beyond already published information in describing the lives of their subjects and seem to think that there may be little of relevance or significance in those lives. In his 'biographical' preface to *A Nightingale's Lament: Selections from the Poems of Parvin*

E'tesami (1985), Heshmat Moayyad observes: 'Parvin's life may be described in a few lines. It was simple, unexciting, and without any significant ... events.' In an essay on the minor poetess Tahereh Saffarzadeh (b. 1937) ... Farzaneh Milani observes: 'Not much is known about Saffarzadeh's life, and it is practically impossible to fully reconstruct it from the meager published information.'[1]

Hillmann goes on to quote several more such comments, with regard to both male and female writers. He then continues:

The fact is that biography and autobiography are almost non-existent in Persian literature. Almost nothing is recorded of the personal lives of Ferdowsi, 'Omar Khayyam, Sa'di, Hafez, and scores of other poets from Rudaki to Jami in the classical period of Persian literature. If one wonders whether this is so precisely because the necessary information is no longer available, there is the more startling fact that not a single biography exists even of [Sadiq] Hedayat or Nima [Yushij], the 'fathers' of modernist Persian prose and verse respectively, about whose lives the necessary information in the form of eyewitness accounts, correspondence, notes and considerable published data is readily available. No published biography exists in Persian for any modernist Iranian writer or poet.[2]

What is really astonishing is not so much that last statement as the fact that Hillmann is actually incorrect in his earlier remark that 'biography and autobiography are almost non-existent in Persian literature'. If we ignore the specifically 'Persian' tag and accept materials written in Iran or by Iranians in both Arabic and Persian, biographical literature is so thick on the ground it is hard to understand how an informed writer like Hillmann missed it.

The biographical dictionary as a literary genre had its birth in the Islamic world, in the form of *tadhkira* or *rijal* literature. It arose in direct response to an originally religious and legal need. The great corpus of Islamic traditions, records of the alleged sayings and doings of the Prophet and his companions grew up in the first

[1] *A Lonely Woman: Forough Farrokhzad and her Poetry*, Three Continents Press/Mage Publishers, Washington D.C., 1987, p. 148.
[2] Ibid, pp. 148–50.

213

three centuries of Islam as a means of providing divine sanction for legal and religious rulings. Each record is introduced by a chain of transmitters: A told me that B told him that he had been told by C, whose father had told him from D, who related from the Prophet – something like that. These chains were crucial to the acceptability of the text. If it could be shown that A had never met B, or that D had been dead when C was born, or that someone was a notorious liar, the entire chain might be broken and the Prophetic saying falsified.

A science of recording the details of the men – the *rijal* – who transmitted traditions developed in tandem with other legal and religious specialisms. By the ninth century, the writing of biography had started to break away from these origins to become a form of literature in its own right. Biographical dictionaries came to be regarded as 'among the most remarkable productions of the later centuries of Islamic culture'. They cover a vast range. There are dictionaries of religious scholars, poets, governors, the famous men of individual cities and regions, soldiers, mystics and women. No library of Arabic or Persian writing would be complete without several shelves of this material.

So what did Michael Hillmann mean when he wrote that 'biography and autobiography are almost non-existent in Persian literature'? I think – and I trust I am not putting words into his mouth – that he may have meant to say that there is no biography or autobiography in the sense that they are understood in Western culture. Certainly, he does go on to attempt to define what he thinks are certain culture-specific attitudes in Iranian life that act against the production of detailed, revealing and informative biography: male protectiveness of females, friendship 'especially of younger critics toward established literary figures', apprehension that candid comment may later prove politically incriminating, and the all-pervasive fear of what *mardom*, 'people', may say or think, with its inevitable descent into self-censorship.

All of that is true, but the real problem lies, I believe, at a deeper level in the very origins of Islamic biographical literature. Franz Rosenthal drew attention to this when he wrote: 'Biography . . . was originally a handmaiden of the religious sciences. As such, it was expected to provide only a limited number of dry data. No matter how elaborate they were, biographies of scholars were inclined to renounce any literary ambition.'[3] The first Islamic biographies were religious in nature and intent: lives of the Prophet and his companions, then the lives of men who had transmitted their words. Biography necessarily began as hagiography.

This tendency can be seen in the biographical writing of Baha'ism, an international religious movement with roots in nineteenth-century Iran. In the case of Baha'i biographies in English, one might have expected the culture-specific reticence of Iranian hagiography to have given way to a more relaxed European or American style. Not a bit of it. One of the worst books I have ever read is a 451-page biography of the Baha'i leader Shoghi Effendi (d. 1957). Written by his Canadian widow, Ruhiyyih, this is a manual on how to say virtually nothing in 180,000 words. Politicians and civil servants could read it to advantage. Extracting personal information of any description is like drawing blood from a block of the white marble Shoghi loved to use in his numerous building schemes. We are provided with elaborate details of expansion plans and religious crusades, organizational developments, books written and translated, official correspondence: everything but the man behind them. The book is the very antithesis of good biography. It conceals more than it reveals.

Here, the religious motives for concealment are blatant. To make such a figure too human, to stress his weaknesses or explore his darker side, would be to strain the faith of the ordinary believer, an eventuality to be avoided at all costs. But once begun, such a process taints all lesser mortals. The biographies of other Baha'is, like those of Muslim clerics or mystics, are generally devoid of meaningful or insightful information or comment. They adhere faithfully to the strict formula of lives of dedicated service and humble sacrifice. There are occasional anecdotes, but nothing that will rock the boat.

Islam, curiously enough, does not seem at first glance suitable soil for such attitudes to take root in. Like Judaism, it is a worldly religion, as concerned with bodily functions as heavenly rewards. Muhammad is not regarded as divine, but as a man like any other, subject to human passions and to error: Christian deification of

[3] In Joseph Schacht and C.E. Bosworth (eds.), *The Legacy of Islam*, 2nd edn, Oxford University Press, 1974, pp. 327–8.

Jesus, by contrast, is looked on askance. There is a well-known saying in which Muhammad admits to having loved three things: prayer, women and perfume. We know many details of his life, including his sexual life, that would be impossible to discover about the founder of any other religion.

I include in that number the Iranian founder of Baha'ism, a man who died as recently as 1892, and whose biographical details are almost as sparse as those of Jesus Christ. Clearly something happened to biography in the Islamic world between the ninth and nineteenth centuries.

That something seems to have been the growth throughout this period of a highly refined sense of personal privacy. The sense of the inviolability of domestic space is immediately obvious to anyone who walks through a traditional Islamic city, whether it be the old Medina in Fez or a more isolated desert town like Yazd in the centre of Iran. The buildings all face inwards. There are few windows opening on to the street. Those that do have, as in old Cairo, elaborate latticework screens or other obstacles to the prying eye. Traditional homes have two distinct arenas within which action takes place: the space known in Persian as the *biruni* or 'exterior', where guests are received, and the *andaruni* or 'interior', where the family (and, in particular, the womenfolk) may carry on their lives without outside interference.

Even in smaller modern homes this distinction is retained by various devices. A male guest may be received inside, but during his visit the women of the house will be kept out of sight, usually in the kitchen, where they will prepare the meal. The sense of separation is preserved in speech. It is impolite to ask after one's host's wife: one must simply enquire about the wellbeing of 'the house'.

Outside the home, this need for privacy is continued by means of the veiling of women. The word for 'veil' in Persian, *chador*, actually means a tent, as though the home itself were somehow transported into the public sphere. This covering of the self is not restricted to women. Tuareg men veil their faces. In traditional painting, the faces of the Prophet and other sacred figures are regularly depicted with a long white veil.

Arabic and Persian speech uses numerous devices to extend this concealment to the verbal sphere. We have already noticed the use of '*bayt*' or 'house' to refer obliquely to a man's wife. In speaking or writing of the Prophet, it is customary, indeed obligatory, to use honorific phrases to demarcate his name from those of other mortals. In literature generally, allusion, euphemism and hyperbole are common rhetorical devices.

The notion of privacy, particularly of female privacy, is closely connected, both semantically and conceptually, to the Islamic legal category of forbiddenness, expressed through the Arabic root *hrm*. This is a complex root from which a wide range of words may be derived. Meanings and usages run into one another in a most intricate and suggestive fashion.

Things that are *haram*, for example, are both 'sacred' and 'prohibited' – 'taboo' in the strict sense. As a noun, the word can refer to a religious sanctuary (such as the Kaaba enclosure at Mecca) or to a wife. The harem is not only a term for an area of a palace reserved for women (or for the women themselves), but may be used for any inviolable place or sacred precinct. *Ihram* refers to the state of ritual consecration into which both male and female pilgrims enter when they make the *hajj* to Mecca, wearing seamless white garments, shaving their heads, and abstaining from sexual intercourse. In Christian Arabic, *hirm* means excommunication.

Three things seem to join forces here to develop the sense of what is *haram*: holiness; impurity (as with pork or wine); and sexual activity (or, by extension, women, in whom sex is invested). All exist within conceptual spaces that mark them off from ordinary life. All define boundaries that may not be crossed, spatial, social and moral circles of inviolability.

Untouchability is a recurrent theme in Islamic thinking and behaviour. On the outside cover of most copies of the Qur'an, you will find the phrase 'let none but the pure touch it'. The pious will perform ablutions before they set hands on the book. They will not hold it below waist height or lay it on the floor or beneath other books. The very pious will pick up scraps of waste paper from the street and place them on walls in case they bear anywhere on them verses from the sacred text. The strict will neither sell nor give the book to non-believers.

Najasa is a term widely used in Islam, particularly among traditional Shi'ites, where it refers to the impurity of things that may contaminate the believer. Pork is *najis*, dogs are *najis*, and, in the strictest legal sense, unbelievers are *najis*. Touching any of these or other unclean objects or persons makes void the purity of the believer, which must be restored before he can again engage in normal activities. The parallel with taboo is obvious.

The world is thus divided into two distinct spheres: that of the unclean and untouchable and that of the clean and touchable. Sex, of course, renders the participants impure. The private world of the bedroom thus partakes of the realm of the untouchable. A man may not pray after sex until he has performed an ablution. Purity is inherently unstable and under constant threat of contamination.

In his study of the *Satanic Verses* debacle, *A Satanic Affair*, Malise Ruthven identified a recurrent use of sexual imagery in the statements of Muslim opponents of the novel. 'What he has written is far worse to Muslims than if he had raped one's own daughter,' one leading protester told the *Guardian*. 'It's like a knife being dug into you – or being raped yourself,' said another.

'The connection between faith and sexuality is, if anything, more entrenched in Islamic cultures than others,' Ruthven observes. The world, he notes, is divided in the Qur'an between the realms of the revealed or exoteric (*al-shahada* or *al-zahir*) and the hidden or esoteric (*al-ghaib* or *al-batin*). The realm of the hidden, he argues, has close connections to that of sexuality. In another context, it is a realm in which the Prophet has been cocooned by his hagiographers. Salman Rushdie's iconoclastic entry into that sacral space was perceived 'as a violation, as a kind of "rape"'.

This argument deserves to be taken further. It is, in fact, precisely the biographical elements in *The Satanic Verses* which caused the greatest outrage. The desacralizing of the Prophet, however noble its intentions, violated several codes of honour. If the character of Mahound is to be assimilated to the Prophet – and it seems reasonable that he should be, though by no means reasonable to pretend that he *is* the Prophet – then, in a sense, he represents all the biographies of Muhammad that have not been and can never be written, the anti-hagiographies that lie beneath the surface of the blandly pious 'real lives'.

The modern novel is, if you like, the most intimate form of

biography or autobiography. Through novels we enter, not only the most private dimensions of other people's lives, but even their thoughts and fantasies. It is the peculiar power of the best novels that they enable us to live vicariously, to partake momentarily of what is otherwise the most hidden of realms, the inner lives of other human beings.

It is here, I think, that the real meaning of the *Satanic Verses* furore must be sought. Traditional Islamic culture made the writing of biography one of its central undertakings, and yet, in doing so, denatured it by declaring out of bounds any hint of the hidden realm of men's real lives. The diary and the confessional narrative never became a part of Arabic or Persian literature. Other men's lives were approached through the same medium as the lives of saints: the bowdlerized and sanitized eulogy. The Prophet's life itself was subjected to revision and pious dehumanizing.

By drawing freely on the prophetic biography while subjecting it to the transformations of the novelistic form, Rushdie brought to light the deepest fears of Muslim culture: the fear that one's own inner self may be brought to view, that hagiography may become biography and biography a vehicle for doubt. The fear that what lurks within the realm of the personal unseen may turn out to be as dark and unsparkling as what lies on the surface. It was, perhaps, Salman Rushdie's error to have attempted to shed light on the inner life of Islam by starting at the very centre, at the heart of the realm of what is untouchable and hidden.

It is one of the functions of art, according to Freud, to heighten man's 'feelings of identification', 'by providing an occasion for sharing highly valued emotional experiences'.[4] Fiction, drama and biography in particular, I believe, provide us with a means to achieve a sense of identification through the glimpses they give us of other people's lives. That some of these lives are fictional and some 'real' is irrelevant. Beyond this, such works of art enable us to obtain insights into the multiple personalities each of us possesses. The novelist is able to express through his characters aspects of his own personality normally suppressed, the

[4] Sigmund Freud, 'The Future of an Illusion', in *Civilization, Society and Religion*. The Pellican Freud Library, vol. 12, London, 1985, p. 193.

reader to obtain an understanding of drives and wishes scarcely recognized.

Until recently, Islamic society was devoid, not only of insightful biography, but of the novel and the drama too. The prohibition of representational art (as a back door for the production of idolatrous images) has all but closed off portraiture, whether in painting or sculpture, leaving Muslim artists with highly stylized, formal renderings of conventional scenes or, in a more strictly religious atmosphere, with the arts of calligraphy and ornament. Music – for some, the most personal of all the arts – has time and again been the object of anathema from the ranks of the *ulama*.

It is difficult to begin to appreciate just what this means. In her scathing study of Islamic sexuality, *Woman in the Muslim Unconscious*, Fitna A. Sabbah describes how a fictive paradise is made the model for life on earth, depriving believers of will and creativity, of anything that may disturb the sacred order God has imposed on His creation:

Paradise, with its food and its houri, is programmed for a consumer-believer deprived of the creative dimension. The believer is fulfilled in Paradise by renouncing all the potentialities that define a human being, all possibilities of making choices not programmed by an external will. The purpose of the believer is to fit himself into the plan organized, conceived, and programmed by another will. The purpose of the believer is to reduce himself to a consumer and annihilate within himself his creative potential, for to create within the paradisal context would be to disturb the order and destroy the plan. The believer is passive: He digests, makes love to a houri deprived of a uterus (for she is a virgin), and relaxes. Like the houri, he forms an integral part of a system where he exists as a thing deprived of will. The only difference is that the houri is consumed as an object by the believer, and he is consumed as an object by the system. In the Muslim Hereafter, where one would expect that the spiritual dimension of the being would be magnified, one witnesses the metamorphosis of the human being into a thing. In the ideal society of Islam, the ideal citizen, the successful believer, is an automaton reduced to a few limited, programmed movements of the digestive tract and genital apparatus.[5]

[5] Fitna A. Sabbah, *Woman in the Muslim Unconscious*, trans. Mary Jo Lakeland, New York, 1984, pp. 96–7.

It is this reification of the believer that lies, I believe, at the heart of our dilemma. By dressing all women in much the same costume, above all by covering the face, the seat of individuality and recognition, it is possible to transform each single woman into a stereotype of 'woman' as she ought to be, as she is prescribed for in the law. A man may go abroad with his face uncovered, but even here the law lays down how he should wear his hair and beard, how he should dress, how he should eat, drink, urinate and make love. There is little room for the individual. The image of rank upon rank of believers praying in unison brings home how powerful is this erasure of man as individual and his replacement by man as believer, as an ordained type.

Of course, the reality of Muslim society has been quite other than this. Muslims are individuals, they are creative, inventive, different. But the pressures are undeniably present. The inculcation of a norm to which each individual must conform, the fear of innovation, the elaboration of rules for all areas of human conduct – all have conspired to render individuality something very close to a sin. Within that context, it can be imagined how disruptive the novel or the closely-observed biography would be. They would show how little the average man or woman does in fact conform to any ideal standard, how complex desires, dreams, fantasies, rebellions and whims reside in all of us and make us what we are as much as or more than external regulations.

One of the most central problems for Muslims in the modern period has been that of identity – of finding old identities or forging new ones. Ironically, the very *shari'a*-mindedness that is looked on as a route to the rediscovery of the Muslim self is more likely to imperil any real formulation of personal identity, precisely because of its stress on conformity to an exaggerated ideal. It is not by reference to hagiographically-determined model types and religiously-prescribed behavioural norms that individual Muslims will find any abiding sense of personal worth, either in themselves or in their colleagues. Would it be presumptuous to suggest that such discoveries might best be made in the arts of the novel and the biography, or in the rounded characterizations of the theatre and the cinema?

Such a development, should it take place, would have profound consequences for everyone. For Westerners, Muslims would emerge from the mist of stereotype as individuals with lives very like our own. And for Muslims, there would be the possibility of an understanding that, to live a life with all the flaws and weaknesses of the individual is not to fall short of a fictive divine standard but simply to be human.

A Faith Spread by the Sword?

In his powerful novel of utopia gone wrong, *One*, the American writer David Karp described the efforts of the 'Benevolent State' to destroy all traces of heresy in one man, a professor of English called Burden. In a series of frightening inquisitions, Burden is stripped of his identity and made to conform. Given a new name, he is sent back into society as an experiment. It is predicted that, if it can root out the heresy of individualism in Burden, the state will endure for ever. If it cannot, heresy will, in the long run, destroy it. Burden, now living under the new name of Hughes, seems at first tamed; but at the end of the book his heresy resurfaces. The chief inquisitor, a man called Lark (himself a heretic at heart), orders him executed. But in that very act we know the state is fated to collapse.

News of Salman Rushdie's 'conversion' to Islam leaves a bad taste in the mouth. Not so much because he has chosen this way out of his impasse – God knows, he deserves any chance to escape his nightmare – but because so many, from Muslim spokesmen to *Times* leader-writers, are acclaiming his recantation as a victory for tolerance and the spirit of compromise. Rushdie himself, writing in *The Times*, speaks of the 'tolerance, compassion and love' at the heart of Islam.

Where, in the name of God, is tolerance when a man is forced on pain of death to embrace a faith? Where is compromise when one man has given his soul and his opponents have not budged an inch? What century are we living in when a self-proclaimed 'moderate' suggests that Rushdie may be brought before panels of religious inquisition in Egypt and Iran? Far from being a victory for Islam, Rushdie's conversion may go down in history as the moment of its greatest shame.

By arguing that Rushdie's life should be spared now that he

has accepted Islam, Hesham el-Essawy (the force behind recent developments) and other Muslim 'moderates' have effectively sanctioned the original death sentence. Real tolerance would be to grant Rushdie his life without requiring that he change his beliefs.

El-Essawy and others have striven for years to unmake the old image of Islam as a faith spread by the sword. But in bringing Rushdie to this pass, they have done much to reinforce old prejudices. More than anything, this bizarre episode conjures up echoes of the earliest period of the Islamic conquests, when Jews and Christians were given three basic choices: to fight and be killed; to convert; or to pay a poll tax known as *jizya*, thereby accepting the subordinate position of 'protected communities'.

I wish to avoid gross simplification. On the whole, conversion to Islam took place as a gradual, peaceful process. Jews, Christians and others embraced the faith because it was in their interest to do so, not because of overt threats. Later, Islam was spread peacefully by traders and Sufi missionaries. Nevertheless, these conversions took place in the wake of military conquest. Nor should the continuing duty of holy war as an obligation binding on all Muslims be ignored. Islamic tolerance is closely linked to Islamic triumphalism.

That may have been acceptable in the past, but today a new kind of tolerance is needed if religious and racial communities are to live in harmony. Muslims, rightly, have demanded open-mindedness and fairness from Christians and secularists; but this is meaningful only if it cuts both ways. When our skylines are dotted with the domes of mosques but US servicemen in Saudi Arabia are forced to describe illegal Christian services as 'mental gymnastics' and hold them in secret, parity goes to the wall.

I have from the beginning sympathized with Salman Rushdie. I shall continue to do so. His decision to convert (if that is what it really is) is a personal matter. What concerns me are the long-term implications of such a public case of forced conversion. Not so long ago, Amnesty International and other agencies voiced deep concern about Baha'is in Iran who were offered their lives provided they converted to Islam. Hesham el-Essawy and other moderate Muslims did not protest then, nor have they done so since. El-Essawy wants Rushdie to plead his case before men who have countenanced, even commended, such behaviour.

Salman Rushdie has been offered a respite at the price of his own conscience. Now he is regarded as a Muslim, he cannot escape: the sentence for apostasy is death. It is one of the strengths of our society that there are no sentences for loss of faith. However much Muslim writers may complain of a 'liberal crusade' against Islam, I know of no forced converts to secularism. We have reached a crossroads for the simplest of freedoms: the freedom to believe or disbelieve.

The Rushdie issue has passed beyond the bounds of a debate about free speech. It has become a test for the freedom of the individual conscience itself.

(First published in the *Independent*, 31 December 1990)

Glossary

Abbasid Muslim caliphal dynasty (749–1258), ruling from Baghdad

'ada 'Custom', 'customary law'

adhan The call to each of the five daily obligatory prayers

ahadith pl. of **hadith**

Ahl al-Dhimma 'People of [God's] protection', i.e. Jews and Christians as protected communities under Islamic rule

Ahmadis Members of a heretical Islamic sect founded in India in the late 19th century by Mirza Ghulam Ahmad

al-ghaib 'the unseen', a hidden realm beyond the world of physical reality

aliya Emigration to Israel

Allahu akbar 'God is greater [than all others]', a widely used rallying-cry

al-wahid 'The One', often used of God

andaruni Persian term for that section of a private house closed to outsiders

Ayurveda The traditional Hindu system of medicine, still used in India and, increasingly, other countries

Babism An extremist millenarian sect of Shi'ite Islam founded in Iran in 1844. Named after its founder, Mirza 'Ali Muhammad Shirazi, the Bab (1819–50). The immediate predecessor of the **Baha'i** movement

Baha'ism An international religious community originating in **Babism**. Its founder was Mirza Husayn 'Ali Nuri, Baha' Allah (1817–92).

batin 'The inward', applied (particularly in **Sufism** and esoteric **Shi'ism**) to the inner meaning or reality of texts or things (in distinction to **zahir**)

bid'a 'Innovation', a term used in Islamic law to signify acts or things not registered in the Qur'an, Traditions, or accepted practice (as distinct from **sunna**)

biruni Persian term for the public quarters of a private house where guests may be received

chador Persian term for the veil worn by Muslim women. In Iran, this is a long garment covering the body from head to foot and gathered by hand at the front

Dajjal An Antichrist figure who, according to Muslim legend, will appear as one of the signs of the Last Day

Dar al-Islam 'The realm of Islam', applied to territory that has come under Muslim rule either by conversion or military conquest

Dar al-Kufr 'The realm of unbelief', applied to territory ruled by non-believers or (in some sectarian applications) by Muslims of a different denomination

Dar al-Harb 'The realm of war', roughly equivalent to **dar al-Kufr**

da'wa 'Summons', generally applied to the act of prozelytization on behalf of Islam, whether among uncommitted Muslims or non-believers

Deus absconditus 'The hidden God', applied to the concept of a divinity who is inaccessible to human beings

dhikr 'Remembrance', 'mentioning', the act of reciting the names of God and related phrases, usually forming part of Sufi ritual practice

al-fana' fi 'llah 'Extinction in God', that stage in Islamic mysticism where the devotee ceases to exist in himself and has his being only in the Godhead

faqih A muslim jurisprudent or lawyer

fatwa A decree issued by a recognized authority in Islamic law, giving a ruling on a legal question

Fedayeen (Fida'iyin, Fida'iyan), 'self-sacrificers', a term applied either generally to Muslims willing to give their lives for the sake of their faith, or specifically to members of extremist movements such as the Fida'iyan-i Islam

fi sabil Allah 'In the path of God', a Quranic phrase which refers to the sacrifice of life or property by believers, usually in a holy war

gomchen (Tibetan, 'sgom-ch'en), the highest degree of hermit in Tibetan Buddhism

hadith A single item from a body of Islamic sacred literature, second to the Qur'an, alleged to represent authentic sayings of the Prophet or eye-witness narratives about him and his companions

hadra The central communal ritual performed in Sufi orders, involving the recital of prayers and a variety of movements and breathing exercises

hajj The Muslim pilgrimage to Mecca, performed during the month of Dhu 'l-Hijja. Pilgrimages to the shrines of saints etc. are termed *ziyara*

halal An Islamic legal category, applied to permitted actions and things

Hanbali One of the four recognized law schools within Sunni Islam. Founded by a famous jurist, Ahmad ibn Hanbal (d. 855)

haram 'Prohibited', a category in Islamic law applied to actions or things prohibited to believers (as distinct from **halal**)

hesychasm An important contemplative practice in the Orthodox Christian church

Hezbollah (Ar. Hizb Allah, 'the Party of God'), an extremist Shi'ite group originating in Iran and active in Lebanon

hijra 'flight', the migration in 622 from Mecca to Yathrib (later Medina) by the prophet Muhammad and his followers, marking the commencement of the Islamic calendar

ihram The state entered into by one embarking on the **hajj** or pilgrimage to Mecca; also applied to the white dress worn by pilgrims

Ikhwan 'Brethren', a term applied to a number of Islamic groups, notably Wahhabi militants in Saudi Arabia in the early 20th century and the Ikhwan al-Muslimin or Muslim Brotherhood of Egypt, Syria, and elsewhere

'ilm 'Knowledge'

Imam In Shi'ism, a male descendant of the Prophet endowed with supernatural qualities and regarded as the legitimate leader of the Islamic community. In Sunnism, a prayer-leader

Islah A principle in Islamic law permitting legislation to the benefit of the community

Ismailis Members of a branch of Shi'ism headed by the Aga Khan and chiefly represented in India and East Africa

i'tikaf 'Seclusion', a minor Islamic practice involving seclusion in a mosque or shrine for limited periods

izzat 'Honour', a broad concept of some importance, mainly among rural and tribal Muslims

jahili Referring or belonging to the period of **jahiliyya**

jahiliyya The 'period of ignorance' or 'barbarism' before the coming of Islam. Also applied by many fundamentalists to the 'unIslamic' nature of modern society, even in the Muslim world

jahl 'Ignorance'

jama'at islamiyya In its plural form, used to describe the modern Islamicist movements in Egypt and elsewhere

jihad Holy war

jinn 'Genies', a species of creature referred to in the Qur'an as intermediate between men and angels

khalwa A form of retreat popular in some Sufi orders

Kharijites An early Muslim schismatic group noted for their readiness to kill their religious and political opponents

khatam al-anbiya' (Also Khatam al-nabiyin), 'Seal of the Prophets', an epithet applied to Muhammad in the Qur'an and taken as evidence for his being the last of God's prophets to be sent to men

Khoda (Persian), 'God'

La ilaha illa 'llh 'There is no god but God'

Lex talionis The law of retaliation, as in 'an eye for an eye'

madhhab A school of Islamic law, chiefly applied to four 'orthodox' schools mutually recognized by Sunni Muslims

Mahdism The belief in the future advent of the Mahdi or 'Guided One', a saviour figure who will bring peace, unite mankind, and ensure the triumph of Islam

madrasa A college of Muslim theological and legal studies

Malamatiyya A form of Sufi mysticism in which public ridicule is sought as a token of the devotee's disdain for the formal, external norms of behaviour and religious practice

Maududist A follower of the Pakistani fundamentalist thinker, Abu 'l-Ala Maududi (1903–79), the originator of the concept of 'Modern Jahiliyya'

mufti A functionary in the Islamic legal system, responsible for the issue of legal rulings (**fatwa**) in response to written requests from litigants or others seeking clarification of the norms of the religious law

Muharram The first month of the Muslim calendar. The 10th is celebrated by Shi'ites as the anniversary of the martyrdom of the third Imam, Husayn

mujaddid 'Renewer', one of several figures identified (differently by Sunnis and Shi'ites) as responsible for the revivification of the faith at the beginning of each century

mujahidin 'Crusaders', a term generally applied to any Muslims fighting in a holy war (**jihad**) or, more recently to members of militant organizations, such as the Iranian Mujahidin-i Khalq

mujtahid An Islamic legal authority entitled to exercise *ijtihad* or independent reasoning in matters of religious law. The only living mujtahids are recognized in Shi'ism, where they are the leading members of the clerical establishment

mukhabarat A term generally used for the intelligence services in several Arab states, usually with further specification (e.g. *mukhabarat 'amma*)

mulla A loose designation for a Shi'ite cleric, usually applied nowadays to the lowest-ranking members of the establishment, but sometimes to any religious figure

muqallidun 'Imitators', a term applied to the mass of Shi'ites, to indicate their dependence in matters of religious law on **mujtahids**

murshid 'Guide', the general Arabic term for the head of a Sufi brotherhood or sub-order

Muslim Brotherhood ('al-Ikhwan al-Muslimun'), a fundamentalist organization founded in Egypt in 1928 by Hasan al-Banna' (1904–49). Cells have been set up in other Arab countries, Pakistan, and elsewhere

nahda 'Renaissance', a common Arabic term for Islamic revivalism

najasa 'Uncleanness', a term applied (mainly in Shi'ism) to things or people whose touch or presence renders the believer impure and unable to perform religious duties such as prayer

Naqshbandi An important Sufi order, founded by Baha' al-Din Naqshbandi (1317–89), and widespread in Central Asia

Nizari Ismailism A militant branch of **Ismaili Shi'ism** that developed in Iran in the 12th century (where adherents acquired the name 'Assassins') and which now represents the chief form of Ismailism, without its former militancy

parousia The future advent of Jesus Christ

pir Persian term for a Sufi shaykh or **murshid**

purdah An Indian term for the veil or the state of seclusion of Muslim women

qisas 'Retribution', the Islamic form of the **lex talionis**

Rifa'iyya A North African Sufi order noted for its unorthodox practices

rijal (Ar. 'men'), a term applied to the transmitters of Islamic traditions

sabb al-nabi (also *sabb al-rasul*, 'denigration of the prophet'), applied to any spoken or written statement deemed insulting to the prophet Muhammad or, by extension, any of the pre-Islamic prophets

salafiyya A modern movement in Islam, seeking to return believers to the thought and practice of the first generation of Muslims, *al-salaf al-salih* ('the pious forebears')

salibiyin 'Crusaders', often applied nowadays to the Americans, British, Zionists, and other 'enemies of Islam'

Sanusiyya An important 19th-and 20th-century militant Sufi brotherhood founded by Sidi Muhammad al-Sanusi (1791–1859), in what is now Libya

Sassanid The name of the Iranian dynasty (224–c.640) which ruled immediately prior to the Arab invasion and the introduction of Islam

shahada 'Act of witness', a term applied, among other things, to the recitation of faith in Islam ('There is no god but God, Muhammad is the Prophet of God') or to martyrdom

shahid A Muslim martyr

shari'a Islamic religious law, sometimes applied more widely to mean the religion in its entirety

shaykh A Muslim religious leader (such as the head of al-Azhar University), often used for the head of a **Sufi** order (see **murshid, pir**)

shema The Jewish testimony to God's singleness from Deut. 6:4, 'Hear, O Israel, the Lord is our God, the Lord is One' (from the first Hebrew word, 'hear'). Used as a prayer in the morning and evening liturgy, it is made up of three separate passages: Deut. 6:4–9, Deut. 11:13, 21, and Num. 15:37–41

shiatsu A form of Japanese medicine combining massage with finger pressure on the points used in acupuncture

Shi'ism The main form of Islam after **Sunnism**, originating in a power conflict after the death of Muhammad in 632. The Shi'a recognize lines of **Imams** (which differ according to sect) as the bearers of religious truth after the prophet. The largest group is that of the Twelvers (Ithna' 'Ashariyya), who are dominant in Iran and have large followings in Iraq, Lebanon, and elsewhere

shirk The act of joining partners to God, whether in the traditional form of polytheism or in the Christian theory of the Trinity

Sufi A Muslim mystic, originally a hermit, later a member of one of many widespread brotherhoods which, until this century, dominated Islamic practice in many countries

sunna The 'path' of orthodox Islamic practice deemed to have been established by the Prophet and his companions and taken as the model for religious law and social behaviour

Sunni A Muslim belonging to the majority branch of the faith, as distinct from a Shi'ite

Swedenborgianism A religio-philosophical system, still active, founded by the Swedish scientist, theologian, and mystic, Emanuel Swedenborg (1688–1772)

tajdid 'Renewal', a common term for religious revival

takfir The act of declaring someone an unbeliever ('*Kafir*'), sometimes used in a formal manner somewhat like excommunication

tanzih The doctrine in Islamic theology which asserts that God is wholly different from His creation

tariqa/tariqat A **Sufi** brotherhood. A sub-order is known as a *ta'ifa*

Tijaniyya A militant **Sufi** order founded in North Africa by Ahmad al-Tijani (1737–1815). The order played an important political role in Algeria, Senegal, and elsewhere in Africa until this century

ulema ('ulama), 'the learned', a general term designating members of the Islamic clerical establishment, who are distinguished (and defined) by their knowledge of the Qur'an, Traditions, theology, and religious law

umma The community of believers in Islam, conceived of as a group originally distinct from Jews and Christians, and now used by fundamentalists to designate a hypothetical pan-Islamic political entity

Umayyads (Bani Umayya), an Arab caliphal dynasty which ruled the early Islamic empire from 661 to 750 and which is today regarded by pious Muslims as having been a 'kingdom' rather than a caliphate. An Andalusian branch of the dynasty ruled independently

Wahhabism A puritanical form of **Sunni** Islam founded by Muhammad ibn 'Abd al-Wahhab (1703–87), now the dominant school in Saudi Arabia

zahir 'Outward', a term used (particularly in **Sufism** and esoteric **Shi'ism**) to designate the exoteric, external meaning or reality of texts or things (in distinction to **batin**)

Zaidi A follower of a branch of **Shi'ism** which has been for many centuries the dominant form of Islam in Yemen

Index

Index

Durkheim, Emile, 109, 137, 149, 152
Dzerzhinskii Square, 195

Easterman, Daniel, 106, 196, 198; *Brotherhood of the Tomb*, 12; *The Last Assasin*, 12, 196; *The Ninth Buddha*, 12; *The Seventh Sanctuary*, 10, 196, 198, 200
economics, 83
Edinburgh, 111; University, 73
education, 38, 45–6, 77, 82–3, 92–3, 111, 171–2, *see also* knowledge
Egypt, 22, 27, 30, 35, 36, 86, 97, 98, 111, 116, 118, 142, 200, 203, 223
Egyptian Supreme Administrative Court, 98
Elementary Forms of the Religious Life, The, 153n
el-Essawy, Hesham, 224
England, *see* Britain
epistemology, 39–40
Europe, 8–9, 27–8, 31, 36–7, 41n, 46, 49, 69, 79, 89–90, 102, 108, 111, 123, 125–6, 161, 178, 181, 185–6, 190, 195–6, 198–201, 205–6, 215
Evangelism, 170–77, 180, 209
'evil empire', Muslims as the, 49–51, 59–60.

faith, 45–8; spread by the sword, 223–5
Falkland Islands, 51
family life, 83–4
Family Protection Court, 52
fana' fi 'llah, 148
faqih, 148, 228
Farrokhzad, Forough, 212
fascism, 70, 124, 198
fatwa, 102, 111, 123, 228, 230
Fedayeen, 22, 228
Ferdowsi, 213
First Congregational Church, Kennebunkport, 207
fi sabil Allah, 149–56, 228
Follett, Ken, 10, 196; *On the Wings of Eagles*, 196
forbidden topics, 171
France, 20, 25, 126–7, 196–7, 200–201, 212
Franciscan monks, 30
'Free Churches', 180
freedoms, 104–5, 106–8, 117, 120, 126, 127–8, 129, 139–40, 209, *see also* civil liberties, human rights
Freemasons, 12, 200
Freud, Sigmund, 219; *Civilization, Society and Religion*, 219 n
Freidson, Eliot, 155
Friends of Homoeopathy, 169
fundamentalism, 7, 31, 33–4, 41–2, 44, 48, 50–51, 108, 110, 117, 124, 142, 209: Christian, 8–9, 17–18, 85, 120, 128, 172, 188, 205; Islamic/Muslim, 17–18, 20–28, 51, 55–8, 69, 73–6, 85–6, 94, 115, 119, 173, 206, 208; Protestant, 133; religious, 69, 92, 95, 102, 104–5, 127, 136, 173–5; 180; scientific, 174; secular, 127–9; Shi'i, 71; Sunni, 71

'fundamentalist liberal Inquisition' 208
Fundamentals, The, 23

Gellner, Ernest, 24
Germany, 59, 126, 161, 162, 190, 191, 200, 201
Ghadhafi, Colonel, 22, 51, 196, 197, 203
Gibbon, Edward, 111
Gilbert Islands, 185
Gilsenen, Michael, 65
God, names of, 59–68
Godard, Jean Luc, 59
gomchen, 147, 228
Gospel Outreach Movement, 183
Greene, Graham, *The Comedians*, 114
Greenville, Tennessee, 17
Guardian, 12, 17, 19, 20n, 45n, 48n, 51, 59, 106, 115, 204, 208, 218
Guatemala, 183, 184
Guatemalan Episcopal Conference, 183
Guevara, Che, 148
Gulf War, 31, 123, 195, 200, 202–4, 208
Guyana, 148

hadith, 82n, 111, 227, 229
hadra, 62–5, 229
Hafez, 213
Hahnemann, Mélanie, 210–11
Hahnemann, Samuel, 210
Haifa, 190
hajj, 55, 217, 229
Hajj Amin al-Husayni, 200
halal, 229
Hallaj (mystic), 151
Hampshire, 171, 172
Hanbali, 83, 229
Handley, Rima, *A Homoeopathic Love Story*, 210–12
haram, 217, 229
Harem, film, 21
Hasan al-Banna, 71, 119
Hassan, Kamal, 83
Hassidic Jews, 29
Hawkins county, 18
Hedayat, Sadiq, 213
Hellenic civilizations, 196
Herbert Read Memorial Lecture, 133
hesychasm, 172, 229
Hezbollah, 21, 162, 209, 229
hijra, 23, 35–6, 229
Hillman, Michael, *A Lonely Woman*, 212–14
Himmler, Heinrich, 162, 164
Hinduism, 74, 83, 92, 95, 99, 112, 117, 120, 128, 142, 149, 157
hirm, 217
Hiro, Dilip, 74, 85–6; *Islamic Fundamentalism*, 85–6
Hiroshima, 12, 160
Hitler, Adolf, 134, 161
Höhne, Heinz, *The Order of the Death's Head*, 163n
Hollywood, 21

235

Index

Knightsbridge, 127
Knipschild, Paul, 170*n*
knowledge, 33–4, 37–42, 47–8, 111, *see also*
  education
Koestler, Arthur, 154, 160, 162
Komei-to, 189
Koran, *see* Qur'an
Korea, 182
Köthen, near Leipzig, 210
Krishna, 171
Kufa, 151
Kuhn, Thomas, 41, 171, 174; *The Structure of
  Scientific Revolution*, 174*n*
Kuwait, 143, 197

la ilaha illa 'ilah, 60, 63, 230
Lalla Rookh, 90
languages, 30, 64, 85, 133
Latin America, 118, 178, 180, 182, 185, 186
law, religious, 52–3, 56
Lebanon, 12, 50, 152, 197
Le Carré, John, 115, 195
Lee, Professor Simon, 132–5, 205
LePen, Jean-Marie, 20
Levant, 49
lex talionis, 53, 230, 232
Liberal Democrat conference, 104
liberalism, 17–19, 20–21, 75, 95, 97, 101–2,
  104–5, 115, 124, 188, 209
Libya, 21, 49, 197
Limits to Medicine: Medical Nemesis, 155*n*
literature, 43, 89–93, 94–5, 101–5, 133–8, 141,
  195–200, 210–20
Lockerbie, 202
London, 55, 111, 196, 202, 208
Lurie, Alison, *Imaginary Friends*, 7
Luxemburg, Rosa, 148

Ma'alim fi'l-tariq, 34
McLuhan, (Herbert) Marshall, 57
madhhab, 36, 230
madrasa, 230
Maharishi Educational Foundation, 181
Maharishi Mahesh Yogi, 179, 180–81
Mahdism, 75, 230
Mahoud, 108, 218
Malamatiyya, 148, 230
Malietoa Tanumafili II, King, 184
Malinowski, Bronislaw, 156
Manzoor, Professor Parvez, 80
Marcos, President, 180–81
mardom, 214
Markus, Gilbert, 180, 184, 186–7
martyrs/martyrdom, 147–56, 158, 161
Marxism, 25, 51, 83, 202
masochism, 157, 161
mass extermination, 163–4
Maududists, 230, 123
Mecca, 35, 55, 150, 217
medicine, 167–8; alternative, 129, 167, 169–76;
  orthodox, 129, 174–6; painful and risky
  treatments, 166–8

Medina, 22, 111, 150, 216
Mennonites, 29
Mesopotamia, 158
Methodists, 129
Middle Ages, 49, 59, 179
Middle East, 8, 28, 196–9, 201, 208
Midgely, Mary, *Perspective on Suffering*, 165
Milani, Farzaneh, 213
Milgram, Stanley, 163; *Obedience to Authority*,
  163*n*
minority groups, 47, 129–30
Mitford, Nancy, 60
Moayyad, Heshmat, *A Nightingale's Lament:
  Selections from the Poems of Parvin E'tesami*,
  212–13
Modern Literary Arabic, 30
modernists, 56–7
Mongol invasions, 24
Mongolia, 12
monks, 204
Monotheism of Islam, 61
Moon, Sun Myung, 95, 139, 179, 181–2
Moonies, 93, 95–6, 129, 179, 181–4, 186,
  189–90, 205
Moon's Unification Church, *see* Moonies
Moral Majority, 18, 51, 180, 189, 209
Morier, J., 93, 95; *Hajji Baba*, 95
Mormons, 93, 95, 96, 128, 129;
  Book of, 110, 189
Morocco, 56, 126, 127, 200, 207
Morrell, David, 10
Moses, 32, 42, 61, 138
Mosques, rise of, in Europe, 126
MOSSAD, 199
mufti, 148, 200, 230
Mughal empire, 37, 79
Muhammad (Prophet), 31–5, 37, 40, 42–3, 51,
  56, 60, 70, 73–4, 79, 89–93, 98, 110–11, 114,
  119–22, 130, 138, 142, 149–50, 171, 213,
  215–19
Muhammad Shah, 43
Muharram, 151, 230–31
Muhyi' I-Din Ibn al-'Arabi, 67–8
mujaddid, 33, 75, 231
Mujahideen, 22
mujahidin, 150, 231
mujtahid, 107, 118, 231
mukhabarat, 196, 231
mulla, 231
Munich, 163
muqallidun, 107, 231
murshid, 36, 231, 232
Muslim Brotherhood, 22, 35, 85–6, 231
Muslim Education, 38
Muslims, 17–19, 20–26, 28, 30–38, 40, 42–4,
  45–8, 49–51, 55–7, 59–61, 63–4, 70–71,
  73–5, 77–84, 89–93, 94–9, 101–5, 107–13,
  114–20, 121–4, 125–30, 133, 135, 137,
  139, 141–3, 149–51, 158, 184, 186, 196–7,
  199–204, 207–9, 215, 218–25
Mussadeq, 50
Mustafa Kamil 'Ali 'Abd Allah, 98

237

Index